STUDY GUIDE

Shelia M. Kennison
Oklahoma State University

Elaine C. Fernandez
Oklahoma State University

UNDERSTANDING HUMAN DEVELOPMENT

GRACE J. CRAIG
University of Massachusetts

WENDY L. DUNN
Coe College

PEARSON

Prentice
Hall

Upper Saddle River, New Jersey 07458

PEARSON

Prentice
Hall

© 2007 by PEARSON EDUCATION, INC.
Upper Saddle River, New Jersey 07458

ISBN 0-13-171031-1

Printed in the United States of America

Table of Contents

Page

Preface   iv

How to Use This Study Guide   vi

Chapter 1   Understanding Human Development   1

Chapter 2   Heredity and Environment   21

Chapter 3   Prenatal Development and Childbirth   38

Chapter 4   Infancy and Toddlerhood: Physical, Cognitive and Language Development 58

Chapter 5   Infancy and Toddlerhood: Personality and Sociocultural Development   76

Chapter 6   Early Childhood: Physical, Cognitive, and Language Development   94

Chapter 7   Early Childhood: Personality and Sociocultural Development   111

Chapter 8   Middle Childhood: Physical and Cognitive Development   128

Chapter 9   Middle Childhood: Personality and Sociocultural Development   143

Chapter 10   Adolescence: Physical and Cognitive Development   158

Chapter 11   Adolescence: Personality and Sociocultural Development   174

Chapter 12   Young Adulthood: Physical and Cognitive Development   190

Chapter 13   Young Adulthood: Personality and Sociocultural Development   208

Chapter 14   Middle Adulthood: Physical and Cognitive Development   226

Chapter 15   Middle Adulthood: Personality and Sociocultural Development   239

Chapter 16   Older Adulthood: Physical and Cognitive Development   253

Chapter 17   Older Adulthood: Personality and Sociocultural Development   267

Chapter 18   Death and Dying   280

Preface

This Study Guide was written to accompany *Understanding Human Development* by Grace J. Craig and Wendy L. Dunn. The purpose of a study guide is to assist you in learning the material presented in each chapter of the textbook.

The most effective use of this study guide is as a knowledge check after you have read a chapter in the textbook. When you are ready to test your knowledge of the material in a chapter, you can work through the corresponding chapter in this Study Guide. Because each chapter of the textbook contains many ideas and concepts that are unfamiliar to you, don't hesitate to reread each chapter after you complete the exercises in this study guide. By rereading the chapter, you will be able to reinforce the material that you know very well and be able to review the material you remembered less well. As you progress through the course, you can become more and more aware of the types of concepts that are easiest for you to learn and the types of concepts that take more time for you to master.

The chapters in the Study Guide contain some or all of the following eight sections:

- ◆ Learning Objectives
- ◆ Multiple Choice Pretest
- ◆ True/False
- ◆ Key Vocabulary Terms
- ◆ Matching (Names or Terms)
- ◆ Programmed Review (fill-in-the-blank)
- ◆ Critical Thinking Essay Questions
- ◆ Multiple Choice Post test

Answer keys are provided at the end of each study guide chapter for the multiple choice question pretest and posttests, some vocabulary items, matching, and the programmed review. Always consult the answer key after completing the exercises because some answers may seem to be intuitively true but turn out not to be the correct answer. In many cases, results from research studies have proven that many assumptions about human development are not correct.

Your performance on the exams and assignments in any class is directly related to how much time and effort you put into studying the class material. Most students who put in adequate time to read each chapter, complete the corresponding study guide chapter, and review the chapter again will excel in the course using the textbook *Understanding Human Development*. Figuring out how much time is adequate can be the challenge. Because the speed at which students can learn new concepts and vocabulary terms varies widely, it is important that you not compare yourself to other students when determining how much time you need to learn the material presented in each chapter. Generally, students do not like to admit how much time it may actually take, so the impression that your classmates may give you about how much time they spend studying is likely to be an underestimation of the time they are actually spending studying the textbook.

In the event that you want to improve your performance in the course using the textbook *Understanding Human Development* and you have completed all the material provided in this study guide, you are encouraged to visit your instructor during his or her office hours. Your instructor can discuss with you how he or she grades assignments and what types of material are emphasized on course exams. The instructor chooses what material from the textbook to include in course lectures and what material appears on course exams. The best way to understand your instructor's idea of what is important in the course is to attend lectures, of course, and to visit office hours.

If you come to believe that your difficulty with the course is related to your difficulty in remembering so much material in a short time, you can seek assistance from your campus's study skills center. Most campuses provide resources to help students develop their reading speed and comprehension. There are typically resources to help students learn how to take good notes and how to improve recall of textbook material.   Because most schools have searchable pages on the Internet, you should have little trouble locating the appropriate office on your campus.

Because textbooks may contain concepts and terminology that are not commonly used in everyday language, you may come across words with meanings that are not familiar to you. We encourage you to take the time to look up such words in a dictionary. Reviewing a dictionary definition of an unfamiliar word will not only help you become more familiar with the meaning of the given word, but it will also help you recall the particular sense of the word that is relevant in the course. There are many free searchable dictionaries on the Internet.

Good luck and enjoy the course!

How to Use This Study Guide

1. Learning Objectives

After you have read and studied each chapter, you should be able to complete the learning objectives listed at the beginning of each chapter in this Study Guide.

2. Multiple Choice Questions (Pretest and Post Tests)

Practice tests are an important way to check your progress. There is a pretest at the start of each chapter and a post test at the end of each chapter in this Study Guide. These tests measure your progress toward your goal of mastering the material. Your scores on the post tests should be higher than your scores on the pretests if you have studied the programmed review.

3. Key Names

Throughout the history of psychology, there have been individuals who have become well known for their areas of research. Some individuals are well known for theories that they have developed. Other individuals are well known for well-designed and informative studies. As a student of psychology, it is important to become familiar with the names of key individuals who have made outstanding contributions to the field. Several chapters in this Study Guide contain sections in which you can match the names of individuals with their contributions to psychology.

4. Key Vocabulary Terms

It is important to learn the definitions of terms as they are used in the field of psychology so you should complete the exercises related to definitions.

5. Programmed Review

The programmed review will help you learn the major points in each chapter. Try to fill in what you can on your own but for those questions that you are unable to answer, feel free to use the text. The act of looking up the material will reinforce your learning of it.

6. Critical Thinking Questions

Many college courses are designed to help you develop your writing skills so completing short essay questions can be useful. This is true if your psychology course will include essay exams. Some of the questions you find in each of these chapters are from the chapters in your text.

Study Tips

Useful Study Techniques

1. Make material meaningful to you by creating associations with what you already know.
2. Learn the material actively.
   a. Imagine vivid pictures.
   b. Recite out loud.
   c. Tell someone about what you have learned.
3. Study in a quiet environment by reducing noise and interruptions.
4. Be aware of your attitude toward the information.
5. Study at spaced intervals – studying the material in manageable blocks as opposed to "cramming" will improve your retention.
6. Remember related information when you are having trouble recalling something.
7. Use mnemonic devices (rhymes or words created from the first letters of each word).

When and How to Study

1. Plan two hours of study time for every hour you spend in class.
2. Study difficult or boring subjects first.
3. Avoid long study sessions.
4. Be aware of the time of day when you are most alert.
5. Use a regular study area.
6. Use a library.
7. Take at least one 10-minute break for every 50 minutes of study time.
8. Avoid noise distractions.
9. Test yourself by explaining what you have learned to a friend. If you can explain the material to another person, you can be sure you know it well.

Studying in Groups

Research has shown that one of the most effective ways to learn is to study with other students. Your grades on exams will be better and you will have a lot more fun doing it.

How to Form a Group

1. Look for dedicated students who share some of your academic goals and challenges.
2. Only study in a group after you have studied individually. This is the same for other group members.
3. Ask your instructor for help in recruiting group members.
4. Limit groups to fewer than six people.
5. Test the group by planning a "one time only" session. If that session works, plan another.

Possible Activities for a Study Group

1. Compare notes.
2. Have discussions and debates about the material.
3. Test each other with questions brought to the group meeting by each member.
4. Practice teaching each other.
5. Brainstorm possible test questions.
6. Share suggestions for problems in the areas of finances, transportation, child care, time scheduling, or other barriers.

Better Test Taking

1. Ask your instructor to describe the test format – how long it will be and what kind of questions to expect.
2. Have a section in your notebook labeled "Test Questions" and add several questions to this section after every lecture and after reading the text. Record topics that the instructor repeats several times or goes back to in subsequent lectures. Write down questions the instructor poses to students.
3. Know the rules for taking the test so you do not create the impression of cheating.
4. Scan the whole test immediately. Budget your time based on how many points each section is worth.
5. Read the directions slowly - then reread them.
6. Answer the easiest, shortest questions first. This gives you the experience of success, stimulates associations, and prepares your mind for more difficult questions.
7. Use memory techniques when you are stuck. If your recall on something is blocked, remember something else that's related.
8. Look for answers in other test questions. A term, name, date, or other fact that you can't remember might appear in the test itself.
9. Don't change an answer unless you are sure because your first instinct is usually best.

Reading for Remembering

1. Skim the entire chapter.
2. Read the outline at the front of the chapter in the text.
3. Read the material.
4. Highlight the most important information.
5. Recite the key points when you finish an assignment.
6. Plan your first review within 24 hours.
7. Reread the chapter summary.
8. Weekly reviews are important. Go over the notes. Read the highlighted parts of your text. Recite the more complicated points.

More About Review

You can do short reviews anytime, anywhere, if you are prepared. If you don't have time to read a whole assignment, review last week's assignment. Conduct 5 minute reviews regularly. Three-by-five note cards work well for review. Write ideas and facts on cards and carry them with you. These short review periods can be effortless.

Effective Note-Taking During Class

1. Review the textbook chapter before class. Instructors often design a lecture based on the assumption that you have read the chapter before class. You can take notes more easily if you already have some idea of the material.
2. Bring your favorite note-taking tools to class.
3. Sit as close to the instructor as possible so that you have fewer distractions.
4. Arrive to class early. Relax and review your notes from the previous class.
5. Focus on understanding what the instructor is saying because that is what you will find on the test. When you hear something you disagree with, make a note about it and ask the instructor for clarification during office hours or after class.
6. Be active in class. Volunteer for demonstrations. Join in class discussions.
7. Relate the topic to an interest of yours. We remember things in which we are most interested.
8. Watch for clues of what is important, such as repetition, summary statements, information written on the board, information that interests the instructor, and information the instructor takes directly from notes.

Chapter 1

Understanding Human Development

CHAPTER OUTLINE

◈ Introduction to Development
 ♦ Lifespan Development
 ♦ Guiding Themes in Human Development

◈ The Nature of Human Development
 ♦ Biology and Environment
 ♦ The Sociocultural Context
 ♦ The Domains of Human Development

◈ Theoretical Frameworks for Human Development
 ♦ The Role of Theory
 ♦ Biological Views of Human Development
 ♦ Psychodynamic Views of Human Development
 ♦ Behavioral Views of Human Development
 ♦ Cognitive Views of Human Development
 ♦ Integrating Theoretical Approaches

◈ The Scientific Approach to the Study of Human Development
 ♦ Descriptive Methods
 ♦ Studying Development Across Time
 ♦ Correlation as a Descriptive Tool
 ♦ Experimental Approaches: The Study of Cause and Effect
 ♦ Summary of Research Methods
 ♦ Ethics in Developmental Research
 ♦ Development in Context

LEARNING OBJECTIVES

After you have read and studied this chapter, you should be able to answer the following questions.

1. What is meant when researchers say that heredity and environment interact during the course of human development?
2. How do biological, environmental, and social factors influence human development?
3. What are the theories of human development that have influenced the researchers?
4. Why is the study of human development considered a scientific endeavor?
5. What are the ethical issues that researchers in developmental psychology routinely encounter?

PRACTICE TEST - PRETEST

Circle the correct answer for each multiple choice question and check your answers with the Answer Key at the end of the chapter.

1. A person experiences a traumatic event during childhood. A developmental psychologist would view the traumatic event as an example of which of the following?
   a. biological factor
   b. random factor
   c. social context
   d. environmental factor

2. At what age is one no longer considered an adolescent, but rather a young adult?
   a. 12-19 years of age
   b. 18-21 years of age
   c. 8-12 years of age
   d. 16-18 years of age

3. A researcher who is interested in understanding the how children develop reasoning and problem solving skills is associated with:
   a. physical domain
   b. sociocultural domain
   c. personality domain
   d. cognitive domain

4. According to Freud, the part of the human mind concerned with following the rules of society that may experience feelings of guilt when one violates social norms:
   a. id
   b. ego
   c. superego
   d. libido

5. Which of the following is NOT a stage in Freud's psychosexual theory?
   a. oral
   b. phallic
   c. latency
   d. puberty

6. According to Freud, at what age does a child enter into the genital stage of development?
   a. 18 months
   b. 6 years
   c. 3 years
   d. 12 years

7. According to Erik Erikson's theory of psychosocial development, what stage of development would a child who is just entering school be starting?
   a. ego identity vs. ego diffusion
   b. initiative vs. guilt
   c. intimacy vs. isolation
   d. industry vs. inferiority

8. Erik Erikson proposed that a person who was involved in the stage of trust vs. mistrust is about how old?
   a. birth to 1 year
   b. 6-12 years old
   c. 3-6 years
   d. 12-18 years old

9. Which researcher believed that human behavior could be best understood in terms of how rewards and punishments exert an influence on people's actions?
   a. Charles Darwin
   b. Mary Ainsworth
   c. Lev Vygotsky
   d. B. F. Skinner

10. Research showing that dogs could learn to anticipate food when a bell was rung was conducted by:
    a. B. F. Skinner
    b. Ivan Pavlov
    c. Lev Vygotsky
    d. Charles Darwin

11. The view that by observing the behavior of others and the resulting consequences can influence our own behavior is known as:
    a. classical conditioning
    b. epigenetic principle
    c. social learning theory
    d. operant conditioning

12. According to Piaget, at what age is a child first able to use logic in his/her thinking?
    a. from birth
    b. 2 years
    c. 7 years
    d. 11 years

13. Piaget's theory of cognitive development suggests that children start out in life relying primarily on their senses and bodily motion. This stage is referred to as:
    a. preoperational
    b. formal operational
    c. concrete operational
    d. sensorimotor

14. A study in which the same participants are studied at various points in time is called:
    a. a cross-sectional design
    b. longitudinal design
    c. interview study
    d. case design

15. Which model emphasizes that human development is a dynamic, interactive process that begins with an individual's genetic endowment and unfolds overtime as a result of interactions with various levels of the environment?
    a. natural selection
    b. psychosexual model
    c. guided participation approach
    d. bioecological model

16. The process by which organisms change in order to become more successful in their environment is:
    a. enculturation
    c. maturation
    b. adaptation
    d. socialization

17. When two variables are not correlated at all, the value of the correlation will be:
    a. -.50 or +.50
    c. -1.00
    b. 0
    d. +1.00

18. If one once became ill after eating pizza and now anytime the person smells pizza the person starts to feel queasy, the person has likely experienced:
    a. adaptation
    c. classical conditioning
    b. assimilation
    d. operant conditioning

19. This field of study attempts to understand how brain function is related to specific human behaviors:
    a. cognitive development
    c. neuroscience
    b. behaviorism
    d. evolutionary psychology

20. Which of the following researchers conducted the classic "bobo doll" experiment?
    a. Jean Piaget
    c. Mary Ainsworth
    b. Lev Vygotsky
    d. Albert Bandura

TRUE/FALSE

For each of the following statements indicate whether the statement is True or False. Check your answers with the Answer Key at the end of this chapter.

___T___ 1.   Developmental psychologists generally focus their study on the common features that typical, rather than atypical, human development.

___F___ 2.   Biological factors influencing development include the specific situations that an individual experiences and that influence behavior and development.

___T___ 3.   In collectivistic cultures, competition is stressed over cooperation.

___T___ 4.   Enculturation occurs when one learns about a culture by being taught.

___T___ 5.   Evolution refers to the process through which species change across generations.

___F___ 6.   Lewis Terman is best known for developing the psychosexual approach to human development.

___T___ 7.   The field of ethology involves the study of animal behavior, especially the behaviors influenced by instinct.

I 8. Freud believed that unconscious processes determine human development.

F 9. Freud showed in his research how logical reasoning developed during childhood.

F 10. Erik Erikson's view of development, like Freud's, focused on the role of unconscious processes on development.

I 11. The approach to psychology known as Behaviorism was primarily focused on the study of consciousness.

T 12. Jean Piaget's view of the child is one of the active scientist who interacts with the physical environment and develops complex thought strategies.

F 13. Lev Vygotsky's view of development influenced the role of biological factors on development.

T 14. In a naturalistic observation, a researcher observes behaviors as they occur in real-life, rather than in a laboratory.

T 15. In the United States, the use of corporal punishment has been completely banned in public schools.

F 16. When a researcher finds a positive correlation between the amount of violent TV watched by school children and the number of violent outbursts by the children, the researcher can safely conclude that TV viewing directly caused the violent outbursts.

T 17. In a case study, a person is observed in their everyday life without their knowledge.

T 18. Freud proposed that the id was involved in pleasure-seeking impulses.

T 19. A representative sample mirrors the population in every important way.

T 20. Erik Erikson believed that the developing stages that people go through are determined by a biological plan also referred to as the epigenetic principle.

KEY NAMES

Match the following names with the appropriate description and check your answers with the Answer Key at the end of this chapter.

1. __d__ Mary Ainsworth   a. bioecological approach

2. __e__ Albert Bandura   b. classical conditioning

3. __a__ Urie Bronfenbrenner   c. cognitive development

4. __g__ Charles Darwin   d. guided participation

5. __j__ Erik Erikson   e. laboratory observation

6. __i__ Sigmund Freud   f. longitudinal research

7. __f__ Jean Piaget   g. natural selection

8. __b__ Ivan Pavlov   h. operant conditioning

9. __c__ B. F. Skinner   i. psychosexual theory

10. __k__ Lewis Terman   j. psychosocial theory

11. __h__ Lev Vygotsky   k. social-cognitive learning theory

KEY VOCABULARY TERMS

Look up the definition and give a specific example of each of the following aspects of development.

1. physical domain 7
2. cognitive domain 5

3. personality domain 6
4. sociocultural domain 8

Label each definition with the appropriate term.

5. An organized, coherent set of ideas that helps us to understand, to explain, and to make predictions.

6. Freud's theory that emphasizes unconscious processes and the importance of early childhood development.

7. The view that the appropriate focus of psychology should be on observable behavior.

8. Piaget's term for the process that requires schemas to change when a new object or event does not fit.

Explain the difference between the following sets of terms.

9. Maturation; Learning
10. Enculturation; Socialization
11. Collectivistic culture; Individualistic culture
12. Classical conditioning; Operant conditioning
13. Longitudinal design; Cross-sectional design
14. Naturalistic observation; Laboratory observation

Give a brief description of each of the following types of research.

25. quasi-experimental research	28. sequential-cohort design
26. longitudinal research	29. cross-sectional research
27. case study	30. baby biography

The following table displays Freud's stages of psychosexual development. Fill in the missing information.

	Stages	**Age**
31.	_____	birth to 18 months
32.	Anal	_____
33.	Phallic	_____
34.	_____	6 years to 12 years
35.	_____	12 years and up

The following table displays Erikson's stages of psychosocial development. Fill in the missing information.

	Age	Stage
36.	Birth to 12 months	_____
37.	_____	autonomy vs. self doubt
38.	_____	initiative vs. guilt
39.	6 years to 12 years	_____
40.	12 years to 18 years	_____
41.	_____	intimacy vs. isolation
42.	_____	generativity vs. self-absorption
43.	65 years and older	_____

The following table displays Piaget's stages of cognitive development. Fill in the missing information.

	Age	Stage
44.	_____	Sensorimotor
45.	_____	Preoperational
46.	7 years to 11 to 12 years	_____
47.	11 or 12 years and up	_____

PROGRAMMED REVIEW

Fill in the blanks in the following programmed review. Then check your answers with the Answer Key at the end of the chapter.

Introduction to Development
Lifespan Development

1. In order to better understand the general patterns of change across an individual's life, psychologists divide the lifespan into _____, where each part corresponds to a segment of the lifespan.

2. The lifespan is usually divided into the _____ period from birth to 18-24 months, the _____ period from 12-15 months to 2-3 years, _____ from 2-3 years to 5-6 years, _____ from 6 years to 12 years, _____ from 12 ears to 18-21 years, _____ from 18-21 years to 40 years, _____ from 40 years to 60-65 years, and _____ from 65 years to death.

Guiding Themes in Human Development

3. Development is a continuous process influenced by both _____ factors and _____ factors.

4. Individuals' development is influenced by family, society, and culture, which is generally referred to as the _____ context.

The Nature of Human Development
Biology and Environment

5. Maturation and learning are both important aspects of human development. Maturational changes are _____ in nature, and changes resulting from learning are _____ in nature.

The Sociocultural Context

6. In _____ cultures, competition is stressed over cooperation. In _____ cultures, the opposite is true.

The Domains of Human Development

7. Psychologists consider changes in human development in four domains. Changes in physical shape and size are in the _____ domain. Changes in thinking, reasoning, and problem solving are in the _____ domain. The acquisition of relatively stable and enduring personal traits are in the _____ domain. Changes related to learning about one's society either through formal schooling or through informal observation are in the _____ domain.

Theoretical Frameworks for Human Development
The Role of Theory

8. Scientific investigations produce _____ that are used to develop explanations or _____ of human development.

Biological Views of Human Development

9. The theory of _____ was first put forth by _____ in his book _____.

10. Animal behaviors, particularly those that are the result of instinct, are of interest to those in the field of _____.

11. The entire arrangement of all human genes is referred to as the _____.

12. Darwin's view of "the survival of the fittest" is also referred to as _____.

Psychodynamic Views of Human Development

13. Freud viewed the human mind as composed of three parts. The _____ is involved in pleasure-seeking impulses and pain avoidance activities. The _____ is involved in one's feelings of conscience and guilt. The _____ is involved in conscious rational choices.

14. According to Freud, when a child experiences difficulty during some stage of development, a _____ may occur, resulting in some primitive behavior from that stage being carried forward into adulthood.

15. Erik Erikson emphasized _____ which is defined as a basic sense of who we are as individuals.

Behavioral Views of Human Development

16. In the area of behaviorism, _____'s work illustrates principles of classical conditioning and _____'s work illustrates the principles of operant conditioning.

17. Learning which occurs when we observe others' behavior and the consequences is referred to as _____.

Cognitive Views of Human Development

18. According to Piaget, children begin to form concepts and to use symbols during the _____ stage of development which occurs between the ages of _____ and _____.

19. Piaget referred to mental structures that process information, perceptions, and experiences as _____.

20. Lev Vygotsky's view of childhood is one of _____ that involves learning about the world through the assistance of others.

Integrating Theoretical Approaches

21. An example of a systems model is Urie Bronfenbrenner's _____ model. In it, the _____ involves activities, roles, and interactions in the person's immediate setting. The _____ is the social settings or organizations beyond the person's immediate experience. The _____ includes the laws, values, and customs of the society in which the person lives.

The Scientific Approach to the Study of Human Development
Descriptive Methods

22. Both Charles Darwin and Jean Piaget kept _____ in which they recorded daily records of a child's early development.

23. Researchers can study human behavior through observation. When observations are carried out in a natural setting in which the behavior typically occurs, it is referred to as a _____. When observations are carried out in a controlled setting, it is referred to as a _____.

24. The primary difference between questionnaires and interviews is that interviews are carried out _____ and questionnaires are carried out _____.

Studying Development Across Time

25. A classic study of "gifted" children was conducted by _____ using a _____ which involved testing the same individuals repeatedly over time.

26. When compared with _____ design , a _____ design is quicker and cheaper to conduct.

Correlation as a Descriptive Tool

27. The more one studies, the higher his or her GPA is exemplifies a _____. The more one attends late-night social parties, the lower his or her GPA is exemplifies a _____.

Experimental Approaches: The Study of Cause and Effect

28. A researcher who wishes to prove that one variable causes a change in another variable should avoid _____ in favor of _____.

29. In an experiment, the variable that is manipulated and believed to cause a change in a second variable is referred to as _____. The second variable that changes as a result of the manipulation is referred to as _____.

30. Researchers repeat experiments which are called _____ in order to determine whether research findings can be observed again.

Summary of Research Methods

31. The _____ refers to cases in which participants cannot be randomly assigned to different groups.

Ethics in Developmental Research

32. Research institutions have committees whose job it is to evaluate the ethical soundness of research studies. These committees are called _____.

33. Volunteers for research studies are routinely provided with a clear statement of the procedures and risks involved in a study and provided with the opportunity to participate or to decline participation. This process is referred to as _____.

CRITICAL THINKING QUESTIONS

To further your mastery of the topics, write out the answers to the following essay questions in the space provided.

1. The nature-nurture debate has received a great deal of attention in developmental psychology. In your own words, explain this debate. Provide one example of an influence on development that represents "nature" and one that represents "nurture."

2. Describe how the attitudes toward children in Western civilization have changed since ancient Greece.

3. Consider the views of Lev Vygotsky and Jean Piaget on cognitive development. How do they differ?

4. Consider the views of Lev Vygotsky and Albert Bandura on social development. What ideas do they have in common?

5. The systems approach offered by Urie Bronfrenbrenner involves five systems: 1) microsystem; 2) mesosystem; 3) exosystem; 4) macrosystem; and 5) chromosystem. What aspects of a person's daily life are included in each of these systems?

6. Discuss how a parent might use B.F. Skinner's idea about rewards and punishments to get children to study more often and to fight with one another less often.

7. Discuss how television viewing can play a role in social learning for young children.

8. In your own words, explain why researchers value replications of studies or experiments.

9. What are the advantages and disadvantages of using either a longitudinal design or a cross sectional design to investigate human development?

10. Current guidelines for the research ethics require participants to be informed about the nature of the research in which they participate. Explain how researchers are required to inform children who are participants and their parents.

PRACTICE TEST – POST TEST

Circle the correct answer for each multiple choice question and check your answers with the Answer Key at the end of the chapter.

1. A child attempts to carry out a stunt involving a skateboard and a ramp that he has seen on television. The knowledge that is involved in doing this was likely obtained through which of the following?
   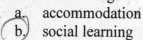
   a. accommodation   c. adaptation
   b. social learning   d. guided participation

2. Freud believed that this part of the human mind played a central role in mediating the part of the mind involved in pleasure-seeking and the part of the mind prone to feelings of guilt when social norms were broken.
   a. super ego   c. id
   b. the unconscious mind d. ego

3. A researcher plans to recruit families for a new research project in which participants will view pictures and be asked to report feelings evoked by the pictures. There is a chance that some of the pictures may bring to mind unpleasant memories or thoughts. The researcher should do which of the following?
   a. refrain from telling participants about this risk until after the study is over
   b. tell participants during the informed consent process
   c. never mention this because it may bias participants' responses in the study
   d. terminate the study because all research evoking negative emotions is unethical

4. Cultures in which individuals are encouraged to put time and energy into projects that will help large groups of people in their own society are best described as:
   a. primitive
   b. collectivistic
   c. individualistic
   d. idealistic

5. Lev Vygotsky's views on human development can be best categorized as which aspect of development?
   a. biological
   b. evolutionary
   c. psychodynamic
   d. social

6. This researcher proposed that children between the ages of 3 and 6 years might develop feelings of guilt if they are severely criticized or punished for their own actions.
   a. Sigmund Freud
   b. Jean Piaget
   c. Erik Erikson
   d. Urie Bronfenbrenner

7. William recalls a time when he was a child when he nearly drowned in a public swimming pool. It was a very frightening experience. Since that time, the smell of chlorine leaves him with a palpable sense of dread. This can be most easily explained by which of the following?
   a. classical conditioning
   b. guided participation
   c. superego
   d. social learning theory

8. According to B.F. Skinner, if you would like to get your child to keep his or her room tidy, which of the following is most likely to work?
   a. having a chat with the child about his or her feelings
   b. showing the child how to clean so the child will learn from observing you
   c. routinely rewarding the child when the child carries out any cleaning
   d. none of the above; nothing is likely to work

9. According to Piaget, when is a child first able to reason about abstract concepts?
   a. not until the age of 11 or 12
   b. not until the age of 7
   c. by the age of 2
   d. from birth

10. A high school student who still sucks his or her thumb when under stress is an example which of the following?
    a. Piaget's notion of accommodation
    b. Bandura's notion of social learning
    c. Darwin's notion of natural selection
    d. Freud's notion of a fixation

11. According the Urie Bronfenbrenner's bioecological model of development, the school that a child attends would be part of his or her:
    a. microsystem
    b. macrosystem
    c. mesosystem
    d. exosystem

12. Gloria plans to spend a semester abroad in Thailand. She looks forward to learning about the culture by living with a local family. She does not plan to attend any formal classes. Her knowledge of the culture will be gained primarily through which of the following?
    a. adaptation
    b. classical conditioning
    c. enculturation
    d. accommodation

13. Which of the following is a reason why one might use a cross-sectional research design instead of a longitudinal research design?
    a. Cross-sectional design can be completed in much less time than longitudinal designs
    b. Cross-sectional designs involve repeated testing of the same individuals over time, so the results are more valid than in longitudinal designs
    c. Cross-sectional designs always involve testing more participants than longitudinal designs, which produces more reliable results
    d. None of the above – the designs are comparable in terms of their pros and cons

14. A researcher plans to investigate how toddlers interact with each other, starting from the first time they meet. In the planned study, toddlers that do not know one another will be placed in a room with many interesting toys. Parents will be nearby. Researchers will record the toddlers' interaction and examine the videotapes at a later time. This type of research is best described as which of the following?
    a. experiment
    b. laboratory observation
    c. naturalistic observation
    d. cross-sectional design

15. According to Erik Erikson, it is typical for individuals to look back on their lives and judge themselves. If they are satisfied with their lives, they may have a sense of integrity. If they are not satisfied with their lives, they may have a sense of despair. At what age are adults likely to experience this stage?
    a. in their 20s
    b. in their 40s
    c. in their 50s
    d. in their 60s or later

16. Which of the following best describes the difference in Freud's and Erikson's views about human development?
    a. Freud emphasized the role of conscious processes; Erikson emphasized unconscious processes
    b. Erikson emphasized the role of social learning; Freud emphasized unconscious processes
    c. Erikson emphasized the role of unconscious processes; Freud emphasized conscious processes
    d. none of the above – their views were very similar

17. According to Freud, children at this stage of development repress sexual interests and instead focus on developing cognitive and interpersonal skills.
    a. genital
    b. latency
    c. phallic
    d. anal

18. A researcher investigated how daily exercise influences memory performance. Memory performance was compared for three groups of participants:1) participants who exercised for 5 minutes or less per day; 2) participants who exercised for 20 minutes per day; and 3) participants who exercised 60 minutes per day. In this research, memory performance is which of the following?
    a. correlational variable   c. dependent variable
    b. independent variable   d. quasi-experimental variable

19. A researcher is interested in investigating the relationship between smiling by a customer and the amount of time a customer service representative spends with the customer. She finds that a smiling customer is dealt with for longer by the customer service representative than a non-smiling customer. This pattern of results is best described as which of the following?
    a. causative result   c. negative correlation
    b. positive correlation   d. zero correlation

20. A researcher wants to investigate how cognitive processes develop. The researcher plans to compare the performance of 2-, 4-, and 5-year-olds on a new test to measure thinking and reasoning. Which of the following best describes this research design?
    a. cross-sectional   c. correlational
    b. longitudinal   d. mixed groups

ANSWER KEYS

Practice Test - Pretest (with text page numbers)

1. d 7	6. d 17	11. c 20	16. b 22
2. b 5	7. d 18	12. c 21	17. b 32
3. d 1	8. a 18	13. d 21	18. c 20
4. c 1	9. d 19	14. b 30	19. c 15
5. d 1	10. b 19	15. d 24	20. d 34

True False

1. T	6. F	11. F	16. F
2. F	7. T	12. T	17. F
3. F	8. T	13. F	18. T
4. F	9. F	14. T	19. T
5. T	10. F	15. F	20. T

Key Names

1. g	5. j	9. i
2. k	6. h	10. h
3. b	7. d	11. f
4. e	8. c	

Key Vocabulary Terms

5. theory
6. psychodynamic approach
7. behaviorism
8. accommodation

9. Maturation refers to physical changes that occur during development; whereas learning refers to changes that occur as a result of a person's interaction with the environment.

11. Enculturation occurs when a person learns about a culture through passive exposure or immersion in the culture; socialization occurs when a person is specifically taught about a culture.

12. Collectivistic cultures emphasize cooperation over competition; individualistic cultures emphasize competition over cooperation.

13. Classical conditioning occurs when an organism learns to respond in a particular way to a neutral stimulus that normally does not bring about that type of response; operant conditioning occurs when an organism learns to produce a voluntary response either more often or less often, depending on its association with positive consequence (reward) or negative consequence (punishment).

14. Longitudinal designs involve the repeated testing of the same participants over time; cross-sectional designs involve the testing of participants of different age groups at a single time.

15. <u>Naturalistic observations</u> are studies of behavior as it occurs in everyday life situations; <u>laboratory observations</u> are studies of behavior in a laboratory setting.

Fill in the missing information
31. oral
32. 18 months to 3 years
33. 3 years to 6 years
34. Latency
35. Genital
36. trust vs. mistrust
37. 12 months to 3 years
38. 3 years to 6 years
39. Industry vs. inferiority
40. Ego identity vs. ego diffusion
41. 18 years to 40 years
42. 40 years to 65 years
43. Integrity vs. Despair
44. birth to 2 years
45. 2 years to 7 years
46. concrete operational
47. formal operational

Programmed Review
1. developmental periods or stages
2. infancy, toddlerhood, early childhood, middle childhood, adolescence, young adulthood, middle adulthood, older adulthood
3. biological, environmental
4. sociocultural
5. biological, environmental
6. individualist, collectivistic
7. physical, cognitive, personality, social
8. data, theories
9. evolution, Charles Darwin, Origin of Species
10. ethology
11. human genome
12. natural selection
13. id, super ego, ego
14. fixation
15. ego identity
16. Ivan Pavlov (also John Watson), B. F. Skinner
17. social learning
18. preoperational, 2 years to approximately 7 years
19. schemes or schemas
20. guided participation
21. bioecological, microsystem, exosystem, macrosystem

22. baby biographies
23. naturalistic observation, laboratory observation
24. in person, in a pencil-paper format
25. Lewis Terman, longitudinal design
26. longitudinal, cross-sectional
27. positive correlation, negative correlation
28. correlational research, experimental research
29. Independent variable (IV), Dependent variable (DV)
30. replications
31. quasi-experimental research
32. Institutional Review Boards (IRBs)
33. informed consent

Practice Test – Post Test (with text page numbers)

1. b 20	6. c 18	11. a 25	16. c 17
2. d 16	7. a 19	12. c 12	17. b 17
3. b 38	8. c 19	13. a 31	18. c 33
4. b 10	9. a 21	14. c 28	19. b 32
5. d 22	10. d 17	15. d 18	20. a 31

Chapter 2

Heredity and Environment

CHAPTER OUTLINE

- ◈ Molecular Genetics
  - ◆ Human Cells
  - ◆ DNA
  - ◆ Genes
  - ◆ Protein Synthesis

- ◈ Genes, Chromosomes, and Cell Division
  - ◆ Cell Division and Reproduction
  - ◆ From Genotype to Phenotype
  - ◆ The Variation of Traits Among Individuals

- ◈ Genetic and Chromosomal Disorders
  - ◆ Sex-Linked Disorders
  - ◆ Autosomal Disorders
  - ◆ Genetic Counseling
  - ◆ Advances in Genetic Research and Treatment

- ◈ Behavior Genetics
  - ◆ Adoption Studies
  - ◆ Twin Studies

- ◈ Environmental Influences and Contexts
  - ◆ Contexts
  - ◆ Basic Processes That Affect Behavior
  - ◆ Conditioning, Behavior Modification, and Life
  - ◆ Social Learning and the Evolving Self-Concept

- ◈ Environment in a Broader Context: Family and Culture
  - ◆ Family Systems
  - ◆ The Family as Transmitter of Culture
  - ◆ Sociocultural Influence on Development Across the Lifespan

LEARNING OBJECTIVES

After you have read and studied this chapter, you should be able to answer the following questions.

1. How are traits inherited from parents?
2. What disorders occur as a result of how genes are inherited?
3. What can the study of twins and adopted children reveal about behavior genetics?
4. How can environmental events exert their influence on the processes involved in development?
5. In what ways does one's family and culture shape the way development unfolds?

PRACTICE TEST - PRETEST

Circle the correct answer for each multiple choice question and check your answers with the Answer Key at the end of the chapter.

1. Although the exact number of genes in the human genome is currently unknown, the number has been estimated to be approximately:
    a. 500 or fewer
    b. 10,000-15,000
    c. 500-1,000
    d. 20,000-25,000

2. Which of the following is not one of the bases of DNA?
    a. nucleases
    b. cytosine
    c. adenine
    d. thymine

3. Humans normally have how many chromosomes?
    a. 2
    b. 46
    c. 4600
    d. scientists do not yet know for sure

4. DNA refers to:
    a. di-nucleic antibody
    b. duonucleic acid
    c. deoxyribonucleic acid
    d. dynonucleic antigen

5. This type of protein functions to protect the body from disease.
    a. collagen
    b. antibody
    c. enzyme
    d. insulin

6. A photograph of a cell's chromosomes arranged in pairs according to size:
    a. genotype
    b. karyotype
    c. phenotype
    d. polypeptide chain

7. These are alternate versions of a gene that perform the same function; one is inherited from the mother and one is inherited from the father.
   a. alleles
   b. chromosomes
   c. autosomes
   d. gametes

8. The number of genetically unique children that a mother and a father can produce has been estimated to be:
   a. thousands
   b. hundreds of millions
   c. hundreds of billions
   d. hundreds of trillions

9. This inherited disorder results in problems with blood clotting.
   a. klinefelter syndrome
   b. turner syndrome
   c. hemophilia
   d. color blindness

10. Colorblindness occurs because of which of the following?
    a. mutation during development
    b. recessive gene
    c. gene imprinting
    d. error during transcription

11. The chance that a child is born with Down syndrome has been shown to be related to which of the following?
    a. father's age
    b. mother's age
    c. parents' ethnic background
    d. mother's diet during pregnancy

12. This technique involves attempting to cure a genetic disorder by directly altering the molecular structure of the patient's DNA.
    a. gene therapy
    b. gene duplication
    c. gene transcription
    d. gene imprinting

13. Which of the following sex-linked disorders occurs most often?
    a. klinefelter syndrome
    b. turner syndrome
    c. hemophilia
    d. color blindness

14. Which of the following disorders is not associated with mental retardation?
    a. cystic fibrosis
    b. prader-willi syndrome
    c. down syndrome
    d. fragile X syndrome

15. The symptoms of this disorder occur around the age of 35, which include a lopsided staggering walk, random jerking movements, dementia, and ultimately death.
    a. cystic fibrosis
    b. huntington's disease
    c. prader-willi syndrome
    d. angelman syndrome

16. Couples wishing to have a child may consult a genetic counselor. Which of the following types of information would NOT be of interest to a genetic counselor?
    a. parents' ages
    b. parents' relatedness to one another
    c. parents' ethnic background
    d. parents' income

17. Some people experience unreasonable fear in certain situations, such as fear of being in closed spaces or fear of spiders. Such unreasonable fears are called:
    a. delusions
    c. phobias
    b. hallucinations
    d. reactivations

18. Parents can reward children for producing desired responses. By systematically reinforcing successes or near successes in producing the desired response, parents can _____ children's behavior.
    a. cancel
    c. prevent
    b. extinguish
    d. shape

19. When researchers refer to an age defined group, such as Generation X-ers or baby-boomers, they are referring to which of the following?
    a. cohort
    c. phenotype
    b. family
    d. genotype

20. Which of the following would NOT be an example of nonnormative influences?
    a. illness
    c. career changes
    b. marrying
    d. divorce

TRUE/FALSE

For each of the following statements indicate whether the statement is True or False. Check your answers with the Answer Key at the end of this chapter.

_____ 1.   We share about 98% of our genes with chimpanzees.

_____ 2.   In the human body, there are approximately 20 different kinds of cells, which are arranged in different ways to create different tissues and organs.

_____ 3.   Scientists have been able to identify markers in the human DNA that distinguish different races of people.

_____ 4.   The inheritance of eye color is determined by a single gene pair.

_____ 5.   Most human traits involve polygenic inheritance (multiple genes) rather than a single gene.

_____ 6.   Blood type is a sex-linked trait, which means that certain blood types are more common in males than in females.

_____ 7.   A mutation occurring during development may result in a miscarriage.

_____ 8.   Each year in the United States congenital anomalies (or birth defects) affect between 10% and 15% of all births.

____ 9.	There is no evidence that one's genetic make-up can influence their behavior.

____ 10.	Females typically have a total of roughly 400,000 ova, which begin to develop in the child before birth.

____ 11.	The studies of twins that have been conducted in the United States have yielded different results than twin studies conducted in other countries, such as Japan and India.

____ 12.	Only the most primitive cultures exhibit ethnocentrism, which is the working assumption that one's own beliefs, perceptions, customs, and values are correct and that those of others are inferior.

____ 13.	Down syndrome is the most common cause of mental retardation in the United States.

____ 14.	Most children born with congenital anomalies (or birth defects) each year do not survive.

____ 15.	Mutations occur frequently during development.

MATCHING

Match the following proteins with the appropriate function and check your answers with the Answer Key at the end of this chapter.

1. ____ Antibodies

a.	Speed(s) up the chemical reactions within cells

2. ____ Collagen

b.	Control(s) the glucose level in the blood

3. ____ Contractile Proteins

c.	Form(s) the basis for connective tissue in the body

4. ____ DNA

d.	Form(s) the muscles

5. ____ Enzymes

e.	Protect(s) the body from disease

6. ____ Hemoglobin

f.	Control(s) physical growth and adjust(s) the body under stress

7. ____ Hormones

g.	Serve(s) in gene expression

8. ____ Insulin

h.	Transport(s) oxygen in the blood

KEY VOCABULARY TERMS

Label each definition with the appropriate term.

1. The reproductive cells (ova and sperm) that are formed by the process of meiosis.

2. A phenomenon in which gene expression and phenotype depend on which parent the genes come from.

3. An alteration in the DNA that usually occurs during mitosis or meiosis and is transmitted to subsequent cells through cell division.

4. This refers to the genetic code of a given individual.

5. A method that uses conditional procedures – such as reinforcement, reward, and shaping – to change behavior.

Explain the difference between the following sets of terms.

6. gene; chromosome
7. mitosis; meiosis
8. dominant; recessive
9. self-concept; self-efficacy
10. normative age-graded influences; normative history-graded influences

PROGRAMMED REVIEW

Fill in the blanks in the following programmed review. Then check your answers with the Answer Key at the end of the chapter.

Molecular Genetics
<u>Human Cells</u>

1. The cell contains many parts. The _____ is the cell's powerhouse, processing nutrients and producing energy. Proteins are produced by these three cell structures: 1) _____; 2) _____; and 3) _____. DNA is contained in the cell's _____.

<u>DNA</u>

2. The molecules contained in DNA are arranged in the shape of a twisted ladder also called _____. The ladder contains building blocks called _____, each of which consists of a phosphate molecule and a _____ molecule and one of four nitrogen-carbon-hydrogen bases, which include _____, _____, _____, and _____.

3. Because bases combine in a restricted way (adenine with thymine and cytosine with guanine), the differences in DNA across species and across individuals within the same species arise because of three types of variation: 1) _____; 2) _____; and 3) _____.

Genes

4. A gene is typically composed of _____ base pairs.

Protein Synthesis

5. Proteins are synthesized (or built) by _____. During protein synthesis, _____ results in a mirror-image copy of the DNA molecule that is "unzipped," which is referred to as _____.

6. When messenger RNA (mRNA) exits the cell, it is called _____ and is processed by _____, resulting in the release of strings of molecules called _____.

Genes, Chromosomes, and Cell Division

7. All human cells, except sperm and ova, contain exactly _____ chromosomes arranged in _____ pairs.
8. The first 22 pairs are referred to as _____. The final pair are _____ chromosomes.
9. Visual inspections of DNA can be carried out on a _____, which is a photograph of a cell's chromosome pairs arranged according to _____.

Cell Division and Reproduction

10. During meiosis, _____ are produced. In males, meiosis takes place in the _____; in females, meiosis takes place in the _____ before _____.

From Genotype to Phenotype

11. The sex chromosomes are the _____ pair. An individual having XX as sex chromosomes is a _____; an individual having XY as sex chromosomes is a _____.

12. A person may inherit a recessive gene for blue eyes and a dominant gene for brown eyes. The trait of eye color is expressed in that person as brown eyes. Brown is the person's _____.

13. A person may inherit a dominant gene for brown eyes and a recessive gene for blue eyes. Such a person is said to be _____ for that trait. On the other hand, if a person inherits two dominant genes for brown eyes or two recessive genes for blue eyes, the person is said to be _____ for that trait.

14. It is possible for a person with one parent with blood type A and the other parent with blood type B to inherit the blood type AB. In this way, blood type is an example of a trait in which alleles can be _____.

The Variation of Traits Among Individuals

15. Individual variation can occur during meiosis when genetic material randomly crosses over and is exchanged between chromosomes, resulting in a unique new _____. Furthermore, in the final stage of meiosis, _____ determines which half of the chromosome pairs will go into which sperm or ovum. This process is called _____.

Genetic and Chromosomal Disorders

16. Prenatal death or _____ can result from _____ that seriously disrupt development.

Sex-linked disorders

17. A recessive gene on the _____ is much more likely to be expressed as traits in males and females because the _____ has an allele that might counteract the gene.

Autosomal Disorders

18. Trisomy 21 refers to the disorder known as _____, which results in mental retardation, characteristic facial features, and health problems.

19. There are complexities in how genetic disorders manifest; the phenomenon of _____ refers to the fact that how an individual's traits (phenotype) express themselves depend on whether the genes were inherited from the mother or the father.

Genetic Counseling

20. The typical person's DNA contained _____ potentially lethal recessive genes.

21. A couple planning on having a child can consult _____ in order to evaluate their chances of having a child with a genetic problem.

Advances in Genetic Research and Treatment

22. Highly sophisticated procedures in which DNA is extracted from cell nuclei and cleaved (cut) into segments by selected enzymes is referred to as _____.

23. Attempts to alter the molecular structure of DNA as a means of curing or treating a disease is referred to as _____.

Behavior Genetics

24. The degree to which a genetic trait is expressed is viewed as being influenced by _____.

Adoption Studies

25. Adoption studies can enable researchers to measure the extent to which children resemble their biological versus adoptive parents. Similarities with adoptive parents are viewed as resulting from _____; similarities with biological parents are viewed as resulting from _____.

26. Research has shown that divorce is disruptive for most children, but it is more problematic for _____ children than for _____ children.

Twin Studies

27. Individuals with identical genetic make-up (identical twins) are more similar in intelligence than fraternal twins and ordinary siblings. Three other traits that have been shown to be inherited are 1) _____; 2) _____; and 3) _____.

Environmental Influences and Contexts

28. When psychologists use the word environment, they are referring to all of the factors, except _____.

Basic Processes That Affect Behavior

29. One of the simplest types of learning involves learning to stop attending to a stimulus in the environment; this type of learning is called _____.

30. The type of learning that occurs through repeated instances of a response co-occurring with some neutral stimulus is called _____.

31. A third type of learning is _____, which involves decreasing unwanted behaviors through the application of _____ and the increasing of desired behaviors through the application of _____.

Conditioning, Behavior Modification, and Life

32. Psychologists use techniques derived from conditioning principles to help individuals reduce undesired behaviors or to increase desired behaviors through applications called _____.

Social Learning and the Evolving Self-Concept

33. Cognitive processes and social learning are intimately involved in one's development of beliefs and feelings about oneself. This is referred to as one's _____. When one believes he or she is capable and competent and can generally accomplish tasks, one is said to have a strong _____.

Environment in a Broader Context: Family and Culture

34. Each child has a unique experience in the world, referred to as the _____, which has three components: 1) _____; 2) _____; and 3) _____.

Family Systems

35. Members of the same family have _____ experiences in common, but also have a significant amount of _____ experiences.

The Family as Transmitter of Culture

36. Individuals are taught to function as members of social groups (e.g., families, communities, work and friendship groups) in a lifelong process called _____.

Sociocultural Influences on Development Across the Lifespan

37. Children and older adults are often more strongly affected by _____ influences; adolescents and young adults are more strongly affected by _____ influences.

CRITICAL THINKING QUESTIONS

To further your mastery of the topics, write out the answers to the following essay questions in the space provided.

1. What has been learned about the composition of human deoxyribonucleic acid (DNA)? What elements make up DNA? How are these elements arranged?

2. What occurs during the process of mitosis and the process of meiosis? How do the processes of mitosis and meiosis differ?

3. What are genes? How are an individual's genes inherited from each of the parents?

4. Describe the relationship between genes and human characteristics. Can single genes produce specific characteristics?

5. What differences exist in the genetic code of males and females? What impact do these differences have on the development of human characteristics?

6. Describe how chromosomal anomalies might affect an individual during development.

7. Discuss how studies of identical twins and fraternal friends have informed our understanding of the role of genetics and environment in aggressiveness, personality, and intelligence.

8. What is the key difference between sex-linked disorders and autosomal disorders?

9. Discuss the difference between dominant and recessive genes. What must occur in order for a recessive gene to be expressed?

PRACTICE TEST – POST TEST

Circle the correct answer for each multiple choice question and check your answers with the Answer Key at the end of the chapter.

1. Which of the following is NOT one of the four nitrogen-carbon-hydrogen bases that make up DNA?
   a. Adrenalin
   b. Thymine
   c. Cytosine
   d. Guanine

2. Human DNA is composed of how many base pairs?
   a. 312
   b. 3,120
   c. 3.12 million
   d. 3.12 billion

3. A single human gene is composed of about how many base pairs?
   a. Anywhere from 1 to several dozen
   b. Anywhere from several dozen to 100
   c. Anywhere from 100 to 1000
   d. Anywhere from several hundred to several million

4. Which of the following is NOT contained in a nucleotide?
   a. base
   b. enzyme
   c. phosphate molecule
   d. sugar molecule

5. What percentage of human DNA is the same for all people (whose development is normal)?
   a. .1%
   b. 50%
   c. 100%
   d. 99.9%

6. Enzymes, Insulin, and Hemoglobin are examples of which of the following?
   a. bases
   b. phosphates
   c. nucleotides
   d. proteins

7. This process results in the formation of gametes, which are the ova in the female and sperm in the male.
   a. meiosis
   b. gene imprinting
   c. transcription
   d. mitosis

8. A mother and a father have four children (biological not adopted). All four children have blue eyes. Which of the following statements must be true?
   a. Each parent has brown eyes, but also has a recessive gene for blue eyes.
   b. Both parents have brown eyes, but only one has a recessive gene for blue eyes.
   c. One parent has blue eyes, and the other has brown eyes, with a recessive gene for blue eyes.
   d. Both parents have blue eyes.

9. All newborns in the United States are routinely screened for this autosomal disorder.
   a. huntington's disease
   b. prader-willi Syndrome
   c. color blindness
   d. phenylketonuria (PKU)

10. When a child's genetic makeup includes features not present in either parent, then a _____ has occurred.
   a. transcription
   b. karyotype
   c. mutation
   d. meisosis

11. Which of the following is NOT a sex-linked disorder?
   a. down syndrome
   b. hemophilia
   c. fragile X syndrome
   d. color blindness

12. Sex-linked traits are determined by genes on which chromosome pair?
    a. 4th   c. 21st
    b. 11th   d. 23rd

13. Individuals with this syndrome have a functional X chromosome, but either a missing or inactive second X chromosome.
    a. klinefelter syndrome   c. superfemale syndrome
    b. fragile X syndrome   d. turner syndrome

14. Which of the following disorders is the most common in the U.S.?
    a. down syndrome   c. cystic fibrosis
    b. sickle-cell anemia   d. huntington's disease

15. Which of the following disorders occurs due to the expression of genes from the mother?
    a. prader-willi syndrome   c. fragile X syndrome
    b. angelman syndrome   d. down syndrome

16. Research suggests that a portion of intelligence is inherited. What percentage of an individual's intelligence is generally believed to be due to genetics?
    a. 10% or less   c. around 75%
    b. around 50%   d. over 90%

17. Sometimes a person will develop a general fear of something, such as bees, after a specific incident, as after a single bee sting. This type of generalization can be the result of which of the following?
    a. classical conditioning   c. operant conditioning
    b. punishment   d. habituation

18. A teenager breaks his curfew, and his parents take away his driving privileges. This parental response is an example of which of the following?
    a. positive reinforcement   c. negative reinforcement
    b. negative punishment   d. positive punishment

19. When one group of individuals view another group of individuals as inferior because of differences in religious views, which of the following has occurred?
    a. normative history-graded influence c. genetic-cultural bias
    b. ethnocentrism   d. nonnormative influence

20. Which of the following is an example of a normative history-graded influence on development?
    a. retirement   c. economic depression
    b. career change   d. unemployment

ANSWER KEYS

Practice Test - Pretest (with text page numbers)

1.	d 47	6.	b 49	11.	b 56	16.	d 58
2.	a 45	7.	a 49	12.	a 59	17.	c 64
3.	b 48	8.	d 52	13.	d 54	18.	d 67
4.	c 45	9.	c 54	14.	a 56	19.	a 71
5.	b 47	10.	b 54	15.	b 56	20.	c 72

True/False

1.	T	6.	T	11.	F
2.	F	7.	F	12.	F
3.	F	8.	F	13.	F
4.	T	9.	F	14.	F
5.	T	10.	T	15.	T

Matching

1.	e	5.	a
2.	c	6.	h
3.	d	7.	f
4.	g	8.	b

Key Vocabulary Terms

1. gametes
2. gene imprinting
3. mutation
4. genotype
5. behavior modification

6. A <u>gene</u> is the basic unit of heritance that may be several hundred to several million base pairs long; a <u>chromosome</u> is a chain of genes visible under a microscope.

7. <u>Mitosis</u> is the process of cell division during which the DNA strands unwind and pull apart, then new base pairs attach to each half of the original chromosome, creating two identical chromosomes; <u>meiosis</u> is the process by which gametes (ova and sperm) are formed, each having one half of a full set of chromosomes.

8. <u>Dominant</u> genes need only to be present in a pair in order to express the trait; <u>Recessive</u> genes are expressed only when the other gene in the pair is also recessive.

9. <u>Self-concept</u> is one's beliefs and feelings about oneself; <u>self-efficacy</u> is what a person believes he or she is capable of doing in a given situation.

10. <u>Normative age-graded influences</u> include those biological and social changes that normally happen at predictable ages during the lifespan; <u>normative history-graded influences</u> include those historical events that affect large numbers of people in similar ways.

Programmed Review

1. mitochondria, ribosomes, Golgi apparatus, endoplasmic reticulum (these three can be in any order), nucleus
2. double helix, nucleotides, sugar, adenine, thymine, cytosine, and guanine (the last four can be in any order)
3. which side of the ladder each base comes from, the order in which the base pairs occur along the ladder, and the overall number of base pairs in the nucleotide (these three can be in any order)
4. several hundred to several million
5. genes, transcription, messenger RNA (mRNA)
6. transfer RNA (tRNA), ribosomes, polypetide chains
7. 46, 23
8. autosomes, sex
9. karyotype, size
10. gametes (ova and sperm), testes, ovaries, birth
11. 23rd, female, male
12. phenotype
13. heterozygous, homozygous
14. codominant
15. recombinant alleles, chance, independent assortment
16. spontaneous abortion, mutations
17. X chromosome, Y chromosome
18. down syndrome
19. gene imprinting
20. 5 to 8
21. genetic counseling
22. recombinant DNA technology
23. gene therapy
24. environmental influences
25. environment, genes
26. biological, adopted
27. emotionality, activity level, and sociability
28. genes
29. habituation
30. classical conditioning
31. operant condition, punishment, reinforcements (or rewards)
32. behavior modification
33. self concept, self-efficacy
34. developmental niche, physical and social setting, childcare and child-rearing customs, and overall psychology of care-givers
35. shared, non-shared
36. socialization
37. age-graded, history-graded

Practice Test – Post Test (with text page numbers)

1. a 45	6. d 47	11. a 54	16. b 62
2. d 46	7. a 49	12. d 52	17. a 64
3. d 47	8. d 51	13. d 54	18. c 65
4. b 45	9. c 56	14. b 56	19. b 70
5. d 46	10. c 52	15. a 57	20. c 72

Chapter 3

Prenatal Development and Childbirth

CHAPTER OUTLINE

◈ Prenatal Growth and Development
- ♦ Trimesters and Periods
- ♦ Conception and the Germinal Period
- ♦ The Embryonic Period
- ♦ The Fetal Period
- ♦ Developmental Trends

◈ Prenatal Environmental Influences
- ♦ Maternal Age
- ♦ Maternal Health and Nutrition
- ♦ Prenatal Health Care
- ♦ Critical Periods in Prenatal Development
- ♦ Teratogens and their Effects

◈ Childbirth
- ♦ Stages of Childbirth
- ♦ Approaches to Childbirth
- ♦ Advances in Technology
- ♦ Complications in Childbirth

◈ Evolving Family
- ♦ The Transition to Parenthood
- ♦ The Arrival of the Neonate

LEARNING OBJECTIVES

After you have read and studied this chapter, you should be able to answer the following questions.

1. What major developmental events take place in each of the three prenatal periods of development?
2. How do various risk factors and protective factors affect the course of prenatal development?
3. What is a "critical period" in development?
4. What sequence of events unfold during a normal childbirth?
5. With the arrival of a new baby, how do mother, father, and newborn adjust?

PRACTICE TEST – PRETEST

Circle the correct answer for each multiple choice question and check your answers with the Answer Key at the end of the chapter.

1. The length of the typical pregnancy is:
   a. 6 months
   b. 8 month
   c. 9 months
   d. 11 months

2. There is a tendency for an infant to react to a stimulus with generalized, whole-body movements at first, with responses becoming more localized later. This trend is referred to as which of the following?
   a. body-in-toto trend
   b. cephalocaudal trend
   c. proximodistal trend
   d. sgross-to-specific trend

3. The fetal period of development occurs during which of the following?
   a. conception through 2 weeks
   b. weeks 2 through 8 weeks
   c. weeks 9 through 38 weeks
   d. weeks 39 through 52 weeks

4. Women who maintain a healthy diet typically gain how many total pounds during their pregnancy?
   a. 25 to 35 pounds
   b. 15 to 25 pounds
   c. 10 to 15 pounds
   d. 8 to 10 pounds

5. When infants reach the age of viability at 24 weeks, they have about a _____ percent chance of surviving outside of the uterus if given high-quality medical treatment.
   a. 90
   b. 70
   c. 50
   d. 10

6. The number of sperm contained in each ejaculation is approximately:
   a. 3 thousand
   b. 30 thousand
   c. 300 thousand
   d. 300 million

7. Major defects in body structures can be caused by exposure to a toxic agent during which stage of pregnancy?
   a. germinal period
   b. embryo stage (3 to 8 weeks)
   c. fetal period (12 to 32 weeks)
   d. pre-birth period (32 to 38 weeks)

8. When does the typical fetus's brain produce electrical activity for the first time?
   a. weeks 1 to 2
   b. around week 16
   c. around week 24
   d. between weeks 36 and 38

9. During this period of fetal development, antibodies are passed from the mother to the fetus.
   a. weeks 1 to 2
   b. by week 16
   c. by week 24
   d. between weeks 36 and 38

10. Which of the following diseases that may affect the unborn child is NOT a sexually transmitted disease?
    a. rubella
    b. gonorrhea
    c. syphilis
    d. herpes simplex

11. During false labor, contractions typically go away or diminish:
    a. when the mother breathes deeply
    b. after 10 minutes
    c. when the mother walks
    d. after several minutes of abdominal massage

12. A midwife is a person who:
    a. is a type of medical doctor (MD) who specializes in the delivery of infants
    b. is a type of registered nurse (RN) who specializes in the delivery of infants
    c. is a type of nursing assistant who specializes in the delivery of infants
    d. is a person with or without formal training who assists in home delivery of infants

13. The term teratogen refers to which of the following:
    a. a toxic agent of any kind that potentially causes abnormalities in the development of the embryo/fetus
    b. a disease-causing bacteria or virus that potentially causes abnormalities in the development of the embryo/fetus
    c. a drug (legal or illegal) that potentially causes abnormalities in the development of the embryo/fetus
    d. an environmental pollutant that potentially causes abnormalities in the development of the embryo/fetus

14. Which of the following is an example of a primitive reflex?
   a. sucking
   b. swimming
   c. breathing
   d. blinking

15. This is the third leading cause of mental retardation in the United States.
   a. narcotic use during pregnancy
   b. malnutrition during pregnacy
   c. exposure to environmental toxins during pregnancy
   d. alcohol use during pregnancy

16. The newborn may suffer _____, which refers to a lack of oxygen that can cause brain damage.
   a. preeclampsia
   b. hypertension
   c. anoxia
   d. toxemia

17. Prior to birth, fetuses may position themselves upside down, causing the head to emerge last rather than first. This position is referred to as:
   a. cesarean
   b. breech
   c. chorionic
   d. preferred

18. The third stage of delivery is the discharging of the afterbirth. When does this typically occur?
   a. 2 days after the infant is born
   b. 1 day after the infant is born
   c. 10-20 hours after the infant is born
   d. 20 minutes after the infant is born

19. Which of the following is NOT a method used for prenatal screening?
   a. Apgar Scoring System
   b. amniocentesis
   c. ultrasound
   d. chorionic villus sampling

20. The reciprocal emotional bond that develops between a child and caregivers is referred to as which of the following?
   a. dependence
   b. attachment
   c. survival reflex
   d. primitive reflex

TRUE/FALSE

For each of the following statements indicate whether the statement is True or False. Check your answers with the Answer Key at the end of this chapter.

F 1.   In the United States, fewer than 10% of all pregnancies are unplanned.

T 2.   A trimester is a period of time equal to three months.

T 3.   Ovulation in the female typically occurs approximately 14 days after menstruation.

F 4.   Sperm can only survive in the vagina for 24 hours.

F 5.   Dizygotic twins have identical DNA.

F 6.   All of the structures that we recognize as human, such as arms, legs, and eyes, develop during the first two weeks of pregnancy.

F 7.   It is not until the 24th week (the end of the sixth month) of the pregnancy that there is electrical activity in the fetus's brain.

F 8.   The lowest risk for miscarriage and congenital anomalies is observed for mothers under the age of 20.

I 9.   Research has demonstrated that providing prenatal education to expectant mothers who otherwise would not receive it can reduce infant mortality rates and premature-birth rates.

I 10.   The brain and nervous system of the infant continue to develop several years after birth.

I 11.   Bacterial infections experienced by the mother during pregnancy have little or no impact on the developing fetus because bacteria cannot cross the placental barrier.

T 12.   Oral contraceptives (also known as the birth control pill) can cause abnormalities to occur in the developing fetus if taken during pregnancy.

F 13.   Even small amounts of alcohol consumption during pregnancy can lead to abnormalities in the fetus.

F 14.   During childbirth, when the mother's "water breaks" urine is involuntarily released.

F 15.   Pain medications do not cross the placental barrier, so women can receive pain medications as needed during childbirth and the infant is unaffected.

T 16.   Expectant mothers over the age of 35 routinely undergo amniocentesis in order to test for genetic abnormalities in the fetus.

I 17.   Many believe that the number of Caesarean sections (C-sections) performed in the United States is too high.

T 18.   Infants who are born prematurely are at higher risk for having learning disabilities and hyperactivity.

T 19.   Although Freud viewed birth as a traumatic experience for the newborn, modern psychologists do not believe that the process of birth places stress on the infant.

I 20. At birth, newborns do not possess any survival reflexes; rather, these reflexes emerge in two weeks following birth.

MATCHING

Match the following proteins with the appropriate function and check your answers with the Answer Key at the end of this chapter.

I 1. Amniocentesis

a. An incision made by the doctor during childbirth to enlarge the vaginal opening

h 2. Caesarean Section

b. A technique that uses sound waves to produce a picture of the fetus in the uterus

d 3. Chorionic Villus Sampling

c. A drug prescribed to expectant mothers for nausea during 1959 and 1960 that caused severe birth defects

A 4. Episiotomy

d. The withdrawal and analysis of cells from the membranes that surround the fetus, carried out with a syringe or catheter

e 5. Fontanel

e. The soft, bony plates of the skull, connected by cartilage

g 6. Forceps

f. A cup placed on the baby's head that is connected to a suction device and used to extract the baby from uterus

J 7. Kangaroo Care

g. Steel or plastic tongs used to grasp the baby's head in order to hasten birth

C 8. Thalidomide

h. Surgical procedure used to remove the baby and the placenta from the uterus by cutting through the abdominal wall

b 9. Ultrasound

i. The withdrawal and analysis of amniotic fluid with a syringe to obtain discarded fetal cells for testing

F 10. Vacuum Extractor

j. A technique used primarily with premature newborns that emphasizes close physical contact between infant and care-giver

KEY VOCABULARY TERMS

Look up the definition for each of the following types of terms.

1. blastula *Fluid Filled Sphere*
2. zygote *Fertilized ovum*
3. embryo *Developing Baby*

4. fetus *Pregnant Fruitful (French)*
5. age of viability *50% chance Survival*
6. neonate

Label each definition with the appropriate key term.

7. The disk-shaped tissue mass that forms along the wall of the uterus through which the embryo receives nutrients and discharges wastes.

8. The "rope" of tissue that connects the placenta to the embryo.

9. A fluid-filled membrane that encloses the developing embryo or fetus.

10. The structure that contains and nourishes the embryo and fetus.

11. In the female, these two passages carry ova from the ovary and allow fertilization to take place.

12. The soft, bony plates of the skull of the newborn that are connected by cartilage and harden relatively late in infancy.

Explain the difference between the following pairs of terms.

13. monozygotic twins; dizygotic twins
14. episiotomy; cesarean section
15. preterm status; small-for-date
16. miscarriage; spontaneous abortion
17. fertilization; differentiation
18. embryonic period; fetal period
19. cephalocaudal trend; proximodistal trend
20. survival reflexes; primitive reflexes

PROGRAMMED REVIEW

Fill in the blanks in the following programmed review. Then check your answers with the Answer Key at the end of the chapter.

Prenatal Growth and Development
Trimesters and Periods

1.   The duration of the normal pregnancy is _____ months, which is divided into _____ 3-month periods referred to as _____.

2.   During pregnancy, prenatal development is divided into three periods: 1) the _____ period; 2) the _____ period; and 3) the _____ period.

Conception and the Germinal Period

3.   The germinal period of prenatal development begins with _____ and ends about _____ later when the _____ is implanted in the wall of the _____.

4.   During ovulation, the _____ travels down one of the two _____ where it can survive for _____.

5.   The typical adult male may produce as many as _____ sperm cells in a day, and as many as _____ may be expelled during a single ejaculation. During sexual intercourse, sperm deposited into the vagina may survive for as long as _____.

6.   About one week following conception, the 1-cell zygote is divided into a ball of many cells, which is referred to as a _____. This ball of cells burrows into the lining of the _____, breaking _____ to obtain nutrients. The cells begin to separate into groups according to their future function. This process is called _____. It is at this point that supporting structures begin to secrete a detectable hormone called _____, which shuts down _____ and prevents the next _____.

7.   During the first two weeks following conception, _____ percent of all fertilized eggs may be lost. In the U.S., for those pregnancies that reach the third week, _____ percent will be lost through miscarriage, _____ will be aborted, and _____ will be carried to full-term and result in a live-birth.

The Embryonic Period

8. The embryonic period extends from _____ to _____. During this period, the supporting structures differentiate into the _____, the _____, and the _____, which serve to provide nourishment to the developing baby.

9. The embryonic disk develops into three distinct layers: 1) the _____ or outer layer, which will ultimately develop into the _____, the _____, and the _____; 2) the _____ or middle layer, which will become _____, ____, and the _____ system ; and 3) the _____ or inner layer, which will develop into the _____, _____, _____, _____, and other organs.

10. Considering the numbers of male and female embryos conceived, females are conceived _____ often than males, and miscarriages (or spontaneous abortions) occur _____ frequently for male embryos and for female embryos.

The Fetal Period

11. The fetal period lasts from _____ to _____. During this time, the developing child may reach the point at which there is a 50 percent chance of survival outside of the womb. This occurs at the _____ week and is referred to as the _____. The chance of survival outside of the womb increases dramatically in the following weeks. By the 25th week, the survival rate is _____ percent. By the 28th week, the survival rate is _____ percent.

Developmental Trends

12. Development occurs in a systematic fashion. Three trends have been identified: 1) _____, which refers to the fact that growth occurs first in the _____ and proceeds _____ in the body; 2) _____, which refers to the fact that growth occurs first at the _____ of the body and proceeds _____; and 3) _____, which refers to the fact that the body reacts to stimulation with _____ movements first and more localized responses later.

Prenatal Environmental Influences

Maternal Age

13. The chance of a miscarriage (or spontaneous abortion) increases dramatically with the age of the mother. For mothers between the ages of 20 and 24, the miscarriage rate was _____ percent. For mothers over the age of 40, the miscarriage rate was _____ percent. For mothers over the age of 45, the miscarriage rate was _____ percent. Children born to older mothers are at a higher risk for having _____.

Maternal Health and Nutrition

14. A mother in good health can expect to gain _____ pounds during a pregnancy. Malnutrition can have a detrimental effect on the developing child, causing _____, _____, _____, and _____. Babies who have suffered fetal malnutrition are predisposed to later health problems, including _____, _____, _____, and _____.

Prenatal Health Care

15. Two predictors of delivering a healthy, full-term baby is _____ and _____ or more visits to a doctor or health-care facility.

Critical Periods in Prenatal Development

16. Toxic agents, such as chemical agents from air or water pollution, diseases, or drugs, are called _____ and can negatively impact the developing child. Major defects in structure, such as the heart, can occur during the _____. Physiological defects and minor defects in structure, such as the neurological system, can occur during the _____.

Teratogens and their Effects

17. Diseases contracted by the mother can be passed along to the developing child by several routes, including 1) through the _____, which occurs in _____ and _____ infection; 2) through the _____, which occurs in _____ and _____ infection; and 3) through exchange of blood or bodily fluids.

18. Unfortunately, it is common for pregnant women to ingest alcohol, in spite of the fact that any exposure to alcohol poses health risks for the unborn child. Research shows that 1 in _____ women of childbearing age reported drinking _____ drinks per week or _____ or more drinks in one sitting. This type of drinking is called _____. Furthermore, 1 in _____ women who knows she is pregnant reports this type of drinking.

19. Children born to mothers who drink alcohol during pregnancy are at higher risk for developing _____, _____, and _____.

20. Smoking during pregnancy can cause abnormalities in the developing child. Heavy smokers are at a higher risk for _____, _____, and _____. Children born to smokers tend to _____ and showed delayed growth when compared to children born to non-smokers. Research shows that smoking can affect blood vessels in the _____, reducing the flow of _____.

21. Children of cocaine-using mothers are at greater risk for developing _____, _____, and _____.

Childbirth

Stages of Childbirth

22. The process of childbirth is generally divided into three separate stages:
1) _____, which begins when the uterus begins to dilate and contractions are spaced _____ minutes apart; 2) _____, which occurs when the cervix is fully dilated and contractions are spaced _____ minutes apart; and 3) _____, which involves the discharging of the _____, _____, and other tissues.

23. Several steps can be taken by medical personnel to help the infant be expelled from the uterus. The region between the mother's vagina and _____ can be cut in order to enlarge the opening. This procedure is referred to as _____. Tongs can be used to grasp the infant's _____. These instruments are called _____. Cups connected to a suction device may also be placed on the infant's _____. This device is called _____.

Approaches to Childbirth

24. In most western nations, the percentage of children born at home was _____ percent in 1930, but decreased to _____ percent in 1990.

25. A modern alternative to traditional childbirth, which takes place in a _____, is _____, which involves the use of a birthing _____, relatively few _____, and a focus on relaxing and _____ control.

Advances in Technology

26. In order to determine whether an unborn fetus is developing normally, _____ may be used. The least invasive technique is the _____, which involves generating and recording high-frequency sound waves that are passed over the abdomen of the mother using a wand. A more risky procedure is _____, which involves the withdrawal of fluid from the amniotic sac.

27. In cases where a serious genetic abnormality is suspected, _____ can be used. At around _____ weeks after conception, cells can be drawn from the membranes surrounding the _____.

28. The use of _____ fetal monitors has been associated with unnecessary _____. When such monitors are used, a _____ containing _____ is inserted into the vagina and attached to the baby's _____ for the purpose of measuring uterine pressure, fetal breathing, head compression, umbilical compression, and fetal oxygen intake.

Complications in Childbirth

29. One common type of complication that occurs during childbirth is when the baby enters the birth canal in a position _____ the mother's abdomen rather than her _____. This position is referred to as _____.

30. As the numbers of cesarean sections in the United States increase, research also shows that mothers who undergo the procedure report experiencing difficulties following delivery, including _____, _____, _____, and _____.

31. In hospitals, the condition of the newborn is measured 1 minute following birth and again 5 minutes following birth using _____. The newborn's pulse, breathing, muscle tone, general reflex response, and general skin tone is scored. A perfect score is _____, with a score higher than _____ considered normal.

32. Infants are considered premature or _____ if delivered before the _____ week of the pregnancy. Infants born prematurely are at higher risk for _____ and _____.

Evolving Family

The Transition to Parenthood

33. Expectant fathers may go through a phase when they identify with their pregnant partner, experiencing _____, _____, _____, or _____.

The Arrival of the Neonate

34. In the last few moments of birth, infants experience a surge of _____ and _____, which are hormones that reduce _____.

35. The hormone _____ helps prepare the _____, which are initially filled with _____, to breathe.

36. Most newborns are alert and reactive for about _____ following birth; at birth, they tend to have _____ levels of a natural pain killer called _____ in their bloodstream.

37. When the newborn begins breathing, the heart no longer needs to pump oxygen-rich blood to the _____. A valve in the baby's _____ closes and redirects the flow of blood to the _____. These changes in the circulatory system are not completed for _____ after birth.

CRITICAL THINKING QUESTIONS

To further your mastery of the topics, write out the answers to the following essay questions in the space provided.

1. Describe the processes involved in the germinal period of a pregnancy from the release of the ovum in the female to implantation of the blastula.

2. Discuss the relationship that has been shown to exist between the age of the mother and risk of miscarriage risk and health of the infant.

3. Discuss how a pregnant woman's exposure to various substances (teratogens and drugs) can influence the development of the developing embryo/fetus.

4. Discuss the differences in traditional childbirth procedures and natural child birth procedures.

5. Describe the multiple stages of childbirth, detailing the major events including initial delivery, labor, delivery and afterbirth.

6. Discuss the three ways by which a disease present in the mother may be passed to the fetus or newborn infant.

7. Describe the various procedures that are used to monitor the health of the unborn child during pregnancy.

8. Describe the differences and similarities in infants who are born prematurely and infants who are full-term, but who are small or underweight.

9. What is the Apgar Scoring System? How are scores computed? What factors are related to an infant receiving a "good" score versus a "bad" score?

10. Discuss how both mothers and fathers differ in their adjustment to the birth of a child.

PRACTICE TEST – POST TEST

Circle the correct answer for each multiple choice question and check your answers with the Answer Key at the end of the chapter.

1. Which of the following milestones occurs last in the developing fetus?
   a. sense of taste is formed
   b. fingers and toes are formed
   c. begins to respond to sounds
   d. eyes are completely formed

2. The typical (normally-developing) fetus weighs over 1 pound by which of the following weeks of pregnancy?
   a. 12 weeks
   b. 24 weeks
   c. 28 weeks
   d. 32 weeks

3. The digestive system, lungs, and other internal organs develop from which of the following layers of cells present in the embryo?
   a. ectoderm
   b. mesoderm
   c. endoderm
   d. zygoderm

4. Approximately _____ percent of all fertilized eggs fail to become implanted in the uterus.
   a. 10
   b. 30 to 50
   c. 50 to 70
   d. 90

5. A fetus delivered at this week of pregnancy can typically survive without intensive medical intervention.
   a. the 16th week
   b. the 20th week
   c. the 24th week
   d. the 32nd week

6. Exposure to toxins during weeks 3 to 5 during a pregnancy may result in which of the following types of defects?
   a. brain
   b. ears
   c. heart
   d. genitalia

7. Which of the following sequences represents the typical infant's development?
   a. baby can control arms first, followed by hands, followed by fingers
   b. baby can control fingers first, followed by hands, followed by arms
   c. baby can control fingers first, followed by arms, followed by hands
   d. baby can control arms first, followed by fingers, followed by hands

8. The typical normal pregnancy has how many trimesters?
   a. 1
   b. 2
   c. 3
   d. 4

9. The germinal period during which the fertilized egg begins to divide begins _____ after fertilization.
   a. 24 hours
   b. 48 hours
   c. 1 week
   d. 2 weeks

10. Which of the following substances when used by a pregnant women has NOT been associated with fetal abnormalities?
    a. tobacco
    b. alcohol
    c. cocaine
    d. none of the above – all are associated with fetal abnormalities

11. Which of the following is the first to develop in the embryo/fetus?
    a. nervous system
    b. digestive system
    c. circulatory system
    d. respiratory system

12. The fetal period of prenatal development occurs:
    a. from conception to birth
    b. from conception to the end of the 2nd month
    c. from the end of the 1st month to birth
    d. from the end of the 2nd month to birth

13. The teeth form under the gums of the unborn embryo/fetus around this week of the pregnancy:
    a. 12th
    b. 24th
    c. 32nd
    d. not until after birth

14. Pregnant mothers who are malnourished are at an increased risk of having a baby with which of the following problems?
    a. deformed genitalia
    b. hyperactivity
    c. deformed eyes
    d. heart disease

15. In sub-Saharan Africa, approximately _____ percent of pregnant women carry the virus that causes AIDS (i.e., HIV).
    a. 100
    b. 40
    c. 10
    d. 60

16. Which of the following poses no risk to the developing child if consumed by the mother during pregnancy?
    a. oral contraceptives
    b. aspirin
    c. cough syrup
    d. none of the above – all pose some risk

17. The typical length of initial labor varies between a few minutes to as many as _____ hours.
    a. 100
    b. 60
    c. 30
    d. 2

18. The procedure referred to as amniocentesis is not performed until this week of pregnancy:
    a. 15th
    b. 20th
    c. 24th
    d. 32nd

19. When infants are held upright with their feet against a surface and are moved forward, they appear to walk in a coordinated way. This reflex is referred to as:
    a. palmar reflex
    b. stepping reflex
    c. babinski reflex
    d. walking reflex

20. Which of the following is NOT a survival reflex present in newborns?
    a. gagging
    b. sneezing
    c. sucking
    d. kicking

ANSWER KEYS

Practice Test - Pretest (with text page numbers)

1. c 80	6. d 81	11. c 97	16. c 94
2. d 86	7. b 89	12. d 97	17. b 101
3. c 81	8. c 84	13. a 89	18. d 97
4. a 87	9. d 84	14. b 108	19. a 99
5. c 83	10. a 91	15. d 93	20. b 107

True/False

1. F	6. F	11. T	16. T
2. T	7. T	12. T	17. T
3. T	8. F	13. T	18. T
4. F	9. T	14. F	19. T
5. T	10. T	15. F	20. F

Matching

1. i	6. g
2. h	7. j
3. d	8 c
4. a	9. b
5. e	10. f

Key Vocabulary Terms

7. placenta
8. umbilical cord
9. amniotic sac
10. uterus
11. fallopian tubes
12. fontanels

13. <u>Monozygotic</u> twins have the same DNA, because they develop from the same single fertilized ovum; <u>dizygotic</u> twins have different DNA, because each twin develops from a unique fertilized ovum.

14. A doctor performs an <u>Episiotomy</u> by cutting the bottom of the vagina to enlarge the opening, allowing the infant to exit; a doctor performs a <u>cesarean section</u> by cutting into the abdominal wall and uterus to remove the infant and placenta.

15. <u>Preterm status</u> is used to describe an infant born before the 35th week of the pregnancy; <u>Small-for-date</u> is used to describe an infant who goes full term (38 weeks), but who weighs less than 5 pounds, 8 ounces.

16. A <u>miscarriage</u> and a <u>spontaneous abortion</u> refer to the same event – the loss or expulsion of a pregnancy before it is viable.

17. <u>Fertilization</u> occurs when the sperm penetrates the ovum; <u>differentiation</u> occurs when the single-celled zygote created from the union of the ovum and sperm begins dividing, drastically increasing the number of cells present.

18. The <u>embryonic</u> period is the second period of prenatal development, lasting from implantation to the end of the second month; the <u>fetal period</u> is the final period of prenatal development, lasting from the end of the second month to birth.

19. The sequence of growth that occurs first in the head and progresses downward is referred to as the <u>cephalocaudal</u> trend; the sequence of growth that occurs from the midline of the body outward is referred to as the <u>proximodistal trend</u>.

20. <u>Survival reflexes</u> are biologically programmed behaviors that are related to the infant's ability to survive, such as breathing, rooting, and sucking; <u>primitive reflexes</u> are also biologically programmed behaviors; however, they do not have a direct link to survival of the infant. Primitive reflexes may be related to survival in the evolutionary past of humans.

Programmed Review
1. nine, three, trimesters
2. germinal, embryonic, and fetal
3. fertilization (or conception), 2 weeks, fertilized egg (or zygote), uterus
4. mature ovum (egg), fallopian tubes, 3 to 5 days
5. one billion, 300 million, 2 to 3 days
6. blastula, uterus, blood vessels, differentiation, human chorionic gonadotropin (hcg), ovulation, and menstrual period
7. 50 to 70, 16, 20, 64
8. implantation of the blastula, the end of the second month, placenta, umbilical cord, amniotic sac
9. ectoderm, skin, sense organs, brain and nervous system, mesoderm, muscles, blood, excretory, endoderm, digestive system, lungs, thyroid, thymus
10. less, more
11. the beginning of the third month, birth, 24th, age of viability, 75, 90
12. the cephalocaudal trend, head, downward, the proximodistal trend, midline, outward, the gross-to-specific trend, whole-body
13. 9, 50, 75, Down Syndrome
14. 25 to 35, miscarriage, stillbirth, prematurity, low birth weight, hypertension, coronary heart disease, thyroid disease, schizophrenia
15. good nutrition, five
16. teratogens, embryonic period, fetal period
17. placenta, HIV, rubella, amniotic fluid, syphilis, gonorrhea,
18. 5, 5 to 7, 5, risk drinking, 30
19. learning disabilities, attention problems, hyperactivity
20. miscarriage, stillbirth, premature delivery, weigh less, uterus, nutrients
21. attention deficit disorder, language delays, learning disabilities.
22. initial labor, 15 to 20, labor and delivery, 2 to 3, after birth, placenta, umbilical cord

23. rectum, episiotomy, head, forceps, head, vacuum extractor
24. 80, 1
25. hospital or medical facility, natural childbirth, coach, medication, breathing
26. prenatal screening, ultrasound, amniocentesis
27. chorionic villus sampling (cvs), 8 to 12, fetus
28. internal, cesarean section, plastic tube, electrodes, head
29. facing, back, breech presentation
30. feeling disappointed or angry, taking longer to choose a name for the baby, having lower self-esteem shortly after delivery, having difficulty feeding infant
31. The Apgar Scoring System, 10, 7
32. preterm status, 35th, learning disabilities, hyperactivity
33. nausea, diarrhea, vomiting, cramps
34. adrenaline, noradrenaline, stress
35. adrenaline, lungs, fluid
36. one hour, high, beta-endorphin
37. placenta, heart, lungs, several days

Practice Test – Post Test (with text page numbers)

1. c 84	6. c 89	11. a 82	16. d 92
2. b 84	7. a 86	12. d 83	17. c 96
3. a 82	8. c 80	13. a 84	18. a 99
4. c 82	9. b 81	14. d 87	19. c 108
5. d 84	10. a 94	15. b 90	20. d 107

Chapter 4

Infancy and Toddlerhood: Physical, Cognitive and Language Development

CHAPTER OUTLINE

◈ The Developing Brain

◈ The Neonatal Period
 ♦ States of Arousal
 ♦ Learning and Habituation
 ♦ Neonatal Assessment

◈ Physical and Motor Development
 ♦ Cultural Influences on Maturation
 ♦ An Overview of Physical and Motor Development: The First 2 Years
 ♦ Nutrition and Malnutrition

◈ Sensory and Perceptual Development
 ♦ Vision and Visual Perception
 ♦ Hearing and Auditory Perception
 ♦ Taste, Smell, and Touch
 ♦ Sensory Integration

◈ Cognitive Development
 ♦ Perceptual Organization and Categories
 ♦ Piaget's Concept of Schemas
 ♦ The Sensorimotor Period
 ♦ Evaluating Piaget's View

◈ Language Development
 ♦ The Structure and Function of Language
 ♦ Language Development in the First Year
 ♦ Words and Sentences
 ♦ The Language Explosion
 ♦ Telegraphic Speech and Early Grammar
 ♦ Theories of Language Development
 ♦ Cultural Aspects of Language Development

LEARNING OBJECTIVES

After you have read and studied this chapter, you should be able to answer the following questions.

1. How does the infant's brain change in the first two years of life?
2. What is habituation? How has researchers' understanding of habituation provided a means for studying how infants think?
3. How do sensory, perceptual, and motor abilities develop during the first two years of life?
4. How do infants develop the ability to think?
5. How do children learn to speak and to understand language?

PRACTICE TEST - PRETEST

Circle the correct answer for each multiple choice question and check your answers with the Answer Key at the end of the chapter.

1. In the classic experiment by Rosenzweig (1969), rats raised in interesting "enriched" environments developed _____ than rats raised in standard cages.
    a. smaller brains
    b. larger bodies
    c. smaller bodies
    d. heavier brains

2. Which of the following is NOT one of the six arousal states of the infant described by Wolf (1966)?
    a. crying
    b. drowsiness
    c. sobbing
    d. sleeping

3. The simple form of learning that allows newborns to ignore meaningless, repetitive sounds in the environment:
    a. habituation
    b. orientation
    c. arousal
    d. regulation

4. An infant's first tooth comes in around:
    a. 1 month
    b. 4 months
    c. 8 months
    d. 12 months

5. The infant develops the ability to control their hands and fingers to grasp objects around the age of:
    a. 2 months
    b. 3 to 4 months
    c. 5 to 8 months
    d. 9 to 12 months

6. Children around this age begin to imitate the behaviors of adults in play, talking on the phone, reading, or sweeping the floor.
    a. 5 to 8 months
    b. 9 to 12 months
    c. 13 to 18 months
    d. 19 to 24 months

7. A study investigating the nutrition of low-income families in the U.S. in 1994 showed that _____ percent of infants suffered from iron deficiency anemia.
   a. 1
   b. 10 to 12
   c. 20 to 24
   d. 90 to 95

8. The process of shifting the infant's diet from breast or bottle-feeding to eating and drinking a wider variety of foods is referred to as:
   a. solidifying
   b. marasmus
   c. de-breasting
   d. weaning

9. Which of the following is true regarding a newborn's visual processes?
   a. they can't see any color
   b. they like to look at faces
   c. near objects are blurry
   d. they tend to experience double vision

10. The translation of a stimulus into a neural impulse by a sense organ is referred to as:
   a. adaptation
   b. perception
   c. sensation
   d. assimilation

11. The Gesell scales summarize which of the following types of abilities?
   a. cognitive
   b. physical
   c. visual
   d. auditory

12. The words used by toddlers are most often:
   a. noun
   b. overextensions
   c. verbs
   d. sound effects, such as *quack quack*

13. Symbolic representation plays an important role in which of the following?
   a walking
   b. language
   c. sensation
   d. all of the above

14. Which of the following is the first to be fully developed in the infant?
   a. color vision
   b. hearing
   c. binocular vision
   d. depth perception

15. For typical children, object permanence is present from this age:
   a. 4 months
   b. 8 months
   c. 12 months
   d. 18 months

16. The neonatal period refers to:
   a. the month prior to an infant's birth
   b. the first month after birth
   c. the three months prior to birth
   d. the three months after birth

17. Regarding Piaget's theories, modern researchers believe he:
    a overemphasized motor development
    b. viewed object permanence as occurring later than it does
    c. viewed infants as less competent than they likely are
    d. all of the above

18. The infant begins babbling around what age?
    a. 2 months   c. 12 months
    b   6 months   d. 18 months

19. This term is used to describe the system of language involving phonemes, morphemes, semantics, and syntax:
    a. receptive language   c. productive language
    b   grammar   d   symbols

20. The view of language acquisition proposed by _____ assumes that children are biologically pre-wired to learn language.
    a. Noam Chomsky   c. Arnold Gessell
    b. Jean Piaget   d. T. Berry Brazelton

TRUE/FALSE

For each of the following statements indicate whether the statement is True or False. Check your answers with the Answer Key at the end of this chapter.

_____ 1.   The size of the brain does not change across the lifespan; the size of one's brain at birth is the size that the his or her brain will be as an adult.

_____ 2.   Before the age of 6 months, infants cry, but typically make no other noises.

_____ 3.   Motor development in infants is strongly influenced by the environment in which they are raised.

_____ 4.   Shaking an infant should never be done because it can result in permanent brain damage.

_____ 5.   Although obesity is a growing problem in the U.S., it is also the case that low-income families experience nutritional deficiencies.

_____ 6.   Across the world, malnutrition affects fewer than 10 percent of people (when all age groups are considered).

_____ 7.   Breast feeding a child until the age of 2 or 3 is extremely rare in countries around the world.

_____ 8. In developing nations, fifty percent of the deaths of children under the age of five are due to malnutrition.

_____ 9. At birth, the newborn's ability to see colors is equal to that of an adult.

_____ 10. At birth, newborns are able to imitate the facial expressions of others, such as sticking out the tongue, pursing the lips, and opening the mouth.

_____ 11. The sense of taste and smell are not fully developed at birth; by the sixth month of life, these senses are functioning at the adult level.

_____ 12. Newborns as young as 2 weeks prefer to look at photos of their mother versus an image of a stranger.

_____ 13. At birth, newborns are unable to hear normally; it takes up to 4 weeks for the anatomical structures in the ear involved in hearing to develop completely.

_____ 14. At birth, newborns are unable to feel pain, which makes procedures like circumcision painless to the child.

_____ 15. According to Piaget, the process of imitation requires the infant to have achieved a symbolic level of representation.

_____ 16. Before a child can produce a complex sentence, it is likely to be able to understand complex sentences.

_____ 17. All human languages have the same basic set of sounds or phonemes, which are arranged in various way to form words.

_____ 18. Researchers generally agree that learning experiences can explain everything about how language develops in children.

_____ 19. Infants who are deaf do not engage in the vocalizations referred to as babbling at all.

_____ 20. Deaf children who are not exposed to either spoken language or signed language can develop their own sign language system.

MATCHING

Match the following types of nutritional deficiency and the associated health affect on the children. Check your answers with the Answer Key at the end of this chapter.

_____ 1. iodine deficiency   a. anemia

_____ 2. iron deficiency   b. visual impairment or blindness

_____ 3. protein deficiency   c. deficits in brain development

_____ 4. calorie deficiency   d. wasting away of muscles

_____ 5. vitamin A deficiency   e. inability to hear or speak

Match the following types of linguistic terms with their definitions. Check your answers with the Answer Key at the end of this chapter.

_____ 6. Phonemes   a. how words are combined in sentences

_____ 7. Morphemes   b. how words and sentences sound

_____ 8. Semantic   c. how meaning is assigned

_____ 9. Syntax   d. basic units of meaning

KEY VOCABULARY TERMS

Label each definition with the appropriate term.

1. Rapid growth during infancy in the size of neurons, the number of glial cells, and the complexity of neural connections.

2. This term is used to refer to a failure to achieve full adult height due to malnutrition during childhood.

3. A grouping of different things that have some feature in common.

4. According to Piaget, the realization by infants beginning at about 8 months that objects continue to exist when they are out of sight.

5. Chomsky's term for an innate set of mental structures that aids children in language learning.

Explain the difference between the following sets of terms.

1. infancy; toddlerhood
2. fine motor skills; gross motor skills
3. sudden infant death syndrome; shaken baby syndrome
4. marasmus; kwashiorkor
5. sensation; perception
6. receptive language; productive language
7. preference paradigm; surprise paradigm
8. holophrastic speech; telegraphic speech

Give a brief description of each of the following techniques and methods.

9. habituation method
10. novelty paradigm
11. preference paradigm
12. surprise paradigm
13. event-related potential recording
14. brain imaging

PROGRAMMED REVIEW

Fill in the blanks in the following programmed review. Then check your answers with the Answer Key at the end of the chapter.

The Developing Brain

1. The child's brain is smaller than the adult brain, but develops rapidly in the first years of life. The adult brain contains approximately _____ neurons. At birth, the brain is _____ percent the size of the adult brain. By the end of the first year of life, the brain is _____ percent the size of the adult brain. By age three, the brain is _____ percent the size of the adult brain.

2. Connections between nerve cells or neurons are called _____. In the brain of the newborn, there are about _____ connections. By the age of 2 or 3, there are about _____ connections.

The Neonatal Period
<u>States of Arousal</u>

3. Wolf (1966) described six arousal states of the infant. These are _____, _____, _____, _____, _____, and _____.

Learning and Habituation

4. Newborns demonstrate _____, which is a simple form of learning that allows them to _____ meaningless, repetitive sounds in the environment.

5. To study the _____ capabilities of infants, researchers _____ infants to certain stimuli, then change the stimuli and observe the response. This technique is called the _____.

Neonatal Assessment

6. The Brazelton's Neonatal Behavioral Assessment Scale consists of _____ measures grouped into _____ clusters, which include habituation, orientation, reflexes, _____, _____, _____, and _____.

Physical and Motor Development

7. The Gesell Scales provide information about when and how average children begin crawling, walking, _____, _____, _____, _____, and _____.

Cultural Influences on Maturation

8. In the 1930s when Gesell conducted his observations of children, the average age of walking for typical children was _____; today children typically start walking _____. The difference in age of first walking is presumably due to changes in _____.

An Overview of Physical and Motor Development: The First 2 Years

9. By the age of _____, infants are able to pick up tiny objects with their thumb and _____, a skill that is referred to as the _____.

Nutrition and Malnutrition

10. The United Nations Children's Fund (UNICEF) has estimated that over _____ percent of children 5 years old or younger experience severe malnutrition known as _____, which refers to malnutrition so severe that it results in the child failing to achieve full adult _____.

11. Severe malnutrition in the first _____ months of life are rarely overcome later. Permanent deficits can be observed in _____. There may be delays in _____ and _____.

12. In populations in which protein malnutrition is observed, one is likely to find parents who are _____ and children who are _____.

13. For the first _____ months of life, _____ is the primary food that infants consume. Most doctors agree that a healthy, well-nourished mother's milk is _____ to that of commercial milk formulas.

14. In developing nations where infant mortality rates are high, bottle-fed babies are _____ times more likely to die from _____ and face a _____ time greater risk for death from _____.

Sensory and Perceptual Development
<u>Vision and Visual Perception</u>

15. Newborns are able to control their eye movements. However, objects more than _____ inches away appear blurred. Until the end of the _____ month of life, they cannot focus both eyes on a single point. By the _____ month, infants focus as well as adults.

16. Newborns are highly responsive to the human face. At _____ months, they look at the internal features of the face. At _____ months, they look more at the _____ of a person who is talking. By _____, they pay attention to the whole face and can distinguish _____.

17. By 3 to 4 months, infants can use _____, _____, and _____ to help define the objects in their world.

<u>Hearing and Auditory Perception</u>

18. The newborn is able to hear at birth, but hearing may be muffled due to _____ which is present in _____.

<u>Taste, Smell, and Touch</u>

19. As early as _____ old, the newborn can recognize the _____ of the mother.

<u>Sensory Integration</u>

20. Studies have shown that infants _____ old can accurately match male and female faces with voices; infants _____ old can accurately match facial expressions with the corresponding vocalizations, and infants as young as _____ can readily learn arbitrary pairings of sights and sounds.

Cognitive Development
Perceptual Organization and Categories

21. Children may be born with the ability to group objects in terms of their similarity. Research shows that children form groups or _____ for men and women's faces and voices as early as _____ of age and for animals and inanimate objects by _____.

Piaget's Concept of Schemas

22. Piaget was one of the most influential developmental theorists in the _____ century. He viewed the infant as an alert, active, and creative individual, who possess mental structures called _____.

The Sensorimotor Period

23. Piaget proposed that the building blocks for cognitive development are the innate, instinctive behavioral schemas, such as _____, _____, and _____.

24. According to Piaget, during the sensorimotor period, _____ schemas are transformed into the early concepts of _____, _____, and _____.

Evaluating Piaget's View

25. Most theorists today view infants as _____ competent than Piaget believed, but perhaps he overemphasized _____ development and did not emphasize enough _____ development.

Language Development
The Structure and Function of Language

26. All human languages contain _____ that are strung together according to each language's specific rules of _____.

Language Development in the First Year

27. By around 6 months, infants begin making nonsense vocalizations that involve the repetition of _____ referred to as _____. This process appears to help the infant learn the _____ of their language.

<u>Words and Sentences</u>

28. Learning new words allows the child to make finer _____ distinctions.

<u>The Language Explosion</u>

29. Around the age of _____ months, children typically experience a language explosion. Prior to the language explosion, children little attention to cues from _____ to determine whether new word is meant for them to learn.

<u>Telegraphic Speech and Early Grammar</u>

30. Toddlers can communicate quite effectively by producing short utterances of one or two words, when they also use _____, _____, and the context of the situation.

<u>Theories of Language Development</u>

31. Learning can explain how children acquire _____, which can be learned through hearing and _____. On the other hand, the development of _____ is difficult to explain.

<u>Cultural Aspects of Language Development</u>

32. Vocabularies of 2-year-olds have been found to be directly related to the amount of time the mother spends _____ and her wide use of _____.

CRITICAL THINKING QUESTIONS

To further your mastery of the topics, write out the answers to the following essay questions in the space provided.

1. Discuss why it is the case that children who suffer brain injuries are sometimes able to make remarkable recoveries.

2. Describe the motor abilities of infants between the ages of 5 to 8 months, specifically those involved in handling objects and in sitting, crawling, and standing.

3. Discuss how the developing infant may be permanently impaired because of lack of calories as well as lack of proper nutrition.

4. Describe the newborn's auditory and visual abilities at birth and how those abilities develop during the first year of life.

5. Children engage in pretend play from a very early age. Discuss when pretend play starts and how it becomes more complex as the child ages.

6. Describe Piaget's view of the child's first two years of life, which he referred to as the sensorimotor period. What do contemporary psychologists think about Piaget's views?

7. Describe how the infant's ability to produce speech develops over the first two years of life.

8. Describe Noam Chomsky's view of how language develops.

9. Discuss how breastfeeding practices vary around the world.

10. Describe the various brain imaging methods that researchers use.

PRACTICE TEST – POST TEST

Circle the correct answer for each multiple choice question and check your answers with the Answer Key at the end of the chapter.

1. These cells function to nourish neurons and enhance communication in the nervous system.
   a. synapses
   b. plasticites
   c. glia
   d. nuclei

2. Researchers use the habituation method to study which of the following capabilities of infants?
   a. perceptual
   b. respiratory
   c. digestive
   d. circulatory

3. Infants are typically sleeping through the night by the age of:
   a. 1 month
   b. 2 months
   c. 4 months
   d. 8 months

4. Which of the following aspects of the newborn's functioning is NOT assessed in the Brazelton Neonatal Behavioral Assessment Scale?
   a. responding to sound
   b. eating
   c. moving
   d. sleeping and waking

5. Infants begin to engage in social games, such as peek-a-boo, bye-bye, and patty-cake at around what age?
   a. 2 months
   b. 4 months
   c. 8 months
   d. 12 months

6. Which of the following skills is NOT typically displayed by the 12 month old?
   a. holding a spoon
   b. kicking a ball
   c. picking up a spoon
   d. holding a drinking cup

7. Which of the following activities would NOT be observed in a typical 13 to 18 month old?
   a. attempting to dress oneself
   b. stacking blocks
   c. imitating adults
   d. throwing a ball

8. When infants are weaned, there is/are:
   a. typically a sharp gain in weight
   b. a risk of malnutrition, due to lack of key nutrients
   c. a tendency for the child to develop multiple new teeth
   d. typically behavioral problems for a short time

9. Infants as young as this age typically refuse to crawl across a "visual cliff."
   a. 2 months
   b. 4 months
   c. 6 months
   d. 12 months

10. An infant is shown an interesting rattle and appears to like it. Then the mother places the rattle under a blanket. The infant appears to forget about the rattle completely. Which of the following is most likely true?
    a. the infant is older than 8 months
    b. the rattle frightened the infant
    c. the infant is younger the 8 months
    d. the blanket was more interesting to the child than the rattle

11. Research with infants has shown that infants can remember visual patterns as early as what age?
    a. 2 months
    b. 8 months
    c. 6 months
    d. 12 months

12. A child that pretends that a tent is a cave is likely to be how old?
    a. 6 to 8 months
    b. 15 to 18 months
    c. 11 to 12 months
    d. 20 to 26 months

13. Piaget proposed that children use these mental structures to organize information about the world.
    a. morphemes
    b. schemas
    c. assimilations
    d. objects

14. Infants begin cooing at approximately what age?
    a.   12 weeks
    c.   18 months
    b.   12 months
    d.   24 months

15. A child typically has a vocabulary of at least 50 words by which of the following ages?
    a.   6 months
    c.   18 months
    b.   12 months
    d.   24 months

16. Most basic aspects of a language are acquired by the typical child by the age of:
    a.   12 years
    c.   6 years
    b.   8 years
    d.   4 years

17. The use of a word, picture, gesture, or other sign to represent past and present events, experiences, and concepts is evidence of:
    a.   adaptation
    c.   deferred imitation
    b.   habituation
    d.   symbolic representation

18. Which of the following utterances is least likely to be used by a toddler?
    a.   throw ball
    c.   eat kitty
    b.   daddy throw
    d.   kitty eat

19. When a child learns a new word, such as *dog,* to describe the family pet and then uses the word to describe any and all animals, the child is producing:
    a.   an adaptation
    c.   an overextension
    b.   holophrastic speech
    d.   telegraphic speech

20. Which of the following accurately describes the relationship between a child's language development?
    a.   the size of a two year old's vocabulary is directly related to how much time the mother spends talking to the child
    b.   the size of a two year old's vocabulary is directly related to how much time the child spends playing with other children
    c.   the size of a two year old's vocabulary is directly related to how much time the child spends watching television
    d.   all of the above

ANSWER KEYS

Practice Test - Pretest (with text page numbers)

1. d 115	6. c 124	11. b 119	16. b 116
2. c 116	7. c 125	12. a 118	17. d 138
3. a 117	8. d 128	13. b 137	18. b 140
4. b 120	9. b 131	14. b 131	19. c 139
5. c 123	10. c 130	15. b 136	20. a 144

True/False

1. F	6. F	11. F	16. T
2. F	7. F	12. T	17. F
3. T	8. T	13. F	18. F
4. T	9. F	14. F	19. F
5. T	10. T	15. T	20. T

Matching

1. e	6. b
2. a	7. c
3. c	8. a
4. d	9. d
5. b	

Key Vocabulary Terms

1. Infancy is the period from about age 4 weeks to about 1 year; toddlerhood is the period from about age 1, when the infant begins walking, until about age 2.

2. Fine motor skills involve the use of the hands and fingers to perform intricate movements; gross motor skills involve the larger muscles or the whole body to perform more general movements.

3. Sudden infant death syndrome (SIDS) is the leading cause of death in infants in the first year of life. Also called "crib death," SIDS occurs when the infants stops breathing. Shaken baby syndrome is the leading cause of death in children in child abuse cases. Shaking a baby causes brain damage, resulting in death or permanent disability.

4. Marasmus is the type of malnutrition caused by an insufficient total quantity of food where muscles waste away and stored fat is depleted. If the duration is short, there may be no long-term negative effects. Kwashiorkor is the type of severe malnutrition caused by insufficient protein. If it occurs in the first 3 years of life, brain development can be directly affected.

5. Sensation is the translation of a stimulus into a neural impulse by a sense organ; perception is the complex process by which the mind interprets and gives meaning to sensory information.

6. <u>Receptive language</u> refers to the repertoire of words and commands that a child understands, even though she or he may not be able to use them; <u>productive language</u> is spoken or written language communication.

7. Using the <u>preference paradigm</u>, a researcher presents two stimuli to a child and monitors which stimuli the child attends to the most; using the <u>surprise paradigm</u>, a researcher measures a child's responses when an unexpected stimuli is presented.

8. <u>Holophrastic speech</u> is the speech that children use during the early stages of language acquisition; they use single words to convey complex thoughts. <u>Telegraphic speech</u> occurs in the utterances of 18 month-olds to 2 year olds. It involves the omission of less significant words and include only words that carry the most meaning.

Programmed Review
1. 100 billion, 25, 70, 90
2. synapses, 2500, 15000
3. waking activity, crying, alert inactivity, drowsiness, regular sleep, irregular sleep
4. habituation, ignore
5. perceptual, habituate, habituation method
6. 28, 7, motor tone and activity, range of state, regulation of state, autonomic stability
7. running, picking up a small pellet, cutting with scissors, managing a pencil, drawing human figures
8. 15 months, between 11 and 13 months, baby care customs
9. 12 months, forefinger, pincer grasp
10. 30, shunting, height
11. 30, physical growth, maturation, learning
12. depressed, inattentive
13. 6, milk, superior
14. 14, diarrhea, 4, respiratory diseases
15. 7 to 10, 2nd, 3rd or 4th
16. 2, 5, mouth, 6 to 7 months, emotional expressions
17. motion, shape, spatial positioning
18. fluid, the middle ear
19. 2 days, smell
20. 6 months, 7 months, a few hours
21. categories, 3 months, 7 or 8 months
22. 20th, schemas
23. sucking, grasping, crying
24. reflexive, objects, people, self
25. more, motor, perceptual
26. words, grammar
27. syllables, babbling, sounds
28. categorical
29. 21, parents and caregivers
30. gestures, tone of voice
31. words, imitation, syntax

32. talking to the child, vocabulary

Practice Test – Post Test (with text page numbers)

1. c 114	6. c 124	11. a 137	16. d 140
2. a 117	7. d 125	12. d 137	17. d 137
3. c 117	8. b 129	13. b 135	18. c 142
4. b 118	9. c 132	14. a 140	19. c 141
5. c 122	10. c 136	15. d 140	20. a 145

Chapter 5

Infancy and Toddlerhood: Personality and Sociocultural Development

CHAPTER OUTLINE

◈ The Foundations of Personality and Social Development
 ♦ Emotional Development
 ♦ Temperament

◈ The Development of Trust
 ♦ Feeding and Comforting

◈ Attachment
 ♦ The Role of Culture in Attachment
 ♦ Studying Infant and Toddler Attachment
 ♦ The Effects of Attachment
 ♦ Explaining Attachment
 ♦ The Relationship Between Attachment and Trust

◈ Separating From the Caregiver
 ♦ Social Referencing and Culture
 ♦ The Development of Autonomy
 ♦ The Development of Prosocial Behavior
 ♦ The Development of the Self
 ♦ Attachment and Separation

◈ The Family System: A Broader Context
 ♦ Fathers
 ♦ Other Family Members as Caregivers
 ♦ The Social Ecology of Child Care

◈ Infants and Toddlers With Special Needs
 ♦ Infants and Toddlers with Visual Impairments
 ♦ Infants and Toddlers with Hearing Impairments
 ♦ Infants and Toddlers with Severe Disabilities
 ♦ When Parenting Goes Awry: Abuse and Neglect

LEARNING OBJECTIVES

After you have read and studied this chapter, you should be able to answer the following questions.

1. What can parents do to ensure that their infant develops a trusting orientation to the world and a strong attachment to them?
2. How does the development of early infant attachment influence later development throughout childhood?
3. How do infants and toddlers develop a sense of their own autonomy without losing their attachment with their caregivers?
4. Can fathers be good "mothers" for their children?
5. What special challenges are faced by the caregivers of infants and toddlers with special needs?
6. How does child abuse or neglect influence development and autonomy?

PRACTICE TEST – PRETEST

Circle the correct answer for each multiple choice question and check your answers with the Answer Key at the end of the chapter.

1. In the first year of life, all of the following emotions emerge in infants, with the exception of :
   a. sadness
   b. guilt
   c. anger
   d. disgust

2. Which of the following is NOT a style of temperament?
   a. anxious
   b. easy
   c. difficult
   d. slow-to-warm-up

3. If an infant's basic needs are met consistently, the infant is more likely to develop a sense of:
   a. trust
   b. guilt
   c. balance
   d. organization

4. Sharing experiences back and forth between the caregiver and the infant in a cooperative manner is called:
   a. orienting
   b. clinging
   c. synchrony
   d. approach

5. The form of attachment where a strong emotional bond between a child and caregiver develops because of responsive caregiving is:
   a. avoidant
   b. secure
   c. resistant
   d. dependent

6. A form of attachment where a child becomes angry when the mother leaves and avoids her when she returns is:
   a. avoidant
   b. secure
   c. resistant
   d. dependent

7. The formation of a bond between some newborn animals (especially birds) and their mothers is called:
   a. flocking
   b. connecting
   c. synchrony
   d. imprinting

8. According to Erikson, the first critical developmental issue that is resolved in the first year of life is:
   a. trust versus mistrust
   b. industry versus inferiority
   c. autonomy versus shame and doubt
   d. integrity versus despair

9. At about what age does an infant develop separation anxiety?
   a. 3 months
   b. 12 months
   c. 7 months
   d. 16 months

10. When infants and toddlers look to caretakers as an indication of how to react to a strange person or situation, it is called:
    a. stranger anxiety
    b. social referencing
    c. collaboration
    d. sharing

11. Most children reliably engage in prosocial behavior (behavior intended to benefit others) by age:
    a. 12 months
    b. 24 months
    c. 18 months
    d. 36 months

12. The overall environment in which child care takes place, both within and beyond the home, is called the:
    a. childhood context
    b. chronosystem
    c. social ecology of child care
    d. total care environment

13. What percentage of U.S. mothers with children under 6 years worked outside the home in 2005?
    a. 12%
    b. 28%
    c. 67%
    d. 92%

14. When fathers hold infants, it is most often for what purpose?
    a. feeding
    b. playing
    c. changing diapers
    d. bathing

15. Which of the following does NOT constitute the "big three" elements of effective fatherhood?
    a. accessibility
    b. responsibility
    c. engagement
    d. reliability

16. How much unpaid leave from work must employers allow parents under the U.S. Family and Medical Leave Act?
    a. 3 weeks
    b. 3 months
    c. 6 months
    d. up to one year

17. The first indication of hearing impairment in 1-year-olds is often their what?
    a. frequent use of hand gestures
    b. rocking back and forth
    c. startled reactions when people approach
    d. interest in vibrations

18. Infants that are small for their age, appear sick, and are unable to digest food properly are said to be suffering from what?
    a. child abuse
    b. sudden infant death syndrome
    c. child neglect
    d. failure-to-thrive syndrome

19. The extent of fussing, crying, and showing distress when desires are frustrated describes what dimension of Rothbart's scale of infant temperament?
    a. irritable distress
    b. fearful distress
    c. soothability
    d. crankiness

20. Which of the following is NOT a variable observed in Ainsworth's strange-situation paradigm?
    a. parent as secure base
    b. reaction to an unfamiliar adult
    c. reaction to confinement
    d. reaction to a reunion

TRUE/FALSE

For each of the following statements indicate whether the statement is True or False. Check your answers with the Answer Key at the end of this chapter.

_____ 1. A child with a slow-to-warm-up temperament has both positive and negative moods, which are usually mild.

_____ 2. Methods of comforting infants vary widely across cultures.

_____ 3. An infant with attentive caregivers is more likely to develop a secure attachment style.

_____ 4. Behavioral problems in childhood may be linked to insecure attachment.

_____ 5. A 2-year-old can be expected to act like a responsible little adult.

_____ 6. When mothers are warm and loving, their children exhibit more empathy during their second year of life.

_____ 7. Toilet training is a major issue in social and personality development.

_____ 8. All infants are born with basically the same temperament style.

_____ 9. A mother's competence with her infant is most likely the result of taking primary responsibility for infant care, rather than because of any innate abilities.

_____ 10. Asking for an older child's help in caring for a new baby can often reduce sibling rivalry.

_____ 11. Parents in the United States receive a great deal of support compared to parents in Sweden.

_____ 12. Lack of sight is usually apparent at birth or shortly after birth.

_____ 13. Blind children develop a responsive smile as early as sighted children.

_____ 14. Grandparents with higher education levels interact more positively with grandchildren with disabilities compared to grandparents with lower education levels.

_____ 15. People who were abused as children will always be child abusers as adults.

_____ 16. Parents should try to create an environment that works with, rather than against, the basic temperament style of the infant.

_____ 17. Attachment with a mother requires only physical presence and the provision of food.

_____ 18. Feedback given to a toddler should focus on the behavior, not the child, as the object of criticism.

MATCHING

Match the following attachment styles with the appropriate description and check your answers with the Answer Key at the end of the chapter.

1. ____ secure attachment

    a.   characterized by contradictory behavior and confusion toward the mother

2. ____ insecure attachment

    b.   a strong emotional bond between a child and a caregiver that develops because of responsive caregiving

3. ____ resistant attachment

    c.   the result of inconsistent or unresponsive caregiving

4. ____ avoidant attachment

    d.   characterized by anger and avoidance of the mother

5. ____ disorganized attachment

    e.   characterized by ambivalence toward the mother

Match each dimension of Rothbart's Scale of Infant Temperament with its description. Check your answers with the Answer Key at the end of this chapter.

6. ____ activity level

    a.   duration of orienting or interest

7. ____ soothability

    b.   extent of fussing, crying, and showing distress when desires are frustrated

8. ____ attention span

    c.   level of gross motor activity

9. ____ fearful distress

    d.   frequency of expression of happiness and pleasure

10. ____ irritable distress

    e.   wariness and distress in response to intense or novel stimuli

11. ____ positive affect

    f.   reduction of fussing, crying or distress in response to calming techniques used by the caregiver or the infant

KEY VOCABULARY TERMS

Label each definition and give a specific example of each.

1. The subtle emotional signals, usually from the parent, that influence the infant's behavior.

2. The formation of a bond between some newborn animals (especially birds) and their mothers, which appears to be present at birth.

3. The back-and-forth interactions between an infant and a caregiver.

4. According to Erikson, the first critical developmental issue that is resolved in the first year of life.

5. The failure of a caregiver to respond to or care for a child.

Explain the difference between the following sets of terms.

6. fearful distress; irritable distress
7. child abuse; child neglect
8. trust; mistrust
9. secure attachment; imprinting
10. stranger anxiety; separation anxiety

PROGRAMMED REVIEW

Fill in the blanks in the following programmed review. Then check your answers with the Answer Key at the end of the chapter.

The Foundations of Personality and Social Development
Emotional Development

1. Babies focus first on managing _____ and _____. Then they begin the process of exchanging signals, sounds, and _____. Gradually, over the first year, basic emotions emerge, such as _____, anger, disgust, _____, and _____.

2. Emotional _____ is a major determinant of children's emotional development.

Temperament

3. Most children can be categorized into one of three temperament styles: _____ (often in a good and predictable), _____ (often irritable and unpredictable), and _____ (moody and resistant to attention).

The Development of Trust
Feeding and Comforting

4. Healthy adjustment requires a _____ in the development of _____ (which allows infants to form secure relationships with others) and _____ (which teaches them to protect themselves when conditions are threatening.

Attachment

5. Mary Ainsworth defined attachment behaviors as those that primarily promote nearness to a _____ person.

6. Such behaviors include _____ (crying, smiling, vocalizing) and _____ (looking).

7. Attachment is _____ : it involves sharing experiences back and forth between the caregiver and the infant in a cooperative manner.

The Role of Culture in Attachment

8. Although the sequence of development of first relationships is fairly _____ across cultures, the details can vary dramatically, depending on the personality of the parents, their specific child-rearing practices, and the _____ and _____ of the baby.

9. In most Western cultures, a typical mother-infant relationship is primarily _____ . In other cultures, however, infants have close _____ contact with caregivers.

Studying Infant and Toddler Attachment

10. Mary Ainsworth's _____ test is often used to assess the quality of infant attachment to the primary caregiver.

The Effects of Attachment

11. Research shows that insecurely attached 2-year-olds often exhibit _____ or _____ , and there is some evidence that such responses may interfere with _____ development.

12. Children of depressed caregivers have been found to display higher levels of _____ behavior during preschool years than their _____ attached peers.

Explaining Attachment

13. Typically, infants who develop secure attachments have caregivers who provide _____ attention to the infant's needs and who interact with the baby with _____ and a _____ attitude.

14. Behaviorists explained attachment as the result of _____, in which infants learn to _____ the presence of the caregiver with the pleasure associated with the satisfaction of _____ needs, such as being fed when hungry.

15. Arguing that attachment-type behavior is often seen in animals, some scientists view attachment more as an _____ that has survival value because it serves to keep newborns close to their mothers where they can be _____ and where they can _____ and _____ her effective behaviors.

16. When monkeys in a lab were raised without their mothers, they often developed _____ behaviors. They were often easily _____, irritable, and reluctant to _____ or _____, despite the fact that they had a nutritious diet and were otherwise well cared for.

The Relationship Between Attachment and Trust

17. When attachment goes awry, _____ is likely to develop. Here, the infant may experience _____, which can be social, emotional, or physical, if the caregiver is _____ or _____.

Separating From the Caregiver

18. By about _____ months of age, babies who have been smiling, welcoming, friendly, and accepting toward strangers suddenly become _____ and _____ of them.

19. According to the discrepancy hypothesis, _____ anxiety results when infants become capable of detecting _____ from the known or the expected.

20. Through _____, parents can assist their infants and toddlers in adjusting to strangers and strange situations by _____ and _____ their own emotional reactions.

Social Referencing and Culture

21. In contrast to many U.S. parents, Kung San parents seemed to pay no attention to their infant's _____ of objects. Instead, they paid close attention to the _____ of objects.

The Development of Autonomy

22. Children who have developed a _____ relationship with their caregivers during the first year of life are better prepared to take the first steps toward _____ than those who are insecurely attached, thereby developing a healthy autonomy from their caregivers.

23. Children who have a strong attachment relationship and whose needs are met through loving interaction with an adult are neither _____ by attention nor _____ or _____ by reasonable limits.

24. Freud believed that toilet training that was begun too early or that was too _____ could produce an _____ that would be carried forward in development, interfering with normal development later in life.

The Development of Prosocial Behavior

25. In studies of cooperation in simple tasks, very few _____-month-old infants cooperate with each other. At _____ months, cooperation is infrequent and appears accidental. At _____ months, with a little coaching, nearly all toddlers can cooperate.

26. The development of empathy may be related to the toddler's sense of _____ versus _____. Indeed, the development of _____ - one's perception of personal identity – is among the more important outcomes of the developmental events in infancy and toddlerhood.

The Development of the Self

27. Later in their first year, infants begin to realize that they can _____ things to happen.

28. Reflective of their growing self-awareness, by the end of the second year, children's language is filled with references to themselves. The words _____ and _____ take on new significance, and the concept of _____ is clearly and strongly acted out.

Attachment and Separation

29. Two fundamental tasks of infancy and toddlerhood are 1) _____ and, beginning around the second year, 2) _____.

The Family System: A Broader Context
Fathers

30. Despite being capable of caring for an infant, most fathers still do not take _____ responsibility for infant care.

Other Family Members as Caregivers

31. Grandparents can be particularly important to the stability of single-parent households, where nearly _____% of U.S. children under age 18 now live, and to the _____% of all families with children under age 3 whose mothers are in the labor force.

The Social Ecology of Child Care

32. Increasingly, mothers with young children are working outside the home, the divorce rate has risen, and caregivers other than the mother are assuming primary infant care. One major impact these changes have produced concerns the _____, which is the overall environment in which child care takes place, both _____ and _____ the home.

Infants and Toddlers With Special Needs
Infants and Toddlers with Visual Impairments

33. One problem that can develop with an infant with visual impairments is that the caregiver may feel the infant is _____.

Infants and Toddlers with Hearing Impairments

34. Without careful attention during infancy, hearing impairment can result in poor _____ during the early childhood years and beyond, which can lead to severe _____, _____, and _____ problems later.

Infants and Toddlers with Severe Disabilities

35. When an infant is born with a severe disability, there is a high risk for parental _____, _____, and _____.

When Parenting Goes Awry: Abuse and Neglect

36. Studies have shown that toddlers who have suffered physical maltreatment experience distortions and delays in the development of their sense of _____ and in their _____ and _____ development.

37. Other than removing a baby from an abusive situation, another option is to have the parents attend _____ programs or _____, which helps to correct the abuse and reduce overall family stress.

CRITICAL THINKING QUESTIONS

To further your mastery of the topics, write out the answers to the following essay questions in the space provided.

1. In your own words, how would you describe the characteristics of a temperamentally "easy" infant? How would you describe a "difficult" infant?

2. Describe some of the ways that cultures can vary in their approach to feeding and comforting infants.

3. Considering the reciprocal relationship between caretakers and infants, how might an infant's temperament affect whether the caretaker develops a secure attachment with the infant?

4. What implications might Harlow's study on infant monkeys have for the importance of synchrony?

5. How is separation anxiety related to the development of the sense of self?

6. In what ways can fathers have a positive or negative influence on infant development?

7. To what are we referring when we use the term "social ecology of child care"? Describe the social ecology of child care in the United States.

8. What are some of the dangers to attachment that come with having an infant or toddler with visual impairments? Why?

9. What are some explanations about why a person might abuse or neglect a baby?

PRACTICE TEST – POST TEST

Circle the correct answer for each multiple choice question and check your answers with the Answer Key at the end of the chapter.

1. Edward Tronick's study on the emotional communication system between infants and caregivers is known as the:
   a. neglect experiment
   b. still-face experiment
   c. funny-face experiment
   d. cooing experiement

2. An infant who is regular in basic routines and easily soothed, but reacts negatively to new people and situations is said to have what temperamental style?
   a. easy
   b. difficult
   c. slow-to-warm-up
   d. other

3. If a parent has a child with a difficult temperament, what should they do?
   a. create a compatible environment   c. send the child to a camp
   b. spank the child when they disobey   d. apply strict, inflexible house rules

4. Feeding, whether by breast or bottle, allows:
   a. the mother to exert control   c. special closeness to form
   b. the baby to regulate temperament   d. development of self

5. Which of the following is NOT an example of infant attachment behavior?
   a. crawling   c. crying
   b. looking   d. clinging

6. Mary Ainsworth's strange-situation test is used to assess what?
   a. stranger anxiety   c. attachment quality
   b. temperament   d. caregiver responsiveness

7. If an infant responds to the mother ambivalently, simultaneously seeking and rejecting affection and not becoming upset when the mother leaves the room, what attachment style does the infant have?
   a. secure   c. avoidant
   b. resistant   d. disorganized

8. Newly hatched goslings will treat the first moving thing they see upon hatching as their mother. This is a striking example of:
   a. imprinting   c. synchrony
   b. disorganized attachment   d. social ecology

9. In Harlow's study, with which artificial surrogate mother did the infant monkeys prefer to spend the most time?
   a. metal with a milk source   c. the monkeys preferred both equally well
   b. terrycloth without a food source   d. the monkeys avoided both artificial mothers

10. What is most likely to foster distrust in an infant?
    a. overstimulation of the senses   c. multiple caregivers
    b. the presence of older siblings   d. inconsistent care

11. Separation anxiety results when infants become capable of detecting departures from the known or expected. This is according to what hypothesis?
    a. disorganization hypothesis   c. discrepancy hypothesis
    b. discernment hypothesis   d. departure hypothesis

12. A toddler bumps his head on a table and then looks at the mother's reaction before getting upset. What is the toddler demonstrating?
    a. social referencing   c. overdependence
    b. autonomy   d. prosocial behavior

13. A mother lets her toddler pick one out of two outfits to wear to the playground, rather than insisting that he wear a particular outfit without his input. What is the mother fostering in her toddler?
    a. empathy
    b. autonomy
    c. narcissism
    d. shame and doubt

14. What did Freud believe results when a parent begins toilet training too early or is too strict?
    a. an Oedipal complex
    b. phobias
    c. anal fixation
    d. introversion

15. One's perception of personal identity is know as:
    a. self-concept
    b. self-esteem
    c. self-efficacy
    d. self-awareness

16. Mothers are more likely to hold infants for ____ , whereas fathers are more likely to hold infants for ____ .
    a. play; caretaking
    b. caretaking; play
    c. social acceptance; self-gratification
    d. self-gratification; social acceptance

17. As many as what percentage of children in the U.S. do not receive consistent, high quality care?
    a. 15-20%
    b. 25-30%
    c. 65-70%
    d. 85-90%

18. What are caregivers of visually impaired infants encouraged to do as often as possible?
    a. move the infant's hands around
    b. play musical instruments
    c. sing to the infant
    d. respond only to cries and smiles

19. Unlike child abuse, child neglect is often
    a. intentional
    b. unintentional
    c. justified
    d. accepted

20. Which of the following is NOT a typical response to child abusers?
    a. assign baby to foster home
    b. assign care to grandparents
    c. have parents attend a parenting skills program
    d. restrict further reproduction

ANSWER KEY

Practice Test – Pretest (with text page numbers)

1. b 150	6. c 157	11. b 163	16. b 170
2. a 152	7. d 158	12. c 168	17. c 173
3. a 154	8. a 160	13. c 169	18. d 174
4. c 155	9. c 161	14. b 167	19. a 153
5. b 157	10. b 161	15. d 166	20. c 156

True/False

1. T	7. F	13. F
2. T	8. F	14. T
3. T	9. T	15. F
4. T	10. T	16. T
5. F	11. F	17. F
6. T	12. T	18. T

Matching

1. b	7. f
2. c	8. a
3. d	9. e
4. e	10. b
5. a	11. d
6. c	

Key Vocabulary Terms

1. Social referencing
2. Imprinting
3. Synchrony
4. Trust versus mistrust
5. Child neglect

6. <u>Fearful distress</u> is wariness and distress in response to intense or novel stimuli. <u>Irritable distress</u> is the extent of fussing, crying, and showing distress when desires are frustrated.

7. <u>Child abuse</u> is the intentional physical or psychological injuries inflicted on a child by an adult. <u>Child neglect</u> is the failure of a caregiver to respond to or care for a child, which is often times unintentional.

8. <u>Trust</u> is the belief a child forms that the world is a safe place, and that they will be secure, and their cares will be met. <u>Mistrust</u> is the opposite: a child experience deprivation (social, emotional, or physical, thereby learning the world is not a safe place.

9. Secure attachment is a strong emotional bond that develops between a child and its caregiver as a result of responsive caregiving. Imprinting is a bond between some newborn animals and their mother, which is the result of biological programming rather than learning.

10. Stranger anxiety is a child's fear of strangers or strange places. Separation anxiety is a child's fear of being separated from its caregiver.

Programmed Review

1. distress, comfort, smiles, sadness, fear, pleasure
2. communication
3. easy, difficult, slow-to-warm-up
4. balance, trust, mistrust
5. specific
6. signaling, orienting
7. synchronous
8. consistent, temperament, personality
9. social, physical
10. strange-situation
11. hyperactivity, chronic stress reactions, brain
12. hostile-aggressive, securely
13. consistent, sensitivity, caring
14. conditioning, associate, biological
15. instinct, protected, observe, imitate
16. maladapted, frightened, eat, play
17. mistrust, deprivation, absent, abusive
18. 7, shy, wary
19. separation, departures
20. social referencing, monitoring, controlling
21. exploration, sharing
22. trusting, independence
23. spoiled, frightened, threatened
24. strict, anal fixation
25. 12, 18, 24
26. self, other, self-concept
27. cause
28. me, mine, ownership
29. forming a secure attachment to the primary caregiver, separating from that caregiver and establishing an independent, autonomous self
30. primary
31. 40, 61
32. social ecology of child care, within, beyond
33. unresponsive
34. communication, social, intellectual, psychological
35. rejection, withdrawal, depression
36. self, language, cognitive

37. parenting skills, counseling

Practice Test – Post Test (with text page numbers)

1. b 151	6. c 156	11. c 161	16. b 167
2. c 152	7. d 157	12. a 161	17. d 170
3. a 153	8. a 158	13. b 162	18. c 173
4. c 154	9. b 159	14. c 163	19. b 174
5. a 155	10. d 160	15. a 163	20. d 175

Chapter 6

Early Childhood: Physical, Cognitive, and Language Development

CHAPTER OUTLINE

◈ Physical Development
- ♦ Changes in the Body
- ♦ Brain Development
- ♦ Human Development: An Interactive and Individual Approach

◈ Motor Skills Development
- ♦ Gross Motor Skills
- ♦ Fine Motor Skills
- ♦ Learning and Motor Skills

◈ Cognitive Development
- ♦ An Overview of Preoperational Thinking
- ♦ Preoperational Substages and Thought
- ♦ Limitations of Preoperational Thinking
- ♦ Conservation
- ♦ Evaluating Piaget's Theory
- ♦ Beyond Piaget: Social Perspectives
- ♦ The Role of Memory

◈ Language Development
- ♦ Words and Concepts
- ♦ Expanding Grammar
- ♦ Mastering the Subtleties of Speech
- ♦ The Influence of Parents' Language Use
- ♦ Multicultural Aspects of Language Development

◈ Play and Learning
- ♦ Play and Cognitive Development

LEARNING OBJECTIVES

After you have read and studied this chapter, you should be able to answer the following questions.

1. What does it mean to say that human development is integrated, interactive, and dynamic?
2. What role does brain maturation play in the major developmental events that characterize early childhood?
3. How do physical development and cognitive development influence each other as children move through early childhood?
4. How do language development and cognitive development interact?
5. What does it mean to say that play both mirrors and encourages cognitive development?

PRACTICE TEST – PRETEST

Circle the correct answer for each multiple choice question and check your answers with the Answer Key at the end of the chapter.

1. Early Childhood is the span of time from:
   a. birth to 2 years
   c. 5 to 7 years
   b. 2 to 6 years
   d. 6 to 11 years

2. Which of the following underlies much of the developmental pattern of early childhood?
   a. biological development
   c. neurological development
   b. social development
   d. physical development

3. The process by which soft tissue or cartilage is transformed into bone is called:
   a. calcification
   c. cartilogenesis
   b. grafting
   d. ossification

4. As development occurs throughout childhood, one's center of gravity:
   a. descends to the pelvic area
   c. causes awkward balance
   b. becomes more pronounced
   d. shifts upward

5. The ability to perform motor behaviors without consciously thinking about them is called
   a. telepathy
   c. self-efficacy
   b. automaticity
   d. ossification

6. A child's general level of activity
   a. declines earlier for girls than for boys
   b. declines earlier for boys than for girls
   c. increases with age

7. A typical child of _____ can tie his/her/its own shoelaces, though he/she/it may still find it difficult.
   a. one year
   b. two years
   c. four years
   d. six years

8. A belief that anything that moves is alive is called _____.
   a. centrism
   b. conservation
   c. reification
   d. animism

9. _____ is the use of actions, images, words, or other signs to represent past and present events, experiences, and concepts.
   a. symbolic representation
   b. concrete operations
   c. egocentrism
   d. reification

10. The understanding that changing an object's shape or appearance does not change its mass, volume, or number is:
   a. conservation
   b. centration
   c. automaticity
   d. egocentrism

11. When a child does not understand that a squashed ball of clay can be re-rolled, and must therefore be the same as the un-squashed ball is experiencing what?
   a. centration
   b. perceptual illogic
   c. scaffolding
   d. irreversibility

12. What term refers to the ability to correctly identify objects or situations that have been previously experienced when they occur again?
   a. metamemory
   b. recognition
   c. scripting
   d. reconnaissance

13. By age 6, most children have a working vocabulary of _____ words, and can understand more than _____.
   a. 250; 5,000
   b. 1,100; 13,000
   c. 2,600; 20,000
   d. 10,000; 45,000

14. Adhering to standard grammar rules, even during exceptions (e.g. using foots instead of feet) is called _____.
   a. hyperregularization
   b. overregularization
   c. literacy
   d. zone of proximal development

15. What is the term used to refer to the language we use when we talk to ourselves?
   a. babbling
   b. recall
   c. collective monologue
   d. private speech

16. Two children who take turns talking, but not necessarily about the same topic, are participating in a _____.
    a. private speech
    b. collective monologue
    c. parallel play
    d. cooperative play

17. The social and cultural aspects of language use are called _____.
    a. grammar acquisition
    b. communication
    c. pragmatics
    d. cultural linguistics

18. According to recent research, growing up bilingual _____ cognitive development.
    a. has no effect on
    b. is detrimental to
    c. is advantageous to
    d. has positive and negative effects on

19. Which of the following is NOT an example of dramatic play?
    a. imitation
    b. lying
    c. pretending
    d. role playing

20. Various age groups allow _____ children to practice teaching and child care.
    a. more favored
    b. less favored
    c. younger
    d. older

TRUE/FALSE

For each of the following statements, indicate whether the statement is True or False. Check your answers with the Answer Key at the end of this chapter.

_____ 1.   Throughout the world, 80% of people are right-handed.

_____ 2.   Fine motor skills include such tasks as writing and handling eating utensils.

_____ 3.   By five years of age, a typical child can throw a ball "overhanded."

_____ 4.   Egocentrism is the tendency of a child to understand things from his own view.

_____ 5.   A 4- to 6-year-old will not change her mind if an adult tells her a story that contradicts her opinion.

_____ 6.   Many limitations of the preconceptual period can be observed by seeing how children respond to Piaget's problems of conservation.

_____ 7.   The lower limit of Vygotsky's zone of proximal development is determined by a child's competence when solving the problem alone.

_____ 8.   Leveling is the progressive structuring of tasks so that the level of difficulty is appropriate.

_____ 9.   The information-processing perspective conceptualizes memory as operating like a computer.

_____ 10.   Young children especially have difficulty remembering information that is organized temporally (in a time-based sequence).

_____ 11.   Beginning at age 18 months, children learn an average of 15 new words a day.

_____ 12.   Many children at the age of six begin to overregularize their speech.

_____ 13.   Many bilingual children at 3 years old show little confusion about the grammar rules of their two languages.

_____ 14.   Constructive play involves a child gaining bits of information to build his understanding of the world.

_____ 15.   Role playing allows a child to experiment with a variety of behaviors and experience the consequences and emotions that come with them.

MATCHING

Match the following with the appropriate answer, and check your answers with the Answer Key at the end of this chapter.

1. _____ myelination

   a. intrinsically motivated behavior that promotes cognitive development

2. _____ functional subordination

   b. the ability to retrieve long-term information and memories with or without cues or prompts

3. _____ preconceptual period

   c. Piaget's period highlighted by the increasingly complex use of symbols

4. _____ intuitive period

   d. Piaget's period highlighted by a child's increasing understanding of causation and more realistic views of the world

5. _____ symbolic representation

   e. when simple motor skills become integrated into more complex, purposeful skills

6. _____ recall   f.   includes imitation, role playing, and pretending

7. _____ play   g.   the formation of sheathing cells that insulate neurons

8. _____ dramatic play   h.   use of actions, images, or words to represent past and present events

KEY VOCABULARY TERMS

Label each definition and give an example of each.

1. The process where specific skills and competencies become localized in either the left or right cerebral hemisphere.

2. Acquiring or developing the necessary prerequisite skills to perform an action.

3. Repeating a skill in order to perfect it.

4. Developing the ability to maintain focus on the skill at hand.

5. Gathering information about how well a skill is being performed to refine the skill.

Explain the difference between the following sets of terms.

6. Gross motor skills; fine motor skills
7. Automaticity; functional subordination
8. working memory; long-term memory
9. private speech; collective monologues
10. rough-and-tumble play; games, rituals, and competitive play

PROGRAMMED REVIEW

Fill in the blanks in the following programmed review. Then check your answers with the Answer Key at the end of the chapter.

Physical Development
<u>Changes in the Body</u>

1. As children's body proportions continue to change throughout childhood, their _____ gradually descends to the _____, which enhances their ability to _____ that are more athletic.

<u>Brain Development</u>

2. The _____ involves both the rapid _____ of interconnections among neurons and the _____ away of connections that are not needed.

3. Maturation of the brain and the central nervous system also includes _____ which is the formation of sheathing cells that _____ the neurons and make transmission of _____ much more efficient.

4. The brain's cerebral cortex is divided into two hemispheres–the _____ and the _____. _____ is the process where specific skills and competencies become localized in a particular cerebral hemisphere.

5. Research shows that left-handed people are more likely to be _____–capable of using either hand with good coordination and fine motor skills.

6. Intervention projects that enroll _____ children in _____ generally have a much greater impact than those that are begun _____ in life.

<u>Human Development: An Interactive and Individual Approach</u>

7. It is important to emphasize that brain development and other aspects of development _____.

Motor Skills Development
<u>Gross Motor Skills</u>

8. The decline in activity occurs earlier for _____ than for _____.

<u>Fine Motor Skills</u>

9. Fine motor skills often require the _____ and _____ use of _____, _____, and _____.

10. Children who are _____ to _____ years of age can typically tie a simple knot, and _____ who wear shoes with laces usually can tie them.

<u>Learning and Motor Skills</u>

11. Sometimes it is clear that actions involve _____, meaning that there are _____ rewards provided for performing an activity.

12. However, much of the behavior in childhood is _____ that is, it is performed for _____.

Cognitive Development

An Overview of Preoperational Thinking

13. When a preoperational child encounters something familiar, they _____. When they encounter something new, they _____ their thinking to incorporate it.

Preoperational Substages and Thought

14. Piaget's preoperational period lasts from about age _____ to age _____. It usually is divided into two parts–the early preoperational or _____ and the _____.

15. Egocentrism refers to children's tendency to _____ and _____ things in terms of their personal point of view; it is a _____ view of the world.

16. The most dramatic cognitive difference between infants and 2-year-olds is in their use of _____, which is the use of _____, images, words, or other signs to represent past and present events, _____, and concepts.

17. Understanding the _____, _____, and _____ of others is crucial to forming close friendships.

18. The sensitivity to others' points of view helps children make the transition to less _____ and more _____ thinking.

Limitations of Preoperational Thinking

19. The limitations on children's thinking include _____; _____; _____; _____; and difficulties with concepts of _____, _____, and _____.

Conservation

20. The term _____ refers to understanding that changing the shape or _____ of objects and materials does not change their _____, _____, _____ and so forth.

Evaluating Piaget's Theory

21. Young children are also better than _____ thought at taking other's perspectives in the context of understanding their _____ and _____.

<u>Beyond Piaget: Social Perspectives</u>

22. The _____ limit of Vygotsky's zone of proximal development is determined by the child's _____ when solving problems _____.

23. The most effective instruction involves _____, which is the _____ structuring of tasks by parents or others so that the level of task difficulty is _____.

<u>The Role of Memory</u>

24. Information that is important is stored in _____, which involves creating _____ in the brain that most likely involve the creation of new _____, which are the connections among _____.

25. It generally has been assumed that young children's difficulties with recall are attributable to poor strategies for _____ and _____.

Language Development

<u>Words and Concepts</u>

26. Early childhood is the period in which children acquire the idea that words can be used to express _____.

<u>Expanding Grammar</u>

27. Much of early language development is _____ across _____, and this consistency extends through early childhood as well.

28. Although their earliest usage of such words is correct, as they learn rules, they begin to use words like _____ instead of went, _____ instead of broke, or _____ instead of feet.

<u>Mastering the Subtleties of Speech</u>

29. Children between the ages of _____ and _____ have been observed talking to themselves about _____% of the time in schools that allow it.

30. Children must also learn to adjust their conversations to reduce _____, _____, and _____.

31. _____ mothers were much more likely than _____ mothers to use evaluative words, such as _____ and _____.

The Influence of Parents' Language Use

32. Play with _____ toys emerges at about age _____, which is the same time that _____ learning accelerates.

Multicultural Aspects of Language Development

33. Language is not only a means of _____; it is also a symbol of _____ or _____ identity.

34. It is also noteworthy that speaking a native language at _____ and a second language at _____ apparently does not interfere with either language.

35. Today, most research supports the conclusion that _____, _____, and probably _____, it is an advantage to grow up bilingual.

Play and Learning

36. _____, according to _____, is child's work.

Play and Cognitive Development

37. Role playing leads to a _____, as well as to a _____.

38. Play both _____ and _____ cognitive development, as well as the refinement of _____ and _____ skills that rapidly advance during the period of early childhood.

CRITICAL THINKING QUESTIONS

To further your mastery of the topics, write out the answers to the following essay questions in the space provided.

1. Why are left-handed people more likely to be ambidextrous than right-handed people?

2. Considering the importance of readiness and practice, what implications do these concepts have for children growing up in poverty?

3. How does scaffolding contribute to a child's ability to understand and solve a problem?

4. Explain why parents who take their young children on a road trip might hear "Are we there yet?" repeatedly.

5. Explain the importance of scripts for memory in young children.

6. What is the purpose of private speech in young children? How is this similar to or different from private speech in adults?

7. How does bilingualism affect cognitive development?

8. How does dramatic play facilitate social knowledge in early childhood?

PRACTICE TEST - POST TEST

Circle the correct answer for each multiple choice question and check your answers with the Answer Key at the end of the chapter.

1. Children who have difficulty with major categories of reality (such as believing in animism and reification) are in which of Piaget's stages?
   a. sensorimotor
   b. preconceptual
   c. precontextual
   d. egocentrifugal

2. A child who believes that objects and people in their thoughts and dreams are real is displaying what?
   a. animism
   b. reification
   c. realism
   d. pseudocognition

3. Which of the following is NOT one of Piaget's types of conservation?
   a. volume
   b. number
   c. energy
   d. mass

4. The ability of the brain to adapt during childhood is referred to as what?
   a. lateralization
   b. myelinization
   c. plasticity
   d. elasticity

5. For most people (and nearly all right-handed people), language is heavily lateralized in which hemisphere of the brain?
   a. right
   b. left
   c. longitudinal
   d. lateral

6. A child who is running and kicking a soccer ball is making use of her what?
   a. intuitive skills
   b. animism skills
   c. fine motor skills
   d. gross motor skills

7. Which of the following is a three-year old more likely to do than a two-year old?
   a. run, turn and stop awkwardly
   b. have a wide stance
   c. walk with a swaying gait
   d. reach for an object with one hand

8. A young child's difficulty with fine motor movements is linked to which of the following?
   a. his immature peripheral nervous system
   b. his immature central nervous system
   c. mental retardation
   d. organic developmental delays

9. On average, what is the youngest a child could be who would use blocks to construct a building?
   a. 1 year
   b. 2 years
   c. 4 years
   d. 6 years

10. Laura must concentrate in order to set a cup of water on the table. She is experiencing which condition involved in learning motor skills?
   a. practice
   b. attention
   c. readiness
   d. competence feedback

11. Joseph needs props similar to the objects he is talking about in order to tell his story. Approximately how old is Joseph?
   a. 2 ½ years
   b. 5 ½ years
   c. 8 years
   d. 11 years

12. Which of the following is NOT a limitation on a child's thinking?
   a. egocentrism
   b. animism
   c. reification
   d. sociocentrism

13. Isabella can explain to you how to walk from her house to her school, but she cannot explain how to walk from her school to her home. What limitation is she experiencing?
   a. reification
   b. irreversibility
   c. symbolic representation
   d. centration

14. Piaget viewed children as which of the following?
   a. little artists
   b. little adults
   c. little scientists
   d. little monsters

15. A child's memory processes reach that of adults at which age?
   a. 2 years
   b. 5 years
   c. 7 years
   d. 10 years

16. Memory scripts about a child's daily routines which contain rules and roles of his family, religion, and culture are the beginnings of the child's what?
   a. egocentric self
   b. historical self
   c. representative self
   d. genealogical self

17. During which stage of grammar acquisition do children learn the "exceptions to the rule?"
    a. stage 1   c. stage 3
    b. stage 2   d. stage 4

18. Which type of speech may help a child develop inner thought and self-direction?
    a. private speech   c. collective monologues
    b. public speech   d. pragmatic speech

19. A child splashing water is engaging in which type of play?
    a. social play   c. rough-and-tumble
    b. sensory pleasure   d. play with motion

20. Sara and James are two years old and are playing near each other. Sara is pretending to be a princess, while James is pretending to be a fireman. What type of play are they engaging in?
    a. dramatic play   c. cooperative play
    b. selfish play   d. parallel play

ANSWER KEY

Practice Test Pretest (with text page numbers)

1. b 180	6. a 185	11. d 193	16. b 199
2. c 180	7. d 186	12. b 195	17. c 199
3. d 181	8. d 188	13. c 197	18. c 201
4. a 181	9. a 189	14. b 198	19. b 204
5. b 184	10. a 191	15. d 198	20. d 205

True/False

1. F	6. F	11. F
2. T	7. T	12. F
3. T	8. F	13. T
4. T	9. T	14. T
5. F	10. F	15. T

Matching

1. G	5. I
2. E	6. B
3. C	7. A
4. D	8. F

Key Vocabulary Terms
1. Lateralization
2. Readiness
3. Practice
4. Attention
5. Competence feedback
6. Gross motor skills are simpler skills such as running, hopping, and throwing; fine motor skills involve more precise tasks such as manipulating a pencil or handling eating utensils.
7. Automaticity is the ability to perform motor behaviors without consciously thinking about them. Functional subordination is the integration of a number of separate, simple actions into a more complex pattern of behavior.
8. Working memory is the section of memory which encodes new information. Actively thinking about something uses working memory. Long-term memory is where our brain stores information that is important enough to be retained.
9. Private speech is the speech patterns people use when they talk to themselves. Collective monologues are conversations among children that include taking turns speaking, but not necessarily about the same topic.
10. Rough-and-tumble play is play (such as wrestling, pushing, and mock fighting) which provides exercise and release of energy. Games, rituals, and competitive play are play (such as Hide and Seek, and Duck, Duck, Goose) that involve cooperation with others and following rules that define appropriate behavior.

Programmed Review

1. center of gravity, pelvic area, perform movements
2. brain growth spurt, development, pruning
3. myelination, insulate, neural impulses
4. left, right, lateralization.
5. ambidextrous
6. high-risk, early infancy, later
7. interact
8. girls, boys
9. coordinated, dextrous, hand, fingers, thumb
10. 5, 6, 6-year-olds
11. extrinsically motivated behavior, explicit
12. intrinsically motivated behavior, its own sake
13. assimilate, accommodate
14. 2, 7, preconceptual period, intuitive period
15. see, understand, self-centered
16. symbolic representation, actions, experiences
17. feelings, thoughts, intentions
18. egocentric, sociocentric
19. concreteness, irreversibility, egocentrism, centration, time, space, sequence
20. conservation, appearance, mass, volume, number
21. Piaget, feelings, intentions
22. lower, competence, alone
23. scaffolding, progressive, appropriate
24. long-term memory, structural changes, synapses, neurons
25. encoding, retrieval
26. concepts
27. universal, cultures
28. goed, breaked, foots
29. 4, 8, 20
30. social friction, conflict, embarrassment
31. English, U.S., bad, good.
32. gender-stereotyped, 2, language
33. communication, social, group
34. home, school
35. linguistically, culturally, cognitively
36. Play, Piaget
37. better understanding of others, clearer definition of self
38. mirrors, encourages, physical, motor

Practice Test Post test (with text page numbers)

1. b 188	6. d 184	11. a 190	16. b 196
2. b 188	7. d 184	12. d 191	17. c 198
3. c 191	8. b 185	13. b 193	18. a 199
4. c 181	9. c 185	14. c 188	19. b 203
5. b 182	10. b 186	15. c 194	20. d 204

Chapter 7

Early Childhood: Personality and Sociocultural Development

CHAPTER OUTLINE

◆ Coping With Feelings and Emotions
- ♦ Fear and Anxiety
- ♦ Emotional Regulation

◆ Aggression and Prosocial Behavior
- ♦ Aggression
- ♦ Prosocial Behavior

◆ Developmental Conflicts
- ♦ Initiative Versus Guilt

◆ Peers, Play, and the Development of Social Competence
- ♦ The Role of Imaginary Companions
- ♦ Cultural Variations in Play
- ♦ Social Competence and the Development of Social Skills

◆ Understanding Self and Others
- ♦ Social Concepts and Rules
- ♦ Self-Concept
- ♦ Self and Gender

◆ Family Dynamics
- ♦ Parenting Styles
- ♦ Discipline and Self-Control
- ♦ Sibling Dynamics
- ♦ Child Maltreatment: Abuse and Neglect

LEARNING OBJECTIVES

After you have read and studied this chapter, you should be able to answer the following questions.

1. Why is learning to control emotions such an important development event in early childhood?
2. Do TV shows, movies, and other media have a negative or positive impact on the development of today's generation of young children?
3. What is the primary developmental task that preschool children must undertake?
4. Does having an imaginary companion bode well or ill for normal development in early childhood?
5. How do children come to understand the concept of gender?
6. What kinds of parenting styles lead to the healthiest adjustments for children?

PRACTICE TEST – PRETEST

Circle the correct answer for each multiple choice question and check your answers with the Answer Key at the end of the chapter.

1. A feeling of uneasiness, apprehension, or fear that has a vague or unknown source is:
    a. anxiety
    b. affection
    c. jealousy
    d. frustration

2. Which of the following is most likely to scare a modern child?
    a. wolves
    b. extraterrestrial creatures
    c. goblins
    d. thunderstorms

3. Learning to deal with a wide range of emotions in socially acceptable ways is called what?
    a. emotional regulation
    b. defense mechanizing
    c. miscellany coping
    d. rationalization

4. Which feeling often occurs in young children when their goals are blocked?
    a. fear
    b. anxiety
    c. frustration
    d. jealousy

5. A child who is frequently punished at home has a tendency to become which of the following?
    a. more aggressive
    b. less aggressive
    c. well-behaved
    d. envious

6. Which of the following types of media is the most pervasive?
    a. internet
    b. television
    c. radio
    d. video games

7. How many hours of television is a U.S. child likely to watch before they enter formal schooling?
   a. 1,000
   b. 2,000
   c. 4,000
   d. 6,000

8. Actions intended to benefit others are called:
   a. programmed benevolences
   b. positive conduct
   c. defense mechanisms
   d. prosocial behaviors

9. The ability to understand the feelings and points of view of others is called what?
   a. egocentrism
   b. empathy
   c. interpersonalism
   d. conscientiousness

10. The peak of conflict between opposing developmental needs (such as independence versus reliance) typically occurs about what age?
    a. 6
    b. 4
    c. 2
    d. 1

11. The dramatic play that children around the age of 4 begin to engage in is referred to as what?
    a. parallel play
    b. theatrical
    c. social pretend play
    d. dynamic play

12. Which of the following do imaginary companions NOT do for their child?
    a. help them deal with fears
    b. provide companionship
    c. provide reassurance
    d. protect against bullying

13. The ability to initiate and maintain satisfying reciprocal relationships with peers is referred to as what?
    a. cultural aptitude
    b. mutual affiliation
    c. social fitness
    d. social competence

14. Young children who are popular are unlikely to do which of the following in their interactions with peers?
    a. force themselves on other children
    b. show helpful behavior
    c. maintain communication
    d. have strategies for resolving conflicts

15. The process by which one incorporates the moral standards and values of one's society into one's self-concept or understanding is called what?
    a. generalization
    b. ingestion
    c. internalization
    d. sensitization

16. A person's own conception of what it means to be male or female is referred to as what?
    a. gender constancy
    b. gender expectation
    c. gender role
    d. gender identity

17. When children are intrinsically motivated to acquire values, interests, and behavior that are in line with their gender, they are experiencing which phenomenon?
    a. self-identification
    b. self-modification
    c. self-socialization
    d. self-actualization

18. A parent who encourages their child's growing autonomy while still setting rules for them to follow is exhibiting which parenting style?
    a. authoritative
    b. authoritarian
    c. permissive
    d. indifferent

19. Which of the following is NOT part of the most productive disciplinary technique?
    a. setting rules that are fairly enforced
    b. establishing a caring environment
    c. giving children freedom from punishment
    d. keeping two-way communication open

20. What percentage of child maltreatment involves child neglect?
    a. 40%
    b. 50%
    c. 60%
    d. 70%

TRUE/FALSE

For each of the following statements, indicate whether the statement is True or False. Check your answers with the Answer Key at the end of this chapter.

_____ 1. A child who experiences a continuous sense of apprehension for no particular reason is experiencing fear.

_____ 2. One of the most effective methods of helping a child cope with anxiety is to reduce the unnecessary stress in his life.

_____ 3. Contemporary developmentalists believe guilt is a more painful and intense emotion than shame.

_____ 4. Around the age of 5, children usually develop a fascination with their genital regions.

_____ 5. Physical aggression is a common childhood response to shame and guilt.

_____ 6. When conditions prevent children from becoming independent, they will often respond by becoming passive or anxious.

_____ 7. Play is a primary means for practicing the values, behaviors, and roles of society.

_____ 8. Young children who are maltreated by their caregivers are more likely to be rejected by their peers.

_____ 9.   On average, when born, males tend to be slightly longer and heavier, but females have slightly more mature skeletons.

_____ 10. Research indicates that many stereotyped gender roles (such as boys being more achievement-oriented, or girls being more social) do exist.

_____ 11. Mothers' influences on their child's ideas of gender are particularly important, and become more influential as the child grows.

_____ 12. An authoritative father might allow his daughter to stay at a friend's house after her normal curfew, if it does not interfere with any of his daughter's other responsibilities (such as school or chores).

_____ 13. When a child is upset and sad, it is often the most effective approach to distract the child from her troubles (such as by putting her in front of the television).

_____ 14. Research indicates that siblings raised in the same family are likely to have very similar personalities.

_____ 15. On average, first-born children tend to have slightly higher IQs than other birth orders and only children.

MATCHING

Match the following with the appropriate answer, and check your answers with the Answer Key at the end of this chapter.

1. _____ Reaction formation

    a. incorporating the values, attitudes, and beliefs of others

2. _____ Repression

    b. unconsciously erasing a frightening event from awareness.

3. _____ Regression

    c. substituting something or someone else for the real source of anger or fear

4. _____ Withdrawal

    d. removing yourself from an unpleasant situation

5. _____ Projection

    e. attributing undesirable thoughts or actions to someone else, thereby distorting reality

6. _____ Rationalization

    f. refusing to admit that a situation exists or that an event happened

7. _____ Displacement

    g. behaving in ways opposite to your inclinations

8. ____ Denial   h. returning to an earlier or more infantile form of behavior as a way of coping with a stressful situation

9. ____ Identification   i. persuading yourself that you do not want what you cannot have

KEY VOCABULARY TERMS

Label each definition and give an example of each.

1. The psychodynamic behaviors that individuals use to reduce the tensions or stress that lead to anxiety.

2. Actions intended to benefit others.

3. The ideas about themselves which define how children think about themselves.

4. A personality type that includes characteristics that are both masculine and feminine traits.

5. The concepts that define how a person thinks about the behaviors and attitudes that are appropriate for males and females.

Explain the difference between the following sets of terms

6. Fear; anxiety
7. Systematic desensitization; participant modeling
8. Shame; guilt
9. Sex; gender
10. Authoritative parenting; Authoritarian parenting

PROGRAMMED REVIEW

Fill in the blanks in the following programmed review. Then check your answers with the Answer Key at the end of the chapter

1. Young children learn the _____, _____, and _____ of their society, and they develop a _____ that may persist throughout their lives.

Coping With Feelings and Emotions

2. One of the earliest tasks that young children must cope with is to learn to manage the wide range of _____ and _____ they experience.

Fear and Anxiety

3. _____ is a state of arousal, tension or apprehension caused by a specific, identifiable _____ or _____ .

4. _____ is a more _____ emotional state, that produces a feeling of _____ , apprehension, or fear that has a _____ source.

5. In contemporary _____ culture, showing _____ is generally frowned upon.

Emotional Regulation

6. Particularly important to the process of emotional regulation is the child's ability to manage feelings of _____ and _____ , which generally develop during the _____ and _____ years of life.

7. Children learn very early that open displays of _____ feelings are usually unacceptable in public places.

Aggression and Prosocial Behavior

8. Aggression is generally viewed as a _____ , one that is displayed across all _____ and _____ .

Aggression

9. By the age of _____ or _____ , children are less egocentric, and better able to understand another child's _____ .

10. One study estimates that by the time children are _____ years old, they will have seen _____ acts of violence on TV, including _____ murders.

Prosocial Behavior

11. When fully developed, prosocial behavior is accopmanied by feelings of _____ , caring, and warmth–including _____ , which is the ability to understand the _____ and _____ of others.

12. Prosocial behavior appears to be a _____ issue that involves not only the child's _____ and ability to make an appropriate response but also the child's _____ of another person's feelings and needs.

Developmental Conflicts
<u>Initiative Versus Guilt</u>

13. _____ refers to the _____ of young children as they ambitiously explore their surroundings.

14. _____ is triggered by the child's newly emerging _____, which is an internal guide that matches the child's behavior to accepted _____.

Peers, Play, and the Development of Social Competence
<u>The Role of Imaginary Companions</u>

15. As a part of their play, many children create _____–invisible characters who may seem real to the child–who become a _____ part of their daily routines.

16. Children who have _____ imaginations have an easier time mastering _____, which is the key to understanding _____ and complex relationships and ideas.

<u>Cultural Variations in Play</u>

17. Even in cultures where there is little time for _____, children frequently create play situations by integrating _____ and _____.

<u>Social Competence and the Development of Social Skills</u>

18. _____, which is the ability to respond to situations with appropriately _____, yet _____ emotions, seems especially important.

19. Socially competent children also have better _____, such as the ability to _____ and participate in _____.

Understanding Self and Others

20. Children put together various specific behaviors to create overall _____ of behavior that are appropriate for their _____, _____, and _____.

<u>Social Concepts and Rules</u>

21. As development proceeds, children begin to incorporate _____ into their thinking, which often involve understanding how _____, as well as other people, _____ and _____.

22. Young children do not acquire a clear understanding of _____ until _____.

Self-Concept

23. Understanding how one _____ to others is an essential step in the development of _____ and _____.

Self and Gender

24. By age _____, the average _____ is well into adolescence, whereas physically the average _____ is still a preadolescent.

25. One cultural shift currently taking place in _____ is a growing acceptance of _____ – the view that all people are capable of developing a wide range of traits.

26. Developing a _____ and a _____ is not just a result of models and rewards.

Family Dynamics
Parenting Styles

27. Two dimensions of parenting that are especially important in characterizing parenting styles are _____ and _____.

28. Traditional _____ parents are often described as _____ and _____, yet the "training" approach they use in child rearing fosters high academic achievement.

Discipline and Self-Control

29. The goal is for children to establish their own _____, not only of their behavior but of their _____ as well.

Sibling Dynamics

30. Siblings can play an important role in helping each other _____ and _____ social concepts and establish appropriate social _____.

31. Despite differences in their situations, young children experience many of the same _____ as they work to develop _____ and _____.

Child Maltreatment: Abuse and Neglect

32. In the United States, official reports of child abuse and neglect total one _____ a year; _____ children die every _____ as a result of physical abuse or neglect.

33. _____ abuse is more often inflicted on girls, _____ abuse more often on boys.

34. Psychological abuse can take _____ forms and can range form mild, unkind treatment to outrageous, _____, and _____ damaging abuse.

35. Programs for _____ child abuse typically focus on providing _____ to parents and teaching them better _____ of discipline.

CRITICAL THINKING QUESTIONS

To further your mastery of the topics, write out the answers to the following essay questions in the space provided.

1. How do history and culture affect what children fear?

2. How would young children be especially vulnerable to violent images and themes in the media?

3. How might the emerging development of self-concept influence play styles?

4. How can parents encourage their children to develop emotional self-control?

5. What effects might child abuse have on the child's emotional regulation?

6. How can an authoritative parenting style contribute to prosocial behavior in children?

7. How might cultural expectations about sex affect a 3-year-old's sense of initiative versus guilt, given their natural curiosity about the genital region at this age?

8. How do gender schemes and gender constancy demonstrate different points in cognitive development?

9. How can having shared goals as a family facilitate social competence?

PRACTICE TEST - POST TEST

Circle the correct answer for each multiple choice question and check your answers with the Answer Key at the end of the chapter.

1. The cognitive-developmental view of early childhood was espoused by which of the following theorists?
   a. Erik Erikson
   b. Lev Vygotsky
   c. Albert Bandura
   d. Karl Jung

2. Mary becomes tense and apprehensive whenever she sees lightning flash; she is experiencing which phenomenon?
   a. dread
   b. phobia
   c. anxiety
   d. fear

3. Xavier is afraid of cats despite the fact that no cat has ever hurt him; what is he experiencing?
   a. phobia
   b. shame
   c. philia
   d. fear

4. Navajo parents believe it is healthy and normal for a child to be afraid. A Navajo child could be expected to have which of the following when compared to children from a Western culture?
   a. the same number of fears
   b. fewer fears
   c. more fears
   d. stronger phobias

5. Abigail tells herself that she would not have had fun at a party to which she was not invited; which defense mechanism is she using?
   a. projection
   b. rationalization
   c. denial
   d. reaction formation

6. Galen watches as his siblings begin fighting; he leaves and plays in his room. Which defense mechanism is he using?
   a. identification
   b. displacement
   c. withdrawal
   d. repression

7. Which of the following affects the core of a child's sense of identity?
   a. shame
   b. guilt
   c. fear
   d. anxiety

8. A child who accidentally hurts another child while playing is exhibiting which type of aggression?
   a. frustration
   b. hostile aggression
   c. instrumental aggression
   d. assertiveness

9. In the United States, what percentage of children between birth age and 3-years-old, have televisions in their rooms?
   a. 27%
   b. 30%
   c. 36%
   d. 40%

10. Megan sees her mother feeling and looking sad. This in turn makes Megan sad. She is experiencing which phenomenon?
    a. empathy
    b. sympathy
    c. frustration
    d. jealousy

11. A child who has an imaginary companion is more likely to be which of the following?
    a. shy
    b. sociable
    c. playful
    d. aggressive

12. Which of the following is NOT a component of social competence?
    a. social regulation
    b. social knowledge
    c. social ramification
    d. social disposition

13. The question "Why did she do that?" is typically asked by a child trying to learn which of the following?
    a. internalization
    b. self-socialization
    c. social concepts
    d. emotional regulation

14. Kathrine says "I am a good girl–I don't hit." She is developing which of the following, which provides guidelines for her behavior?
    a. gender roles
    b. personal stereotypes
    c. personal script
    d. self-knowledge

15. Byron has recently come to understand that his gender does not change despite superficial alterations. Approximately, what is his age?
    a. 3 years
    b. 5 years
    c. 7 years
    d. 9 years

16. Which of the following is the most recently classified parenting style?
    a. authoritative
    b. authoritarian
    c. permissive
    d. indifferent

17. A parent who often makes statements like "a rule is a rule" most likely subscribes to which parenting style?
    a. authoritative
    b. authoritarian
    c. permissive
    d. indifferent

18. A parent helping a child achieve emotional self-control directly corresponds to all of the following except which?
    a. longer attention spans
    b. higher scores in math and reading
    c. higher IQs
    d. slower heart rates

19. How many times more likely is a stepfather to abuse his female children than a biological father?
    a. 5
    b. 6
    c. 8
    d. 10

20. Alfred does not have his needs met, is not allowed to have friends, is often called "loser" in public, and is forced to watch while his father beats his mother. Which of the following forms of abuse has he NOT endured?

a. degradation
b. terrorization
c. isolation
d. exploitation

ANSWER KEYS

Practice Test – Pretest (with text page numbers)

1. a 211	6. b 218	11. c 225	16. d 230
2. b 212	7. c 218	12. d 225	17. c 232
3. a 213	8. d 200	13. d 226	18. a 234
4. c 217	9. b 200	14. a 227	19. c 236
5. a 217	10. c 223	15. c 229	20. c 239

True/False

1. F	6. T	11. F
2. T	7. T	12. T
3. F	8. T	13. F
4. F	9. T	14. F
5. F	10. F	15. T

Matching

1. g	6. i
2. b	7. c
3. h	8. f
4. d	9. a
5. e	

Key Vocabulary Terms

1. Defense mechanisms
2. Prosocial behaviors
3. Self-concepts
4. Androgynous personality
5. gender schemes

6. Fear is a state of arousal, tension, or apprehension caused by a specific and identifiable stimulus or situation. Anxiety is a feeling of uneasiness, apprehension, or fear that has a vague or unknown source.

7. Systematic desensitization is a technique for coping with phobias where the subject works through a hierarchy of fears starting with a minimal version of the feared object or situation and working up to the real thing. Participant modeling is a technique for coping with phobias where the subject watches another person interact with the object feared, or exist in the feared situation, without harm; the subject is then encouraged to follow the model's example.

8. Shame is an intense and painful emotion that reflects negatively on the one that feels it; it causes a desire to change oneself. Guilt involves acknowledging that one has been involved in a morally wrong act; it causes a desire to change a behavior, but not oneself.

9. <u>Sex</u> is the genetic and biological determination of whether one is male or female. <u>Gender</u> is a conceptual understanding of being male or female, which is largely defined by culture.

10. <u>Authoritative parenting</u> combines a high degree of warmth, acceptance, and encouragement of autonomy, with firm, but flexible, control. <u>Authoritarian parenting</u> involves having high degrees of control, showing little warmth, and strictly adhering to rigid rules.

Programmed Review
1. norms, rules, cultural meanings, self-concept
2. feelings, emotions
3. Fear, stimulus, situation
4. Anxiety, generalized, uneasiness, vague
5. Western, fear
6. shame, guilt, second, third
7. negative
8. natural response, cultures, historical periods
9. 6, 7, point of view
10. 18, 200,000, 40,000
11. friendship, empathy, feelings, perspectives
12. complex, willingness, appreciation
13. Initiative, purposefulness
14. Guilt, conscious, moral standards
15. imaginary companions, regular
16. active, symbolic representations, abstract concepts
17. play, chores, fun
18. Emotional regulation, controlled, flexible
19. social skills, take turns, conversations
20. patterns, gender, family, culture
21. social concepts, they, think, act
22. friendship, middle childhood
23. appears, self-knowledge, self-concept
24. 12, girl, boy
25. the United States, androgyny
26. gender role, gender identity
27. control, warmth
28. Chinese, authoritarian, highly controlling
29. self-control, emotions
30. identify, learn, roles
31. conflicts, autonomy, competence
32. million, three, day
33. Sexual, physical
34. multiple, demeaning, emotionally
35. preventing, social support, methods

Practice Test – Post test (with text page numbers)

1. b 210
2. d 211
3. a 211
4. c 212
5. b 213

6. c 213
7. a 215
8. c 217
9. b 219
10. a 220

11. b 225
12. a 226
13. c 229
14. c 230
15. b 232

16. c 234
17. b 235
18. c 237
19. a 239
20. d 240

Chapter 8

Middle Childhood: Physical and Cognitive Development

CHAPTER OUTLINE

◈ Physical and Motor Development
- ♦ Physical Growth and Change
- ♦ Internal Changes
- ♦ Motor Skills Development
- ♦ Health, Fitness, and Accidents

◈ Cognitive Development
- ♦ Piaget and Concrete Operational Thinking
- ♦ Memory and Metacognition
- ♦ Language and Literacy Development
- ♦ Individual Differences in Intelligence

◈ Learning and Thinking in School
- ♦ New Demands and Expectations
- ♦ Developing Competent Learners and Critical Thinkers
- ♦ Success in School

◈ Developmental Disorders
- ♦ Mental Retardation
- ♦ Learning Disorders
- ♦ Attention-Deficit/Hyperactivity Disorder

LEARNING OBJECTIVES

After you have read and studied this chapter, you should be able to answer the following questions.

1. What overarching principles guide development through the period of middle childhood?
2. Why are asthma and obesity becoming more prevalent among grade school children in the United States?
3. How do the thought processes of a grade school child differ from those of a preschool child?
4. What is the best way to define intelligence?
5. What are the most important adjustments children face when they begin school?
6. What is the best way to meet the educational challenges faced by children with special needs?

PRACTICE TEST – PRETEST

Circle the correct answer for each multiple choice question and check your answers with the Answer Key at the end of the chapter.

1. Compared to growth in the first 2 years of life, growth during middle childhood is:
   a. slower and steadier
   b. faster and more abrupt
   c. faster but less obvious
   d. about the same pace

2. What are the episodes of stiffness and aching that are produced by periods of rapid growth?
   a. arthritis
   b. mood swings
   c. growing pains
   d. growth blights

3. Most children from 6 to 12 years old experience relatively few:
   a. accidents
   b. illnesses
   c. vision problems
   d. friendships

4. What is the most prevalent chronic disease in children in the U.S.?
   a. cancer
   b. heart disease
   c. asthma
   d. ear infections

5. Physical fitness involves regular exercise involving four aspects of conditioning. Which of the following is NOT one of those four aspects?
   a. flexibility
   b. cardiovascular efficiency
   c. muscle endurance
   d. weight loss

6. What is the term used to refer to children who must care for themselves after school?
   a. latchkey
   b. rugrat
   c. neglected
   d. loners

7. What does "BMI" stand for?
   a. body-mind indicator
   b. bone muscle index
   c. body mass index
   d. brain myelination index

8. What is the number one cause of death in middle childhood?
   a. pneumonia or influenza
   b. accidents
   c. birth defects
   d. cancer

9. Which of Piaget's stages of cognitive development allows children to perform mental operations on objects that are concrete and can be directly experienced?
   a. sensorimotor
   b. preoperational
   c. concrete operational
   d. formal operational

10. At about what age do children begin to develop theories about abstract concepts, thoughts, or relationships?
    a. 3 or 4
    b. 6 or 7
    c. 11 or 12
    d. 14 or 15

11. What is the name of the intellectual process that enables people to monitor their thinking and memory?
    a. mneumonics
    b. metacognition
    c. recognition
    d. neurosupervision

12. Control processes are strategies and techniques that enhance:
    a. memory
    b. self-control
    c. empathy
    d. overall intelligence

13. The recognition that oral and written language learning are interconnected has led to what approach in literacy?
    a. phonics
    b. word-sound association
    c. whole language
    d. emergent literacy

14. Which of the following is NOT one of the conditions that promote literacy?
    a. a print-rich environment
    b. rote memorization
    c. symbolic representation
    d. firsthand experiences of interest

15. What two types of age are used to calculate intelligence according to the Stanford-Binet Intelligence Scale?
    a. mental and chronological
    b. social and chronological
    c. social and psychological
    d. biological and psychological

16. What is an intelligence test designed to measure?
    a. current intellectual functioning
    b. intellectual potential
    c. academic capability
    d. societal functioning

17. Which of the following is NOT one of Gardner's seven intelligences?
    a. linguistic
    b. musical
    c. neurological
    d. interpersonal

18. Comparing a child's intellectual abilities to that of peers of the same chronological age is known as the:
    a. peer approach to IQ
    b. function approach to IQ
    c. comparison IQ
    d. ratio approach to IQ

19. If a child were to take the same test more than once and receive the same score, that test could be said to be highly:
    a. reliable
    b. static
    c. valid
    d. economical

20. Which of the following is not a real IQ test?
    a. WPPSI
    b. WAIS
    c. WASP
    d. WISC

TRUE/FALSE

For each of the following statements, indicate whether the statement is True or False. Check your answers with the Answer Key at the end of the chapter.

_____ 1. Physical pain associated with rapid growth is both common and normal in adolescence.

_____ 2. Highly muscular athletes will always have a low BMI.

_____ 3. Childhood obesity is associated with serious social and psychological consequences.

_____ 4. By around 7 years of age, a child can perform the same mental tasks as an adult.

_____ 5. Language learning is not yet complete in middle childhood.

_____ 6. Intelligence tests are an objective measure of a child's intellectual potential.

_____ 7. Even when social and economic disparities are taken into account, there are numerous IQ score differences between minority and majority groups.

_____ 8. It is not unusual for a teacher to spend only 10 to 15% of a 30-minute class period on academic work.

_____ 9. Children tend to succeed when their parents provide support and guidance.

____ 10. Most people with mental retardation fall into the category of moderate retardation.

____ 11. Sometimes mental retardation is not identified until the child enters formal education.

____ 12. Children with learning disorders tend to have below-average general intellectual ability.

____ 13. Most children with dyslexia have problems with their visual system.

____ 14. Children with learning disorders often have difficulty with social skills.

____ 15. ADHD has a strong genetic link.

MATCHING

Match the following types of intelligence with their definition.

1. ____	Linguistic	a.	ability to appreciate pitch, rhythm, and timbre
2. ____	Logical-mathematical	b.	ability to correctly understand one's own feelings
3. ____	Spatial	c.	ability to classify plants and animals
4. ____	Bodily-kinesthetic	d.	facility for numerical operations and complex reasoning
5. ____	Musical	e.	sensitivity to the sounds, rhythms, and meanings of words
6. ____	Interpersonal	f.	ability to correctly interpret and appropriately respond to the moods, temperament, and motivations of other people
7. ____	Intrapersonal	g.	ability to control one's own movements and to handle objects skillfully
8. ____	Naturalist	h.	ability to perceive the visuo-spatial world accurately and to manipulate those perceptions

KEY VOCABULARY TERMS

Label each definition and give a specific example of each.

1. Strategies and techniques that enhance memory.

2. Disorder that is characterized by significantly sub-average intellectual functioning and self-help skills.

3. Disorders associated with difficulty in acquiring some specific academic skills but not others despite normal intelligence and the absence of sensory or motor disabilities, may occur in areas such as reading, writing or math.

4. Disorder that involves the inability to keep focused on something long enough to learn it, which is often accompanied by poor impulse control.

5. For Piaget, the third stage of cognitive development; begins at age 5 to 7 and allows the child to perform mental operations, such as conservation, decentration, and reversibility, on objects that are concrete and that can be directly experienced.

Explain the difference between the following sets of terms.

6. perceptual problems; logical problems
7. preoperational; concrete operational
8. mental age; chronological age
9. mental retardation; learning disorder
10. gross motor skills; fine motor skills

PROGRAMMED REVIEW

Fill in the blanks in the following programmed review. Then check your answers with the Answer Key at the end of the chapter.

Physical and Motor Development
Physical Growth and Change

1. Gradual, regular growth continues until about age 9 for girls and age 11 for boys; at that point, the _____ _____ _____ begins.

Internal Changes

2. Between the ages of 6 and 8, the forebrain undergoes a temporary growth spurt; by age 8, the brain is _____ to _____% of its adult size.

3. Parents should be aware that because the _____ and _____ of the school-age child are not mature, overly stringent physical training may cause injuries.

Motor Skills Development

4. At age _____, a boy can typically throw a ball about 34 feet. By age _____, he can probably throw it twice as far; by age _____, three times as far.

5. Most of the fine motor skills required for writing develop between the ages of 6 and 7, although some quite normal children cannot draw a _____ or master many _____ _____ until age 8.

Health, Fitness, and Accidents

6. Vision problems begin to _____ during middle childhood: by the sixth grade, _____% of White middle-class children in the United States have been fitted with glasses or contact lenses.

7. Currently, 12% of U.S. children under the age of 18 have been diagnosed with _____.

8. A better measure of health than absence of illness is _____ _____; that is, the optimal functioning of the heart, lungs, muscles, and blood vessels.

9. National health objectives call not only for physical education classes to meet every day, but also for programs that engage students in active physical exercise – preferably _____ activities such as _____ and _____ – for at least 50% of the time devoted to physical education.

Cognitive Development
Piaget and Concrete Operational Thinking

10. Piaget referred to middle childhood as the _____ _____ period.

11. Unlike preoperational children, concrete operational children can also _____ about the world around them.

12. Because most children learn most readily when working with concrete examples, many educational curricula teach these arithmetic operations by having children _____ _____, such as adding to one pile while subtracting from another.

Memory and Metacognition

13. Early in the period of concrete operations, children's ability to recall lists of items _____ significantly, in part because they begin making _____ efforts to memorize information.

Language and Literacy Development

14. In middle school, children's vocabulary begins to expand, and they master increasingly complex grammatical structures and more sophisticated language usage. For example, they begin to use and understand the _____ _____, although their _____ may still be shaky.

15. _____ and _____ are natural outgrowths of the child's growing language skills.

16. Whole-language theorists focus on the concept of _____ _____.

17. Parents make a major contribution to their children's literacy and are especially effective when they focus on _____ what is being read, rather than on _____ and _____ specific reading skills.

Individual Differences in Intelligence

18. IQ is assumed to be normally distributed around an average score of 100, with about _____ _____ of the general population scoring between 85 and 115 and almost _____% of the population scoring between 70 and 130.

19. Although some intelligence tests define intelligence as a _____ _____, the majority of tests define it as a _____ of abilities.

20. According to Sternberg's triarchic theory of intelligence, _____ intelligence involves adaptation to the environment and what we might call common sense; _____ intelligence involves the ability to cope with new tasks or situations as well as with old ones; and _____ intelligence corresponds roughly to the intellectual abilities measured by commonly employed IQ tests.

21. Perhaps the best way to understand the differences in average IQ scores that exist between minority and majority groups relates to the disparity in their _____ and _____ circumstances.

Learning and Thinking in School
<u>New Demands and Expectations</u>

22. Regardless of the school, there is always a gap between what is expected at home and what is expected in the classroom. The _____ the gap, the more _____ the child's adjustment will be.

<u>Developing Competent Learners and Critical Thinkers</u>

23. Educational psychologist generally recommend a range of teaching strategies to develop thinking skills, and these often require students to practice several different types of skills, such as _____, _____, _____, _____, _____, and _____.

<u>Success in School</u>

24. Girls tend to outperform boys on _____ skills, and boys tend to do better in _____ and _____ tasks.

25. The parents of African-American children who excel academically tend to stress the importance of _____ and to encourage the development of _____ and belief in personal _____.

Developmental Disorders

26. _____ identify the learning goals appropriate for each individual and note the support services that will be provided to help these children meet their goals.

<u>Mental Retardation</u>

27. In many cases, the causes of mental retardation are _____.

28. Mental retardation, especially when it is mild, often is not diagnosed until several _____ after the child's birth and sometimes is diagnosed only when the child begins _____ _____.

<u>Learning Disorders</u>

29. For reasons that remain unclear, up to 80% of children with learning disorders are _____.

30. One common type of reading disorder is _____, which involves incorrectly perceiving letters and words.

31. ADHD may result when a child's nervous system is chronically _____.

32. For those children with ADHD who do not respond to drugs or whose parents choose to avoid using them, an alternate form of treatment is _____ _____, which generally is implemented both at home and at school.

33. Studies of identical and fraternal twins suggest that ADHD has a strong _____ link.

CRITICAL THINKING QUESTIONS
To further your mastery of the topics, write out the answers to the following essay questions in the space provided.

1. What are some differences in cognitive ability between a child in the preoperational stage and a child in the concrete operational stage?

2. Describe emergent literacy. What are some examples?

3. What are some of the reasons why an intelligence test score might not be completely accurate?

4. What are some factors that might account for gender differences in academic success?

5. If one of the symptoms of ADHD is hyperactivity, why does the treatment for ADHD include stimulants?

6. Why do accidents cause the majority of deaths in middle childhood?

7. Even though cognitive development proceeds without formal education, what can be done to speed up the process of thinking and problem solving?

8. Why are small-group projects and activities an effective way to encourage critical thinking?

PRACTICE TEST – POST TEST

Circle the correct answer for each multiple choice question and check your answers with the Answer Key at the end of the chapter.

1. Growing pains can occur as early as what age?
    a. 4 years old   c. 8 years old
    b. 6 years old   d. 0 years old

2. What kind of motor skills eventually leads to the ability to form letters or other symbols if practiced?
    a. fluid motor skills   c. fine motor skills
    b. concrete motor skills   d. gross motor skills

3. Which of the following BMIs falls within the normal range?
   a. 18
   b. 23
   c. 26
   d. 31

4. A child watches as water from a short, wide container is poured into a tall, thin container. Based on the higher level of the water level in the new container, the child concludes that there is now more water. In which stage of cognitive development is the child?
   a. sensorimotor
   b. preoperational
   c. concrete operational
   d. formal operational

5. Drawing, scribbling, nonphonetic writing, and invented spelling are all examples of what literacy-promoting condition?
   a. pressure-free experimentation with writing
   b. a rich oral-language environment
   c. a print-rich environment
   d. symbolic representation

6. Susie is 4 years old and has an IQ of 100 according to the Stanford-Binet intelligence scale. What is her mental age?
   a. 3 years
   b. 4 year
   c. 5 years
   d. 6 years

7. Which of the following is NOT one of Gardner's eight types of intelligence?
   a. charismatic
   b. intrapersonal
   c. linguistic
   d. spatial

8. According to the triarchic theory of intelligence, which type of intelligence might we call "common sense"?
   a. experiential
   b. componential
   c. contextual
   d. logical

9. Which of the following is NOT one of the six "Rs" representing the types of thinking children need to learn?
   a. remembering
   b. repeating
   c. reporting
   d. relating

10. An internalized need to persist toward success and excellence is called:
    a. self-efficacy
    b. goal orientation
    c. stubbornness
    d. achievement motivation

11. If children of both sexes cannot name 10 famous women in American history, this may be evidence of:
    a. outdated textbooks
    b. a gender-biased curriculum
    c. gender discrimination by teachers
    d. lack of critical thinking skills

12. Local schools include children with special needs in regular classrooms and activities as much as possible. This is called providing them with:
    a. upward comparisons
    b. group-learning opportunities
    c. the least restrictive environment
    d. environmental challenge

13. An IQ score of between 25 and 40 indicates what level of mental retardation?
    a. mild
    b. moderate
    c. severe
    d. profound

14. Which of the following is NOT one of the three main categories of learning disorders?
    a. reading disorder
    b. disorder of verbal expression
    c. disorder of written expression
    d. mathematics disorder

15. There are many possible causes of ADHD. Which of the following is NOT one listed by your text?
    a. malnutrition
    b. caffeine
    c. heredity
    d. organic brain damage

16. What area of the brain becomes more mature, improving communication between the brain's left and right hemispheres, during middle childhood?
    a. corpus callosum
    b. prefrontal cortex
    c. temporal lobes
    d. medulla oblongata

17. At what age do children begin to lose their baby teeth?
    a. 2 or 3 years
    b. 4 or 5 years
    c. 6 or 7 years
    d. 9 or 10 years

18. Timmy is of above-average intelligence but has trouble with comprehending and remembering written material. He often confuses similar letters or reads *star* as *rats*. From what developmental disorder is Timmy suffering?
    a. autism
    b. schizophrenia
    c. ADHD
    d. dyslexia

19. Jill is extremely inattentive, has poor impulse control, and is highly active. Based on these symptoms, what developmental disorder might Jill have?
    a. autism
    b. schizophrenia
    c. ADHD
    d. dyslexia

20. What act mandates that students with special needs no longer be sent to special schools but rather they should be included in mainstream classes and activities to the greatest extent possible?
    a. Handicapped Students Act
    b. No Child Left Behind Act
    c. Maximum Student Independence Act
    d. Individuals with Disabilities Education Act

ANSWER KEYS

Practice Test – Pretest (with text page numbers)

1.	a 248	6.	a 252	11.	b 257	16.	a 261
2.	c 249	7.	c 252	12.	a 257	17.	c 262
3.	b 250	8.	b 252	13.	c 259	18.	d 261
4.	c 250	9.	c 254	14.	b 259	19.	a 261
5.	d 251	10.	c 256	15.	a 260	20.	c 261

True/False

1.	T	6.	F	11.	T
2.	F	7.	F	12.	F
3.	T	8.	T	13.	F
4.	F	9.	T	14.	T
5.	T	10.	F	15.	T

Matching

1.	e	5.	a
2.	d	6.	f
3.	g	7.	b
4.	g	8.	c

Key Vocabulary Terms

1. control processes
2. mental retardation
3. learning disorders
4. Attention Deficit Hyperactivity Disorder
5. concrete operational

6. Perceptual problems are resolved using sensory information such as height or width (i.e., one row of matches is shorter, therefore it has more matches); logical problems are resolved by thinking differently about states and transformations (i.e., there are still the same number of matches even though one row is longer because one row has more space between the matches).

7. Preoperational thought is characterized as rigid, irreversible, centered on one dimension, egocentric, and focuses on perceptual evidence; concrete operational thought is reversible, flexible, multidimensional, less egocentric, and uses logical inferences.

8. Mental age is the child's level of cognitive ability; chronological age is the expression of how old the child is in years and months. They may or may not correspond with each other.

9. Mental retardation is characterized by significantly sub-average level of intellectual functioning; a child with a learning disorder has average or above-average intelligence.

10. <u>Gross motor skills</u> involve large, broad movements such as running or hopping; <u>fine motor skills</u> involve more complex movements such as painting or drawing shapes.

Programmed Review
1. adolescent growth spurt
2. 90, 95
3. skeleton; ligaments
4. 7, 10, 12
5. diamond, letter shapes
6. emerge, 25
7. Asthma
8. physical fitness
9. lifelong, jogging, swimming
10. concrete operational
11. theorize
12. manipulate objects
13. improves, conscious
14. passive voice, syntax
15. reading and writing
16. emergent literacy
17. discussing, drilling, correcting
18. two thirds, 96
19. single attribute, composite
20. contextual, experiential, componential
21. social, economic
22. greater, difficult
23. remembering, repeating, reasoning, reorganizing, relating, reflecting
24. verbal, quantitative, spatial
25. education, self-esteem, efficacy
26. Individual Education Plans (IEPs)
27. unknown
28. months, formal education
29. boys
30. dyslexia
31. understimulated
32. educational management
33. genetic

Practice Test – Post test (with text page numbers)

1.	a 249	6.	b 260	11.	b 268	16.	a 249
2.	c 250	7.	a 262	12.	c 269	17.	c 250
3.	b 252	8.	c 262	13.	c 270	18.	d 273
4.	b 255	9.	c 266	14.	b 271	19.	c 274
5.	a 259	10.	d 267	15.	b 274	20.	c 269

Chapter 9

Middle Childhood: Personality and Sociocultural Development

CHAPTER OUTLINE

◈ Personality Development in an Expanding Social World
   ◆ Three Perspectives on Middle Childhood
   ◆ Self-Concept
   ◆ Industry Versus Inferiority
   ◆ Self-Esteem

◈ Social Knowledge and Reasoning
   ◆ The Development of Social Cognition
   ◆ The Development of Morality

◈ Peer Relationships
   ◆ Functions of Friendship
   ◆ Developmental Patterns in Friendship
   ◆ Peer Groups
   ◆ In-Groups, Out-Groups, and Prejudice

◈ Family Influences in Middle Childhood
   ◆ Parent-Child Interactions and Relationships
   ◆ The Changing Nature of the Family

LEARNING OBJECTIVES

After you have read and studied this chapter, you should be able to answer the following questions.

1. What events in middle childhood enhance or detract from the child's developing self-concept?
2. How is a child's social world influenced through interactions with others?
3. How do children of different ages think about questions of right versus wrong?
4. What influences do peers have on development during the grade school years?
5. How does a child come to develop a sense of ethnic identity?
6. When family structures change, such as when parents divorce or remarry, what developmental issues are posed for children?

PRACTICE TEST – PRETEST

Circle the correct answer for each multiple choice question and check your answers with the Answer Key at the end of the chapter.

1. The period of development called middle childhood last, roughly, from the age of six until when?
   a. 13
   b. 12
   c. 11
   d. 10

2. Stable personality characteristics are referred to as which of the following in your text?
   a. features
   b. qualities
   c. attributes
   d. traits

3. Which of the following does self-esteem add to your ideas about self?
   a. who you are
   b. whether you see yourself positively or negatively
   c. what you can do
   d. whether you are proud of your choices

4. A person's knowledge and understanding of the social world makes up her what?
   a. social inference
   b. social cognition
   c. social responsibility
   d. social regulations

5. By which of the following are the customs that govern social interactions referred?
   a. social inference
   b. social cognition
   c. social responsibility
   d. social regulations

6. An individual's unique ideas about right and wrong is called which of the following?
   a. ethics
   b. righteousness
   c. morality
   d. quality

7. Which of the following is NOT the name of one of Kohlberg's three levels of moral development?
   a. Preconventional
   b. Conventional
   c. Metaconventional
   d. Postconventional

8. Under which of Selman's stages of friendship development is friendship seen as a stable, continuing relationship based on trust?
   a. 1
   b. 2
   c. 3
   d. 4

9. At approximately which age does the peer group take on greater significance for its members?
   a. 7
   b. 8
   c. 9
   d. 10

10. A child who pays special attention to what they do and say and how their behavior affects others is said to do which of the following?
    a. self-reflection
    b. self-examination
    c. self-observation
    d. self-monitor

11. Which of the following implies an in-group and an out-group?
    a. discrimination
    b. bigotry
    c. bias
    d. prejudice

12. Excluding or mocking members of a particular group are examples of which of the following?
    a. discrimination
    b. bigotry
    c. bias
    d. prejudice

13. Which of the following is NOT a factor of popularity mentioned in the book?
    a. emotional control
    b. athletic ability
    c. academic performance
    d. physical attractiveness

14. During middle childhood, which of the following is the most important socializing influence on children?
    a. peers
    b. family
    c. school
    d. teachers

15. Children's ability to control and direct their own behavior and to meet the requirement placed on them is referred to as which of the following?
    a. self-monitoring
    b. self-scaffolding
    c. self-control
    d. self-regulation

16. When parents develop sense of shared responsibility with their children, they are engaging in which of the following?
    a. co-administration
    b. cooperation
    c. co-direction
    d. coregulation

17. In 2002, which of the following percentages of mothers of school-aged children worked outside the home?
    a. 52%
    b. 68%
    c. 76%
    d. 84%

18. Children who are able to overcome difficult environments and lead socially competent lives are called what type of children?
    a. forceful
    b. strong-willed
    c. resilient
    d. lucky

19. Which of the following is the best way in which parents can make divorce easier for their child after a divorce?
    a. find a stepparent for the child
    b. distract them with toys
    c. stick to familiar routines
    d. imply the other parent will come back

20. Which of the following is NOT a factor that affects a child's reaction to divorce?
    a. amount of change in the child's life
    b. nature of parent-child relationship
    c. knowledge or understanding of divorce
    d. amount of hostility in the divorce

TRUE/FALSE

For each of the following statements, indicate whether the statement is True or False. Check your answers with the Answer Key at the end of this chapter.

_____ 1.   Social concepts such as morality are more often directly taught than learned from interpreting real world situations.

_____ 2.   Children in the first grade tend to have very realistic perceptions of their abilities and competences.

_____ 3.   When family, peers, and the community view a child in a positive light, the child is likely to develop high self-esteem.

____ 4.   Used in excess, praise can be quite effective at building realistic self-esteem.

____ 5.   Social cognition involves guesses about what other people are thinking and feeling.

____ 6.   All aspects of social cognition–inference, responsibility, and regulations–are involved in developing a child's sense of fairness, justice, and right and wrong.

____ 7.   Kohlberg himself concluded that his sixth stage of moral development may not apply to all people in all cultures, but merely reflect Western values.

____ 8.   In making moral decisions, traditional U.S. culture teaches boys to strive for a perspective of justice, while caring for others is taught to girls.

____ 9.   During middle childhood, both boys and girls tend to want to share intimate thoughts and secrets with their friends.

____ 10.   Children with stable, satisfying friendships tend to achieve more in school.

____ 11.   Within individual peer groups, there are rarely status differences between the members; all members share the roles of leader and follower.

____ 12.   The way that a group is defined in one community may be radically different from the way that same group would be defined in a different community.

____ 13.   It sometimes occurs that African-American students view any academic achievement as being disloyal to the group, because school is seen as a white institution.

____ 14.   Most children whose parents both work felt that their parents gave too much priority to their work.

____ 15.   In severe cases, children who live with constant violence may develop post-traumatic stress disorder.

MATCHING

Match the following with the appropriate answer, and check your answers with the Answer Key at the end of this chapter.

1. ____ Social responsibility

a.   a person's ideas about right and wrong

2. ____ Psychodynamic view

b.   though, knowledge, and understanding that involves the social world

3. ____ Morality

     c. holds that children develop habits through observing and imitating models

4. ____ Social cognition

     d. an individual's obligations to family, friends, and to society

5. ____ Social-learning view

     e. an individual's guesses about what another person is feeling, thinking, or intending

6. ____ Cognitive-developmental view

     f. holds that children develop more mature thinking skills which can be applied to solving social problems

7. ____ Social regulations

     g. holds that children turn their emotional energies toward peers, creative efforts, and learning culturally proscribed tasks

8. ____ Social inference

     h. the customs and conventions that govern social interaction

KEY VOCABULARY TERMS

Label each definition and give an example of each.

1. One's attitude toward oneself, which can range from positive to negative.

2. Any theory of morality that disregards cultural differences in moral belief.

3. A group of three or more people of similar age who interact with each other and who share norms and goals.

4. Children who are able to overcome difficult environments to lead socially competent lives.

5. A family where a mother or a father with children has remarried to produce a new family.

Explain the difference between the following sets of terms.

6. industry; inferiority
7. social inference; social perspective taking
8. moral realism; moral relativism
9. prejudice; discrimination
10. self-regulated behavior; coregulation

PROGRAMMED REVIEW

Fill in the blanks in the following programmed review. Then check your answers with the Answer Key at the end of the chapter

Personality Development in an Expanding Social World
<u>Three Perspectives on Middle Childhood</u>

1. Among these are perspectives of human development within the _____, the _____, and the _____ traditions.

<u>Self-Concept</u>

2. Studying the topic of _____ helps us understand the overall development during middle childhood, in that self-concept interweaves _____ and _____.

<u>Industry Versus Inferiority</u>

3. When children succeed in school, they typically incorporate a sense of _____ into their self-image–they learn that _____ produces results, and they continue to progress toward _____ their environment.

<u>Self-Esteem</u>

4. For children raised in cultures where formal _____ is expected, self-esteem is significantly correlated with _____ achievement.

5. Too much praise or praise that does not reflect real _____ can prevent children from developing an accurate sense of their _____ as well as their _____.

Social Knowledge and Reasoning
<u>The Development of Social Cognition</u>

6. All three aspects of social cognition–_____, _____, and _____– are involved in the child's developing ability to make moral judgments.

<u>The Development of Morality</u>

7. A young child will think that a child who _____ breaks a stack of dishes while setting a table is much _____ than a child who _____ breaks one dish out of _____.

8. Kohlberg's research assesses moral _____, not moral _____.

9. One is based primarily on the concept of _____, the other primarily on human _____ and _____.

Peer Relationships

Functions of Friendship

10. With a friend, children can share their _____, their _____, and every detail of their lives.

Developmental Patterns in Friendship

11. The stage model that _____ proposed provides a means for understanding how _____ advances set the stage for _____ and _____ development.

12. Friendship is conceptualized today as a _____, _____ series of _____.

Peer Groups

13. If children believe that another child _____ them, this may lead to a _____ response, especially if low _____ is involved.

14. Children also are actually more likely to conform to peer pressure when it is _____ than when it involves _____, such as _____, _____, or using _____.

In-Groups, Out-Groups, and Prejudice

15. _____ and _____ often are directed at people identified with particular _____ or _____ groups.

16. African-American children who succeed at school may be perceived as being _____ on grounds that school itself is a _____ institution.

Family Influences in Middle Childhood

17. Despite the time children spend with _____ and in school, the _____ normally continues to be the most important _____ influence during middle childhood.

Parent-Child Interactions and Relationships

18. A _____ parenting approach leads to more _____ and to better compliance with _____.

The Changing Nature of the Family

19. In 1948, only _____ of the mothers of school-age children worked outside the home; in 1975, the figure was _____; and in 2002, it was over _____.

20. Many life situations are inherently stressful for children and their families, including _____, _____, _____, suffering a serious illness or injury, and growing up in a dangerous environment.

21. The first day of school can be a _____ event in a child's life. A child who knows what to expect and who interprets this milestone as a sign of increasing _____ will experience less stress in making the transition than will a child who is not prepared or who associates school with _____ outcomes.

22. When marriages end in _____, children and parents must cope with the _____ and _____ stresses associated with the breakup of the family.

23. Children often _____ the rules to see if the _____ still works the way it did before.

24. Parents can help their children adjust by setting clear _____ and sticking to familiar _____ as much as possible.

25. Children may feel divided _____ to their original parents and feel _____ about abandoning the noncustodial parent by giving _____ to the stepparent.

26. When parents' divorce occurs in _____, children often have difficulty adjusting to the changes that take place.

CRITICAL THINKING QUESTIONS

To further your mastery of the topics, write out the answers to the following essay questions in the space provided.

1. How does a child's newfound social cognition lead to the crisis of industry versus inferiority?

2. How do inference, responsibility, and regulations contribute to the child's ability to make moral judgments?

3. Referring to Kohlberg's theory, distinguish between moral attitudes and moral behavior.

4. Distinguish between the preconventional, conventional, and postconventional levels of moral reasoning.

5. Describe how men and women may display differences in what they consider when determining whether something is moral.

6. How is peer group conformity a result of increased social cognition?

7. How can a person exhibit prejudice without discrimination? How might a person discriminate without being prejudiced?

8. How does coregulation encourage self-regulated behavior?

9. What are some increased risks for children whose parents are divorced? Why?

PRACTICE TEST – POSTTEST

Circle the correct answer for each multiple choice question and check your answers with the Answer Key at the end of the chapter.

1. During middle childhood, which of the following groups becomes highly influential on how a child views himself and the world?
   a.   his parents   c.   his siblings
   b.   his teachers   d.   his peers

2. Which of the following conditions helps lead a child to a clear sense of right and wrong?
   a.   excessive praise   c.   praise for trivial accomplishments
   b.   too little praise   d.   praise for true accomplishments

3. Teddy realizes that he is very bad at baseball. To help his self esteem, which of the following should his parents do for him?
   a.   introduce him to other activities   c.   punish him if he keeps playing badly
   b.   force him to keep trying harder   d.   give him subtle hints to try harder

4. Which of the following choices is a trait of middle childhood?
    a. begin learning emotional regulation
    b. remain egocentric
    c. become less self-centered in focus
    d. remain ignorant of prejudice

5. Which of the following is NOT a component of social cognition?
    a. social identity   c. social regulations
    b. social influence   d. social responsbility

6. Karen notices that even though her mother is smiling, she is not really happy; instead she appears to be distraught about something. Karen is experiencing what?
    a. social regulation   c. social referencing
    b. social empathy   d. social perspective taking

7. Which of the following developmental theories has provided the central context for the current understanding of moral development?
    a. cognitive-developmental c. social-learning
    b. psychodynamic   d. emotio-cognitive

8. According to your text, a man stealing medicine for his sick wife because he cannot afford to buy it legally is an example of what?
    a. moral dilemma   c. moral absolutism
    b. moral realism   d. moral ambiguity

9. Robert chooses to go along with William's suggestion that they skip school, because he wants William to be his friend. In which of Kohlberg's stages of moral development is Robert?
    a. 3   c. 5
    b. 4   d. 6

10. How many levels of moral reasoning were proposed by Kohlberg?
    a. 1   c. 3
    b. 2   d. 4

11. Which of the following is NOT mentioned in the text as a critique of Kohlberg's study?
    a. its stance on moral relativism
    b. its model is too inflexible
    c. it studied moral attitudes, not moral behaviors
    d. it is difficult to score a child's response

12. When discussing morals, Charlie's father ignores the fact that different cultures have different moral standards. Charlie's father is engaging in which of the following?
   a. moral absolutism
   b. moral realism
   c. moral relativism
   d. moral superiority

13. Chantal is 8 years old and her friendships are based on her awareness of others' feelings. In which of Selman's stages of friendship development is she?
   a. 1
   b. 2
   c. 3
   d. 4

14. According to the text, what percentage of girls bullied other children because they annoyed her?
   a. 60.7%
   b. 58.4%
   c. 57.6%
   d. 55.0%

15. Gia and her friends actively avoid being with or near Sarah because she is in the drama club. This is an example of which of the following?
   a. prejudice only
   b. discrimination only
   c. both prejudice and discrimination
   d. none of the above

16. In the study described in your book, where school children picked certain labels to describe themselves, which type of label was picked the least?
   a. gender
   b. religion
   c. color
   d. family role

17. Brian's mother asks him to keep her informed about where he is going and what he is doing with his friends. Brian's mother is doing which of the following?
   a. regulating
   b. monitoring
   c. snooping
   d. watching

18. Which parenting style is more likely to have children who comply with adults' demands while in their presence, but not when the adults are absent?
   a. authoritarian
   b. authoritative
   c. permissive
   d. indifferent

19. What percentage of single-parent households is headed by men?
   a. 5%
   b. 10%
   c. 15%
   d. 20%

20. Mae's mother recently married a man with two children. Her family's situation is best described as which of the following?
   a. rejoined
   b. reconstituted
   c. extended
   d. adoptive

ANSWER KEYS

Practice Test – Pretest (with text page numbers)

1. b 280	6. c 284	11. d 292	16. d 296
2. d 281	7. c 286	12. a 292	17. c 297
3. b 282	8. d 289	13. d 294	18. c 298
4. b 284	9. d 290	14. b 296	19. c 301
5. d 284	10. d 292	15. d 296	20. c 301

True/False

1. F	6. T	11. F
2. F	7. T	12. T
3. T	8. T	13 T
4. F	9. F	14. F
5. F	10. T	15. T

Matching

1. d	5. c
2. g	6. f
3. a	7. h
4. b	8. e

Key Vocabulary Terms

1. self-esteem
2. moral absolutism
3. peer group
4. resilient children
5. reconstituted family or stepfamily

6. Industry is the idea that hard work produces results. Inferiority is a negative sense of worth that can affect a person's personality throughout life.

7. Social inference involves an individual making guesses and assumptions about what another person is feeling, thinking or intending. Social perspective taking is the understanding that a person comes to about other people through the use of social inference.

8. Moral realism is Piaget's first stage of moral development where children believe in rules as real, indestructible things, not abstract principles. Moral relativism is Piaget's term for the second stage of moral development where children realize that rules are created and agreed upon cooperatively by individuals and can change if necessary.

9. Prejudice is a negative attitude formed without adequate reason and usually directed toward people because of their membership in a certain group. Discrimination is the act of treating others in a prejudiced manner.

10. Self-regulated behavior is behavior that is controlled and directed by the child, rather than by parents, teachers, or other external forces. Coregulation is the development of a sense of shared responsibility between parents and their children.

Programmed Review
1. social-learning, psychodynamic, cognitive-developmental
2. self-concept, personality, social behavior
3. industry, hard work, mastering
4. education, academic
5. accomplishments, weaknesses, strengths
6. inference, responsibility, regulations
7. accidentally, guiltier, intentionally, anger
8. attitudes, behavior
9. justice, relationships, caring
10. feelings, fears
11. Selman, cognitive, social, personality
12. complex, multifaceted, relationships
13. dislikes, reciprocal, self-esteem
14. positive, misbehavior, stealing, drinking, illegal drugs
15. Prejudice discrimination, racial, ethnic
16. disloyal, white
17. peers, family, socializing
18. reasoning-based, prosocial behavior, social rules
19. 26%, 51%, 76%
20. poverty, divorce, moving to a new town
21. traumatic, maturity, negative
22. divorce, psychological, economic
23. test, world
24. limits, routines
25. loyalties, guilty, affection
26. middle childhood

Post test (with text page numbers)

1.	d 280	6.	d 284	11.	a 287	16.	b 293
2.	d 283	7.	a 284	12.	a 287	17.	b 296
3.	a 283	8.	a 286	13.	b 289	18.	a 296
4.	c 284	9.	b 286	14.	a 291	19.	c 299
5.	a 284	10.	c 286	15.	c 293	20.	b 302

Chapter 10

Adolescence: Physical and Cognitive Development

CHAPTER OUTLINE

◈ Adolescent Development in a Cultural and Historical Context
  ◆ Adolescence in the United States

◈ Physical Development and Adaptation
  ◆ Physical Growth and Change
  ◆ Puberty
  ◆ Body Image and Adjustment

◈ Gender Identity and Sexual Practices
  ◆ Four Decades of Changes in Sexual Practices
  ◆ Factors That Influence Early Sexual Relationships
  ◆ Consequences of Adolescent Sexual Behavior

◈ Cognitive Changes in Adolescence
  ◆ Brain Development in Adolescence
  ◆ Piaget's Period of Formal Operations
  ◆ The Scope and Content of Adolescent Thought

LEARNING OBJECTIVES

After you have read and studied this chapter, you should be able to answer the following questions.

1. Do adolescents in cultures around the world experience the period of adolescence in much the same way?
2. Why do adolescents focus so intensely on issues of body image, and in what ways are their concerns about their appearance expressed?
3. Is it better to sexually mature before or after most of one's peers?
4. How does the brain's development during adolescence influence the thinking and behavior of teenagers?
5. What is adolescent egocentrism, and how is it linked to the changes in cognitive development that teenagers typically experience?

PRACTICE TEST – PRETEST

Circle the correct answer for each multiple choice question and check your answers with the Answer Key at the end of the chapter.

1. A symbolic event or ritual to mark a life transition, such as from childhood to adult status, is known as:
   a. hazing
   b. transitional attainment
   c. social transcendence
   d. rite of passage

2. Adolescence is a transitional period in which individuals typically plan for:
   a. career
   b. their adult lives
   c. cognitive decline
   d. their own families

3. In terms of speed of biological change, which period of life does adolescence most closely match?
   a. late adulthood
   b. middle childhood
   c. infancy
   d. early adulthood

4. Which of the following is NOT a secondary sex characteristic?
   a. body hair
   b. increased fat and muscle
   c. maturation of genitalia
   d. reproductive organs

5. What controls most physical changes in adolescence?
   a. hormones
   b. environmental factors
   c. glucocorticoids
   d. neurotransmitters

6. What is a period of rapid growth in physical size and strength called?
   a. pubescent jump
   b. massa intermedia
   c. growth spurt
   d. secondary growth

7. Which of the following is an example of an androgen? ·
   a. estrogen
   b. testosterone
   c. progesterone
   d. estrodiol

8. Which of the following are the hormones found in women in the greatest quantity?
   a. estrogen and progesterone
   b. estrogen and testosterone
   c. testosterone and progesterone
   d. androgen and progesterone

9. Which gland is known as the "master gland," producing growth hormone and regulating other glands?
   a. hypothalamus
   b. hippocampus
   c. pituitary
   d. gonad

10. What is a girl's first menstrual period called?
    a. ovariogenesis
    b. anovulatorium
    c. monarch
    d. menarche

11. Production of mature eggs in women and of sperm in men are:
    a. primary sex characteristics
    b. secondary sex characteristics
    c. gonadotropic mechanisms
    d. secondary mechanisms

12. What is the average age at which a girl has her first period?
    a. 6 years
    b. 8 ½ years
    c. 12 ½ years
    d. 15 years

13. What term is used to describe a group between cultures or on the fringe of a dominant culture that typically exhibits an intensified need to conform?
    a. outband
    b. delinquent
    c. subsidiary
    d. marginal

14. What is the name of an eating disorder in which a person is obsessed by thoughts of an unattainable image of "perfect" thinness?
    a. bulimia nervosa
    b. anorexia nervosa
    c. obsessive-compulsive disorder
    d. gordophobia

15. On average, when do girls mature?
    a. 2 years earlier than boys
    b. 6 months earlier than boys
    c. about the same time as boys
    d. 2 years later than boys

16. What is the term for sexual attraction toward members of one's own sex?
    a. sexual double standard
    b. same-sex orientation
    c. heterosexuality
    d. intimate similitude

17. Approximately what percent of sexually active teenagers have a sexually transmitted disease?
    a. 5%
    b. 10%
    c. 15%
    d. 20%

18. Which of Piaget's cognitive stages of development is associated with adolescence?
    a. sensorimotor
    b. preoperational
    c. concrete operational
    d. formal operational

19. What term describes an adolescent's assumption that others are focusing a great deal of critical attention on them?
    a. negotiation
    b. personal fable
    c. imaginary audience
    d. moral reasoning

20. Even though John has seen other people get into car accidents, he does not believe it will ever happen to himself. What is this an example of?
    a. negotiation
    b. personal fable
    c. imaginary audience
    d. moral reasoning

TRUE/FALSE

For each of the following statements, indicate whether the statement is True or False. Check your answers with the Answer Key at the end of this chapter.

_____ 1.   Some societies fail to recognize the attainment of adulthood.

_____ 2.   Even when they have a choice, adolescents often prefer the company of people their own age.

_____ 3.   How a parent reacts to their child's physical changes can greatly affect adolescent adjustment.

_____ 4.   Some developmental trends are the same for boys and girls.

_____ 5.   In both males and females, fat is deposited in the breast area during adolescence.

_____ 6.   Only males produce testosterone.

_____ 7. In many parts of the world, puberty is associated with major religious, cultural or economic significance.

_____ 8. In boys, the first indication of puberty is a change in voice.

_____ 9. A boy's first ejaculation usually contains fertile sperm.

_____ 10. In some parts of the world, menarche occurs considerably later than in the United States.

_____ 11. A girl's own positive body image is not usually correlated with her mother's body image.

_____ 12. About 50% of 15-17 year olds have engaged in sexual intercourse.

_____ 13. The age at which adolescents first have sex varies by ethnic group.

_____ 14. Good students are just as likely to engage in sex as poor students.

_____ 15. Adolescent marriage is more likely to lead to dropping out of high school than is adolescent pregnancy.

_____ 16. Brain development is complete by the time a person reaches the teenage years.

_____ 17. Adolescents sometimes fail to distinguish between their own concerns and those of others.

MATCHING

Match the following biological terms with their description, and check your answers with the Answer Key at the end of this chapter.

1. _____ Hormones

   a. the first menstrual period

2. _____ Androgens

   b. physical changes necessary for reproduction

3. _____ Pituitary gland

   c. physical changes associated with sexual maturation but not directly involved in reproduction

4. _____ Puberty

   d. biochemical substances secreted into the bloodstream in very small amounts by endocrine glands

5. ____ Progesterone
e. male sex hormones

6. ____ Menarche
f. a female sex hormone

7. ____ Primary sex characteristics
g. the part of the brain that produces several varieties of hormones

8. ____ Secondary sex characteristics
h. the attainment of sexual maturity

KEY VOCABULARY TERMS

Label each definition and give a specific example of each.

1. Symbolic events or rituals to mark life transitions, such as from childhood to adult status.

2. The historical trend toward earlier sexual maturation.

3. The view that activity is more permissible for boys than for girls.

4. A group between cultures or on the fringe of a dominant culture that typically exhibits an intensified need to conform.

5. For Piaget, the final stage of cognitive development, which begins at about age 12 and is characterized by the ability to reason hypothetically and think about abstract concepts.

Explain the difference between the following sets of terms.

6. primary sex characteristics; secondary sex characteristics
7. anorexia nervosa; bulimia nervosa
8. androgens; estrogens
9. imaginary audience; personal fable
10. first-order thinking; second-order thinking

PROGRAMMED REVIEW

Fill in the blanks in the following programmed review. Then check your answers with the Answer Key at the end of the chapter

Adolescent Development in a Cultural and Historical Context

1. Any serious attempt to understand adolescence must be considered in the broader _____ context in which development occurs.

<u>Adolescence in the United States Today</u>

2. Although some theorists, such as Erikson, take a more positive view, seeing adolescence as a time when individuals are allowed to _____ and _____ with various roles before taking on the responsibilities of the adult world, adolescents more often find their economic situation _____ and _____.

3. Although positive images also are presented, adolescents tend to gravitate to the more _____, _____ aspects of media programming.

Physical Development and Adaptation

4. Physiologically, adolescence ranks with the _____ period and _____ as a time of extremely rapid biological change.

<u>Physical Growth and Change</u>

5. Some developmental trends are the same for boys and girls, such as increased _____, improved _____, and _____.

6. The growth spurt is accompanied by an increase in _____ - especially for boys – as the body seeks the nutrients necessary for such rapid growth.

7. Maintaining the balance in the production of hormones, including the sex hormones, is the job of two areas of the brain – the _____ and the _____.

8. In females, the sex glands secrete _____ and regulate _____; in males, the sex glands secrete _____ and produce _____.

<u>Puberty</u>

9. Regardless of _____ importance, puberty is accompanied by several changes, including those related to _____ _____.

10. The extensive production of _____ _____ _____ may be one factor in the average superior strength and athletic ability of adolescent boys.

11. In many cases, the early cycles are irregular and _____; that is, a mature ovum is not produced. However, it is thoroughly unwise for a young teenage girl to assume that she is _____.

12. Premenstrual tension is common and is often accompanied by _____, depression, _____, _____, and breast tenderness.

164

Body Image and Adjustment

13. For boys, the primary concern is _____ _____ and _____, and in particular their height and musculature are most important. Girls, in contrast, more often worry about being too _____ or too _____.

14. Like _____ maturing boys, _____ maturing girls experience higher psychological stress, and they exhibit high rates of _____ behavior.

Gender Identity and Sexual Practices
Four Decades of Changes in Sexual Practices

15. Before the mid-1960s, most young people felt that premarital sex was _____, although peer pressure often impelled _____ adolescent boys to gain sexual experience before marriage.

16. By the late 1970s, the _____ _____ was in full swing. Numerous studies reported an increased trend toward sexual _____, reflected both by an increase in sexual activity among adolescents and by a change in social attitudes.

17. During the 1980s, when adolescents were asked what they thought about the sexual attitudes of the 1960s and 1970s, a sizeable proportion viewed them as _____.

18. Throughout the 1990s and into the first decade of the 21st century, cultural values in the United States regarding sexuality have largely _____, partly as a result of the _____ of those who initiated the sexual revolution and who now find themselves squarely in _____.

Factors That Influence Early Sexual Relationships

19. Sexual activity generally begins at an earlier age for adolescent boys and girls who identify themselves as _____, and also for adolescent boys who identify themselves as _____. On average, _____ girls begin their sexual activity at an older age than other groups.

20. Both overly _____ and overly _____ parenting are associated with earlier sexual activity in adolescents.

Consequences of Adolescent Sexual Behavior

21. Although AIDS is still rare among adolescents, in part because it often takes _____ for symptoms to appear and therefore goes _____, adolescents do have a high rate of other _____.

22. Presently, about _____% of adolescent girls and _____% of adolescent boys do not use contraception at first intercourse.

23. The impact of parenthood on the lives of teenage boys may be negative and long lasting. Because of the pressures they feel to _____ their new family, many teenage fathers also tend to leave school and take _____, _____ jobs.

24. Young parents are more likely to _____ or _____ their children, most likely because these parents are often _____ and _____.

Cognitive Changes in Adolescence
<u>Brain Development in Adolescence</u>

25. MRI studies reveal that important changes continue to occur within the brain long past _____, through _____, and perhaps even into early _____.

26. A person's ability to exercise mature _____ _____, to appraise _____, and to make difficult decisions that involve multiple perspectives is most likely not fully elaborated until perhaps as late as early _____.

27. During adolescence, when _____ behavior is highly activated, the more _____-oriented parts of the brain are still maturing.

28. During adolescence, there is normally an expansion in the capacity and style of thought that broadens the young person's _____, _____, _____, and _____.

<u>Piaget's Period of Formal Operations</u>

29. Formal operational thought requires the ability to _____, _____, and _____ hypotheses.

30. Whereas _____-order thinking involves discovering and examining relationships between objects, _____-order thought involves thinking about one's thoughts, looking for links between relationships, and maneuvering between _____ and _____.

31. A certain level of _____ appears to be necessary for formal thought.

<u>The Scope and Content of Adolescent Thought</u>

32. Because the adolescent can now deal with contrary-to-fact situations, reading or viewing _____, _____, or _____ is a popular pastime.

33. Research indicates that teenagers who had the strongest sense of themselves as individuals were more likely to have grown up in families where the parents offered _____ and _____ but also permitted their children to develop their own _____.

34. Adolescents tend to jump to conclusions about the reactions of those around them and to assume that others will be as _____ or as _____ of them as they are of _____.

35. The perception that they are constantly on stage also can lead adolescents to be very sensitive to criticism and to see even innocuous questions from parents as _____, _____, and overly _____.

36. Adolescents do not develop the _____ framework and _____ skills to effectively deal with _____ pressures until well into adolescence or even into early adulthood.

CRITICAL THINKING QUESTIONS

To further your mastery of the topics, write out the answers to the following essay questions in the space provided.

1. How does mass media make adolescents more vulnerable to the crises of their time?

2. How do gender differences in body image comparison relate to the social effects of being an early or late maturing girl or boy?

3. What factors may have contributed to the return to more conservative attitudes about sexual matters in the 1980s?

4. How might an improved understanding of the causes and consequences of teen pregnancy lead to less social stigma and more social support for teenage mothers?

5. What changes in the brain underlie teenagers' emotional outbursts and overly emotional responses?

6. How might an adolescent's entry into formal operational thought contribute to an overestimation of his or her ability to successfully deal with real-world problems?

7. In what way might media such as movies and television shows prolong the adolescent concepts of imaginary audience and personal fable?

PRACTICE TEST - POST TEST

Circle the correct answer for each multiple choice question and check your answers with the Answer Key at the end of the chapter.

1. Adolescence in many agriculturally-based cultures begins when children enter:
   a. the work force
   b. industrialized society
   c. their reproductive years
   d. school

2. What term describes an educational system in which adolescents interact mostly with other adolescents and much less with younger children or adults?
    a. age segregated
    c. heterogeneous groups
    b. age immersed
    d. marginal groups

3. Which of the following is a characteristic of adolescence?
    a. unemotional thought
    c. social confidence
    b. economic dependence
    d. objective reasoning

4. The development of the reproductive organs in men and women are known as:
    a. primary sex characteristics
    c. gonadogenesis
    b. secondary sex characteristics
    d. menarche

5. Hormones are secreted into the bloodstream by what internal organ(s)?
    a. frontal lobe
    c. endocrine glands
    b. capillaries
    d. kidneys

6. What is another term for an oil-producing gland?
    a. trophic gland
    c. fatty gland
    b. endocrine gland
    d. sebaceous gland

7. Which part of the brain initiates eventual reproductive capability in adolescence?
    a. hypothalamus
    c. hippocampus
    b. pituitary gland
    d. frontal lobe

8. Which of the following is present in males?
    a. estrogen
    c. androgens
    b. testosterone
    d. all of the above

9. Which physical change is NOT typical of adolescent girls?
    a. growth of pubic hair
    c. change in voice
    b. body growth
    d. growth of underarm hair

10. What is considered to be the most dramatic and symbolic sign of a girl's changing status?
    a. body growth
    c. increased output of sweat glands
    b. menarche
    d. growth of underarm hair

11. What term describes a menstrual cycle in which a mature ovum (egg) has not been produced?
    a. sebaceous
    c. marginal
    b. anovulatory
    d. counterfactual

12. Which of the following factors does NOT affect the onset of menstruation?
   a. nutrition and general health
   c. socioeconomic background
   b. genetics
   d. personality type

13. What disorder is characterized by a cycle of bingeing and purging?
   a. bulimia nervosa
   c. emotional eating
   b. anorexia nervosa
   d. obesity

14. Which of the following is NOT likely to be experience by an early-maturing girl?
   a. pressure to have sex
   c. teasing by peers
   b. maturing at the same time as boys
   d. deviant behavior

15. What is the term for the view that sexual activity is more permissible for boys than for girls?
   a. sexual double standard
   c. sexual revolution
   b. sexual orientation
   d. gender script

16. In what decade did the revolution in changing sexual norms begin to decline?
   a. 1960s
   c. 1980s
   b. 1970s
   d. 1990s

17. Which of the following is at the highest risk of engaging in adolescent sexual behavior?
   a. Hispanic girl with good grades
   c. Black boy with good grades
   b. Hispanic girl with poor grades
   d. Black boy with poor grades

18. Which of the following represents the least desirable situation for an adolescent girl?
   a. single, not pregnant
   c. single and pregnant
   b. married, not pregnant
   d. married and pregnant

19. Which part of the brain is associated with the increased problem-solving abilities in adolescents?
   a. frontal lobe
   c. pituitary gland
   b. thalamus
   d. hypothalamus

20. What type of thought process involves thinking about one's thoughts, looking for links between relationships, and maneuvering between reality and possibility?
   a. first-order
   c. pre-operational
   b. second-order
   d. concrete operational

ANSWER KEYS

Practice Test – Pretest (with text page numbers)

1. d 304	6. c 307	11. a 308	16. b 313
2. b 304	7. b 307	12. c 309	17. d 315
3. c 306	8. a 307	13. d 310	18. d 322
4. d 306	9. c 307	14. b 311	19. c 325
5. a 307	10. d 308	15. a 312	20. b 326

True/False

1. F	6. F	11. F	16. F
2. T	7. T	12. F	17. T
3. T	8. F	13. T	
4. T	9. F	14. F	
5. T	10. T	15. T	

Matching

1. d	5. f
2. e	6. a
3. g	7. b
4. h	8. c

Key Vocabulary Terms

1. Rite of passage
2. Secular trend
3. Sexual double standard
4. Marginal group
5. Formal operations

6. <u>Primary sex characteristics</u> are necessary for reproduction; <u>secondary sex characteristics</u> are associated with sexual maturation but do not directly involve reproduction.

7. <u>Anorexia nervosa</u> is an eating disorder in which a person is obsessed by thoughts of an unattainable image of "perfect" thinness; <u>bulimia nervosa</u> is an eating disorder characterized by bingeing and purging.

8. <u>Androgens</u> are male hormones; <u>estrogens</u> are female hormones.

9. <u>Imaginary audience</u> is the adolescent assumption that others are focusing a great deal of Attention on them; <u>personal fable</u> is the belief that they are so special that nothing bad can ever happen to them.

10. <u>First-order thinking</u> involves discovering and examining relationships between objects; <u>second-order thinking</u> involves looking for links between relationships, thinking about one's own thoughts, and maneuvering between reality and possibility.

Programmed Review
1. social
2. explore, experiment, limiting, frustrating
3. grizzly, counterculture
4. fetal, infancy
5. size, strength, stamina
6. appetite
7. hypothalamus, pituitary gland
8. estrogens, ovulation, androgens, sperm
9. cultural, sexual maturation
10. red blood cells
11. anovulatory, infertile
12. irritability, crying, bloating
13. physical size, strength, fat, tall
14. early, early, deviant
15. immoral, older
16. sexual revolution, liberalization
17. irresponsible
18. stabilized, aging, middle age
19. Black, Hispanic, Hispanic
20. restrictive, permissive
21. years, undetected, STDs
22. 75, 82
23. support, low-skilled, low-paying
24. neglect, abuse, stressed, frustrated
25. childhood, adolescence, adulthood
26. problem solving, risk, adulthood
27. risk-taking, control
28. awareness, imagination, judgment, insight
29. formulate, test, evaluate
30. first, second, reality, possibility
31. intelligence
32. science fiction, fantasy, horror
33. guidance, comfort, points of view
34. approving, critical, themselves
35. prying, critical, personal
36. moral, cognitive, real-world

Practice Test – Post test (with text page numbers)

1. c 304	6. d 307	11. b 309	16. c 314
2. a 305	7. a 307	12. d 311	17. d 316
3. b 305	8. d 307	13. a 311	18. d 317
4. a 306	9. c 308	14. b 312	19. a 321
5. c 307	10. b 309	15. a 313	20. b 322

Chapter 11

Adolescence: Personality and Sociocultural Development

CHAPTER OUTLINE

- Developmental Tasks of Adolescence
  - Self-Regulation and Interdependence
  - Forming an Identity
  - Identity Formation, Culture, and Context

- Family Dynamics
  - Intergenerational Communication

- Peer Relationships During Adolescence
  - Social Comparison
  - Cliques and Crowds
  - Dating
  - Peers and Parents: A Clash of Cultures

- Risk and Resilience in Adolescence
  - Risk Taking
  - The Use of Tobacco, Alcohol, Marijuana, and Other Drugs
  - Delinquency
  - Sexual Abuse of Adolescents

- Stress, Depression, and Coping
  - Depression
  - Risk Factors for Psychological Problems
  - Protective Factors and Coping Responses

LEARNING OBJECTIVES

After you have read and studied this chapter, you should be able to answer the following questions.

1. Why is forming an identity often considered the most important task of adolescence?
2. What are the most important roles that parents play during the teenage years?
3. Why do adolescents place so much importance on how their peers regard them?
4. Is risky behavior a normal part of adolescence for most teenagers?
5. How do adolescents typically cope with the pressures they feel during the teenage years?

PRACTICE TEST – PRETEST

Circle the correct answer for each multiple choice question and check your answers with the Answer Key at the end of the chapter.

1. What percentage of adolescents is estimated to experience psychological disturbances?
   a. 1-2%
   b. 10-20%
   c. 40-50%
   d. 65-70%

2. Making your own judgments and regulating your own behavior is known as what?
   a. self-confidence
   b. self-efficacy
   c. self-regulation
   d. self-consciousness

3. What term describes reciprocal dependence, where both parties depend on each other?
   a. interdependence
   b. intradependence
   c. identity fusion
   d. identity formation

4. What term describes a period during which individuals grapple with the options available and ultimately make a choice and commitment as to which path their lives will take?
   a. identity crisis
   b. identity commitment
   c. identity forbearance
   d. identity availability

5. In what type of society does the good of the individual subordinate to the good of the group?
   a. individualistic
   b. collectivistic
   c. idealistic
   d. imperialistic

6. Which of the following groups has the highest suicide rates?
   a. adolescent white females
   b. adolescent single parents
   c. adolescent gang members
   d. adolescent gay males

7. What parenting style is characterized by providing little structure or control?
   a. authoritarian
   b. permissive
   c. authoritative
   d. traditional

8. What is it called when parents discuss, give advice, and supervise adolescents, but only to the extent that the teen is willing to disclose?
   a. parental monitoring
   b. parental control
   c. authoritarianism
   d. parental dismissal

9. Evaluating yourself and your situation relative to others is known as:
   a. peer review
   b. proximal assessment
   c. social comparison
   d. group contrast

10. To whom are teenagers most likely to turn for advice?
    a. parents
    b. friends
    c. siblings
    d. school counselors

11. Which of the following is NOT an example of a clique?
    a. jocks
    b. brains
    c. druggies
    d. loners

12. Which interaction scenario would be the least preferable among 15-year-olds?
    a. standing on a street corner
    b. milling around a shopping mall
    c. sitting around chatting in a pizzeria
    d. going out on a date

13. All of the following are functions of dating except:
    a. education
    b. status
    c. recreation
    d. mate selection

14. Which of the following is an adolescent most likely to consider before drinking alcohol?
    a. the need for a designated driver
    b. the dangers of alcohol poisoning
    c. the benefits of higher peer status
    d. the increased risk of unprotected sex

15. What is the most common of high-risk behaviors among adolescents?
    a. driving at high speeds
    b. use of alcohol and other drugs
    c. engaging in petty shoplifting
    d. involvement in gang activity

16. On average, by how many years does moderate smoking shorten a person's life?
    a. 3 years
    b. 12 years
    c. 7 years
    d. 5 years

17. Approximately what proportion of high school seniors have tried smoking?
    a. 50%
    b. 15%
    c. 25%
    d. 80%

18. Which of the following is NOT an effect of large doses of alcohol?
    a. hallucinations
    b. distorted vision
    c. slurred speech
    d. death

19. Which of the following are adolescents most likely to abuse?
    a.   heroin   c.   marijuana
    b.   cocaine   d.   LSD

20. What is the best course of action if you suspect someone you know is depressed?
    a.   tell them to "snap out of it"   c.   give examples of how others are less fortunate
    b.   advise them to be less weak   d.   urge them to seek treatment

TRUE/FALSE

For each of the following statements indicate whether the statement is True or False. Check your answers with the Answer Key at the end of this chapter.

____ 1.   The majority of adolescents are emotionally healthy.

____ 2.   Parental influence must be rejected in order for a teenager to obtain autonomy.

____ 3.   Interdependence is a characteristic of most adult relationships.

____ 4.   Most students immediately establish a clear sense of identity upon entering college.

____ 5.   The timing at which different identity statuses emerge varies from culture to culture.

____ 6.   Conflicts between parents and adolescents are usually about core economic, religious, social, and political values.

____ 7.   Alliances among family members are unnatural and unhealthy.

____ 8.   Both girls and boys generally discuss their ideas and concerns with their fathers.

____ 9.   In the early teenage years, most activities involve just a few close friends.

____ 10.   Adolescents who have been raised abroad and return to their home country generally have little problem adjusting.

____ 11.   Dating serves different functions for boys and girls.

____ 12.   Teenagers with a strong sense of ethnic identity and derive their status in part from ethnic group membership tend to have higher self-esteem than those who do not.

____ 13.   It is possible to create a truly safe environment for one's children.

____ 14.   The long-term effects of marijuana use are comparable to smoking cigarettes.

_____ 15. Many drugs, such as methamphetamine, can be produced from commonly available products.

_____ 16. At some point in their lives, most children engage in some sort of delinquent behavior.

_____ 17. Sexual abusers of young boys are most likely to be males who are not family members.

_____ 18. There are structural differences in the way male and female brains develop during adolescence.

MATCHING

Match each of Marcia's identity terms with their description and check your answers with the Answer Key at the end of the chapter.

1. _____ commitment

   a. the identity status of those who have made commitments without going through much decision making or through an identity crisis

2. _____ foreclosure

   b. the identity status of those who are currently in the midst of an identity crisis or decision-making period

3. _____ diffusion

   c. the part of identity formation that involves making a personal investment in the paths one chooses

4. _____ moratorium

   d. the identity status of those who have neither gone through an identity crisis nor committed to an occupational role or moral code

5. _____ identity achievement

   e. the identity status of those who have gone through an identity crisis and have made commitments

KEY VOCABULARY TERMS

Label each definition and give a specific example of each.

1. A period during which individuals grapple with the options available and ultimately make a choice and commitment as to which path their lives will take.

2. Evaluating yourself and your situation relative to others.

3. Making one's own judgments and regulating one's own behavior.

4. Reciprocal dependence, where both parties depend on each other.

5. Narrow or broad groups with which people identify, and in so doing, help to define themselves.

Explain the difference between the following sets of terms.

6. identity achievement; foreclosure
7. clique; crowd
8. authoritarian parenting; authoritative parenting
9. parental control; parental monitoring

PROGRAMMED REVIEW

Fill in the blanks in the following programmed review. Then check your answers with the Answer Key at the end of the chapter.

Developmental Tasks of Adolescence

1. Although the emotional distance between teenagers and their parents tends to increase in early adolescence, this does not necessarily lead to _____ or to _____ of parental values.

Self-Regulation and Interdependence

2. When parents are able to encourage their teenage children toward _____ and _____ relationships, they are preparing them well for their future as adults.

Forming an Identity

3. Roles that are _____ must be integrated into a personal identity, and this process is harder when role models represent _____ values.

4. In Erikson's view, adolescence is a period in which young people _____ various alternative identities as they attempt to sort through the available options and forge their _____ senses of who they are.

5. When adolescents are confused about their future roles, they often cope by _____, becoming _____ from their friends and family, or by _____ to the expectations of whatever individuals or groups exert the greatest power over their lives.

6. Identity formation sometimes proceeds from one stage to another: For example, there are far more high school adolescents in _____ and _____ status than in _____ and identity _____, and the proportion of people in identity achievement status naturally _____ with age.

7. Identity status may also _____ according to what _____ of identity is under consideration.

Identity Formation, Culture, and Context

8. In collectivist societies, for the most part, the good of the _____ is subordinated to the good of the _____ – where group can refer to family, peers, neighborhood, town, or society at large.

9. It is no accident that adolescent males have one of the highest _____ rates of any group because the _____ often experienced by gay teens can be overwhelming, especially when their peer groups judge this central aspect of their identity to be unacceptable.

Family Dynamics

10. On the one hand, successful parents provide their children with a sense of _____ and _____ in an environment in which the children feel loved and accepted. On the other hand, successful parents encourage their children to become _____ adults who can function _____ in society.

Intergenerational Communication

11. An older brother who dominated his younger brother during _____ will probably have the same influence in _____.

12. Authoritative parenting takes into account the adolescent's increased _____ ability.

Peer Relationships During Adolescence
Social Comparison

13. Often, in their early teenage years, adolescents focus on their _____ and on those personality characteristics that make them _____.

Cliques and Crowds

14. When aloneness is _____, it can provide a welcomed opportunity for creativity, relief from pressures, or psychological renewal.

Dating

15. Older adolescents are less _____ in their attitudes towards dating; they are more concerned about _____ characteristics and the person's _____ for the future.

Peers and Parents: A Clash of Cultures

16. Conflicts occur when Hindu values about _____ and _____ clash with the more _____ values of the U.S. adolescent culture.

Risk and Resilience in Adolescence

17. Although only a minority of adolescents engage in seriously _____ high-risk behaviors, most adolescents take more risks than their _____ would prefer.

Risk Taking

18. Adolescent judgment may be less than fully _____: Teenagers may get into trouble because they do not _____ the risks they are taking.

The Use of Tobacco, Alcohol, Marijuana, and Other Drugs

19. In the United States, the use of legal drugs, such as alcohol and tobacco, is illegal for teenagers because they are _____. Thus, these drugs are particularly problematic for adolescents because they are widely _____, as well as highly _____.

20. Smoking, often of _____, also is used by some teens as a way of covering up their use of other _____, especially _____.

21. Although alcohol abuse is found in _____ category of teenagers, the typical alcohol-abusing adolescent is a _____ with low _____ and a family _____ of alcohol abuse.

22. The short-term effects of marijuana include impaired _____, memory, _____, and perception, along with a rise in heart rate and _____.

23. Teenagers, like adults, sometimes turn to _____ or _____ to obtain the money needed to buy addictive drugs.

Delinquency

24. Some adolescents become delinquent mainly because they seek to be members of a delinquent _____.

Sexual Abuse of Adolescents

25. Sometimes the victim's mother is _____ that the abuse is taking place. At other times, the mother steadfastly _____ to believe her child's claims or does _____ to protect her daughter against further abuse if she does believe her.

Stress, Depression, and Coping

26. Adolescents who need help may not be taken _____ because their behavior and feelings are considered part of a _____ developmental phase.

Depression

27. A reasonable estimate is that at any given point in time about _____% of adolescents suffer from moderate to severe depression, with _____ to _____% of college students reporting having had a period of serious depression at some point in their teens.

28. Lesbians and gay male adolescents show higher rates of depression and are _____ to _____ times more likely to commit suicide than heterosexual adolescents. This presumably is because of the extremely negative _____ _____ they often encounter.

29. Suicide is the _____ leading cause of death among adolescents after _____ and _____.

30. Suicides typically occur within the context of _____ personal or family problems.

Risk Factors for Psychological Problems

31. Research shows that, in the United States, many girls emerge from early adolescence with poor _____, relatively _____ expectations of life, and much less _____ in themselves and their abilities than is true of boys.

Protective Factors and Coping Responses

32. Some individuals appear to be more resilient to negative pressures and risks. Those with such positive attributes as good _____ functioning and appealing _____, who experience solid and positive family _____, and who live in neighborhoods with good _____ and other favorable organizations are more likely to confront the risks associated with adolescence and to deal effectively with them.

CRITICAL THINKING QUESTIONS

To further your mastery of the topics, write out the answers to the following essay questions in the space provided.

1. What kinds of thoughts might go through an adolescent's mind if they were offered five million dollars to play a game of Russian Roulette (a game in which a person places a single bullet in the barrel of a handgun, spins the barrel, then pulls the trigger with the gun pointed at their head)? What conclusion might they reach? Why?

2. How could an authoritarian parenting style contribute to prolonging an adolescent's time spent in a foreclosure identity status?

3. How does an authoritative parenting style contribute to the major adolescent task of achieving autonomy and independence?

4. How are cliques and crowds related to identity formation in adolescence?

5. What changes in decision-making abilities might be contributing to the developmental trends in dating preferences from early adolescence to late adolescence?

6. Why is marijuana referred to as an "egalitarian" drug?

7. How can media portrayal of violence and sex contribute to delinquent behaviors?

8. How can one distinguish between normal "blues" and clinical depression?

9. What can be done to help young people move through adolescence with a minimum of trauma?

PRACTICE TEST – POST TEST

Circle the correct answer for each multiple choice question and check your answers with the Answer Key at the end of the chapter.

1. What are the two major tasks adolescents must confront?
    - a. choose a career; earn money
    - b. start a family; earn money
    - c. achieve autonomy; form an identity
    - d. avoid drugs; stay physically active

2. What question is best answered by identity formation?
    - a. Who am I?
    - b. Am I loved?
    - c. What do others think of me?
    - d. Why are we here?

3. Judy was raised by Republican parents and so she considers herself a Republican, but she has never considered the issues behind her political commitment. What best describes Judy's political identity status?
    - a. identity achievement
    - b. foreclosure
    - c. diffusion
    - d. moratorium

4. Mark is a college freshman who has not declared a major. He is actively exploring several possible career paths, but has not settled on any particular one just yet. What best describes Mark's identity status on this matter?
    - a. identity achievement
    - b. foreclosure
    - c. diffusion
    - d. moratorium

5. Maria grew up attending Catholic church with her family. Upon entering high school she began to question her beliefs and carefully considered a variety of alternative belief systems. Eventually she concluded that she agrees with her original beliefs. What best describes Maria's religious identity status
    - a. identity achievement
    - b. foreclosure
    - c. diffusion
    - d. moratorium

6. Which of the following is least likely to be a topic of conflict between an adolescent and their parent?
    - a. curfew hours
    - b. religious values
    - c. eating habits
    - d. personal appearance

7. Which parenting style is associated with the most positive outcome for adolescent behavior?
    - a. authoritarian
    - b. authoritative
    - c. permissive
    - d. neglectful

8. Compared to families in which the mother is the homemaker, how much do teenagers in dual-income families help out around the house?
    - a. less
    - b. more
    - c. about the same
    - d. it depends on household income

9. What term is used to describe the diverse group of peers that teenagers use to explore various roles and define who they are and who they want to become?
    a. cohort comparison
    b. comparative colleagues
    c. peer arena
    d. friend circuit

10. About which of the following is an adolescent least likely to seek advice from their parent?
    a. education
    b. finances
    c. sex
    d. career plans

11. An adolescent peer group with between 3 and 9 members is known as a:
    a. clique
    b. crowd
    c. gaggle
    d. pack

12. When an adolescent's friends are different from those the parents would prefer, this is known as:
    a. nostalgia
    b. a generational gap
    c. idealistic discord
    d. a clash of cultures

13. Which of the following is NOT a hallmark of adolescence?
    a. defining and redefining oneself
    b. becoming established in a career
    c. experimenting with different attitudes
    d. moving away from parental control

14. All of the following are short-term effects of cigarette smoking except:
    a. increased heart rate
    b. constricted blood vessels
    c. lung cancer
    d. throat irritation

15. Which of the following is NOT a potential long-term effect of cigarette smoking?
    a. brain damage
    b. heart attack
    c. lung cancer
    d. emphysema

16. Adolescent girls are more likely than boys to report daily smoking for what purpose?
    a. weight control
    b. sex appeal
    c. peer intimidation
    d. control of depression

17. What percentage of non-smoking adolescents reports drinking alcohol at least occasionally?
    a. 10%
    b. 15%
    c. 20%
    d. 35%

18. Compared to males, how likely are females to experience depression?
    a. half as likely
    b. just as likely
    c. twice as likely
    d. four times as likely

19. What term is used to describe people under age 16 who commit criminal acts?
    a. cocaine bugs
    b. raves
    c. rugrats
    d. delinquents

20. Who is most likely to be a sexual abuser to an adolescent girl?
    a. the girl's biological father
    b. the girl's stepfather
    c. a male sibling
    d. an adult male stranger

ANSWER KEYS

Practice Test – Pretest (with text page numbers)

1. b 333	6. d 339	11. d 345	16. c 349
2. c 333	7. b 340	12. d 345	17. a 349
3. c 334	8. a 341	13. a 346	18. a 351
4. a 335	9. c 343	14. c 348	19. c 352
5. b 337	10. b 344	15. b 348	20. d 357

True/False

1. T	7. F	13. F
2. F	8. F	14. T
3. T	9. F	15. T
4. F	10. F	16. T
5. T	11. F	17. T
6. F	12. T	18. T

Matching
1. c
2. a
3. d
4. b
5. e

Key Vocabulary Terms
1. Identity crisis
2. Social comparison
3. Self-regulation
4. Interdependence
5. Social reference groups

6. Identity achievement involves both crisis and commitment; foreclosure involves commitment, but not crisis.

7. Cliques involve 3 to 9 people; crowds involve 15 to 30 people.

8. Authoritarian parenting involves high levels of control with inflexible rule; authoritative parenting is also high in control, but it involves warmth and negotiation.

9. Parental control is associated with earlier adolescence, in which the parents control the activities and flow of information between themselves and the adolescent; in parental monitoring, parents give advice, discuss, and supervise, but only to the extent to which the teen is willing to disclose, and is associated with later adolescence.

Programmed Review

1. rebellion, rejection
2. self-regulation, interdependent
3. accepted, conflicting
4. try out, unique
5. withdrawing, isolated, conforming
6. diffusion, foreclosure, moratorium, achievement, increases
7. vary, aspect
8. individual, group
9. suicide, guilt
10. security, roots, self-directing, independently
11. childhood, adolescence
12. cognitive
13. appearance, popular
14. voluntary
15. superficial, personality, plans
16. dating, premarital sex, liberal
17. destructive, parents
18. developed, understand
19. underage, available, addictive
20. cigars, drugs, marijuana
21. every, male, grades, history
22. coordination, attention, blood pressure
23. stealing, prostitution
24. peer group
25. unaware, refuses, nothing
26. seriously, normal
27. 8, 15, 20
28. 2, 3, social pressures
29. third, accidents, homicides
30. long-standing
31. self-image, low, confidence
32. intellectual, personalities, support, schools

Practice Test – Post test (with text page numbers)

1. c 333	6. b 340	11. a 344	16. a 350
2. a 334	7. b 340	12. d 346	17. a 351
3. b 335	8. a 341	13. b 347	18. c 356
4. d 335	9. c 343	14. c 349	19. d 353
5. a 335	10. c 344	15. a 349	20. b 354

Chapter 12

Young Adulthood: Physical and Cognitive Development

CHAPTER OUTLINE

- Perspectives on Adult Development
  - Age Clocks and Social Norms
  - Contextual Paradigms

- General Physical Development
  - Strength and Stamina
  - Fitness and Health

- Sex and Sexuality
  - Fertility
  - Sexually Transmitted Diseases
  - Sexual Attitudes and Behavior
  - Sexual Identity and Sexual Orientation

- Cognitive Development in Adulthood
  - Beyond Formal Operations
  - Postformal Thought
  - Emotional Intelligence
  - Schaie's Stages of Adult Thinking

- Frameworks for Understanding Adult Development
  - Stages and Contexts
  - Havighurst's Developmental Tasks
  - Erikson's Theory of Development
  - Levinson's Seasons of a Man's Life
  - The Limitations of Normative Models
  - Gould's Transformations in Early Adulthood
  - A Closing Comment

LEARNING OBJECTIVES

After you have read and studied this chapter, you should be able to answer the following questions.

1. Are adults who were born in the same year always of the same *age*?
2. In recent decades, have young adults in the United States become more or less physically fit?
3. How does sexual orientation affect how a person experiences young adulthood?
4. How do the thought processes used by young adults differ from those that guide adolescent cognition?
5. What are the primary developmental tasks most young adults confront?

PRACTICE TEST – PRETEST

Circle the correct answer for each multiple choice question and check your answers with the Answer Key at the end of the chapter.

1. Which of the following is NOT a force to which the major markers of adulthood are linked?
   - a. personal
   - b. social
   - c. cultural
   - d. emotional

2. Events that occur at relatively specific times in the life span, which most people in an age cohort experience, are referred to as which of the following?
   - a. idiosyncratic events
   - b. normative events
   - c. motivational events
   - d. age clocks

3. Events that are unexpected, such as a child's death or winning the lottery, are called what?
   - a. idiosyncratic events
   - b. normative events
   - c. motivational events
   - d. age clocks

4. The term "middle adulthood" often refers to which of the following spans of years?
   - a. 80s and up
   - b. 60s and 70s
   - c. 40s and 50s
   - d. 20s and 30s

5. Which of the following terms refers to theories that emphasize the interaction of numerous environmental, social, psychological, and historical factors that influence development?
   - a. effective perspectives
   - b. contextual paradigms
   - c. contextual perspectives
   - d. effective paradigms

6. Compared to other age ranges, all of the following reach their peak during young adulthood except what?
   a. vitality
   b. strength
   c. endurance
   d. flexibility

7. Major league baseball players tend to reach their peak performances during what ages?
   a. 17-20
   b. 21-23
   c. 24-26
   d. 27-30

8. The average woman is born with approximately how many ova?
   a. 100,000
   b. 200,000
   c. 400,000
   d. 800,000

9. What term refers to the sex to which a person is physically attracted as well as which sexual partners with which one might wish to become involved emotionally?
   a. sexual orientation
   b. sexual intimidation
   c. same-sex orientation
   d. sexual reference

10. A person who is attracted to both males and females is called which of the following?
    a. homosexual
    b. heterosexual
    c. bisexual
    d. hermaphrodite

11. When a same-sex-oriented individual lives with a sense of shame and a lowered self-esteem due to their sexual orientation, they have done what with society's prejudiced view of them?
    a. accommodated
    b. internalized
    c. assimilated
    d. externalized

12. The prejudice, fear, and aversion held by individuals and directed against lesbians, gay men, and bisexuals is called what?
    a. homophobia
    b. agoraphobia
    c. xenophobia
    d. heterophobia

13. A large-scale study found that what percentage of gay men, in a California city, has been the victim of a hate crime in the year prior to the study?
    a. 15%
    b. 20%
    c. 25%
    d. 30%

14. Which of the following is the term that describes thought that seeks to integrate opposing or conflicting ideas and observations?
    a. normative thought
    b. dialectical thought
    c. preformal thought
    d. postformal thought

15. What term describes the type of thought that is heavily contextualized and includes consideration of not only logic, but also social and interpersonal issues?
    a. contextual thought
    b. postformal thought
    c. dialectical thought
    d. preformal thought

16. Which of the following is the term given to those aspects of the intellect that relate to understanding others' and one's own emotions and emotional responses?
    a. emotional quotient
    b. intelligence quotient
    c. emotional intelligence
    d. empathetic intelligence

17. Which of Schaie's stages of adult thinking allows the adult to address complex, multi-dimensional issues?
    a. social responsibility period
    b. executive period
    c. achieving period
    d. reorganization period

18. The overall pattern that underlies and unifies a person's life is called their what?
    a. life construct
    b. life hierarchy
    c. life structure
    d. life context

19. "Life is simple and controllable, and there are no significant coexisting contradictory forces within me" is the major false assumption during which age range?
    a. ages 16 to 22
    b. ages 22
    c. ages 28 to 34
    d. ages 34 to 45

20. Which theorist believed that the major task of early adulthood is starting a family and establishing a career?
    a. Schaie
    b. Havighurst
    c. Levinson
    d. Gould

TRUE/FALSE

For each of the following statements, indicate whether the statement is True or False. Check your answers with the Answer Key at the end of this chapter.

_____ 1.   Adults generally have less in common with each other than children do.

_____ 2.   Idiosyncratic events often create considerable stress and a need for reorganization in one's life.

_____ 3.   It is easy to pinpoint stages of adult development solely on the basis of age.

_____ 4.   Contextual paradigm theories only apply to adults; before that only stage theories are applicable.

_____ 5. The average decline of biological systems during the 30s and 40s is much smaller than most people think.

_____ 6. In a comparison, younger athletes from the 1896 Olympics ran a marathon faster than all "master" athletes (ages 40 to 69) from the 1996 Olympics.

_____ 7. Due to new combinations of effective drugs, AIDS has dropped from the second to the sixth leading cause of death in early adulthood in the United States.

_____ 8. Sub-Saharan Africa has the highest percentage of AIDS cases, ranking at 80% of infections world-wide.

_____ 9. A study by the University of Illinois suggests that sexual satisfaction is not linked to having an orgasm.

_____ 10. The popular idea of an effeminate gay man or a macho lesbian is for the most part false.

_____ 11. Homophobia is not a true phobia.

_____ 12. Skills involving speed and rote memory are typically at their highest in early adulthood.

_____ 13. The major task of early adulthood according to Schaie is starting a family and establishing a career.

_____ 14. Studies have found that for women, the early phase of adulthood is more likely to involve role conflict, because many women want both a family and a career.

_____ 15. Around ages 46 to 50 adults finally cast off false assumptions and become fully involved in adult life.

MATCHING

Match the following with the appropriate answer, and check your answers with the Answer Key at the end of this chapter.

1. _____ Havighurst

2. _____ Handling relationships

3. _____ Levinson

4. _____ Gould

5. _____ Developing emotional self-awareness

6. _____ Erikson

7. _____ Schaie

8. _____ Managing emotions

9. _____ Reading emotions

a. controlling emotional responses

b. developing an early life structure

c. understanding the emotional reactions of others

d. starting a family and establishing a career

e. solving relationship problems effectively

f. flexibly applying intellectual, cognitive abilities to accomplish personal and career goals

g. casting off erroneous assumptions about dependency, developing competence, acknowledging personal limitations, and accepting responsibility for one's own life

h. separating feelings from actions

i. establishing a meaningful relationship that involves intimacy while continuing to develop a secure personal identity

KEY VOCABULARY TERMS

Label each definition and give an example of each.

1. A form of internal timing used as a measure of adult development.

2. An individual's current ability to cope with and adapt to social and environmental demands.

3. Which sex you are physically attracted to, as well as with which sexual partners you might wish to become involved emotionally.

4. Prejudice, aversion, fear, and other negative attitudes held by individuals and directed toward lesbians, gay men, and/or bisexuals.

5. The term given to those aspects of the intellect that relate to understanding others' and one's own emotions and emotional responses.

Explain the difference between the following sets of terms.

6. Idiosyncratic events; normative events
7. Lesbian; gay; bisexual
8. Dialectical thought; postformal thought
9. Stage models; context models
10. Intimacy; isolation

PROGRAMMED REVIEW

Fill in the blanks in the following programmed review. Then check your answers with the Answer Key at the end of the chapter.

1. The major markers within adulthood are more closely linked to _____, _____, and _____ forces or events–such as getting married, starting a job or career, or having a child.

Perspectives on Adult Development

2. In recognition of both _____ expectations and individual lifestyle choices, we often turn to the concepts of _____ and _____ to explain adult development.

<u>Age Clocks and Social Norms</u>

3. Cultural norms and expectations define in important ways how we _____ our lives based on whether or not significant life events _____ to what our _____ specify.

4. In _____only about _____ of U.S. women reached age 80 or older; now more than _____ of the female population is expected to reach that age.

5. To more accurately describe the age of individuals, it is often useful to consider their _____, _____, and _____ ages.

<u>Contextual Paradigms</u>

6. Contextual paradigms focus on _____ forces as a whole, including those forces that are _____ as well as _____ to the individual.

7. Death during _____ was once a normal and expected event; it is now an _____ part of the social script.

General Physical Development
<u>Strength and Stamina</u>

8. Our responses to life events are determined by our physical capacity–our _____, _____, _____, and _____.

<u>Fitness and Health</u>

9. Those who establish _____ levels in early adulthood tend to persist in that lifestyle with clear risks of _____ and _____ and consequent health problems later in life.

10. A full _____ of women diagnosed in the United States with HIV in 2002 identified themselves as _____ or _____.

11. People age _____ to _____ have the highest rates of alcohol use, _____, and illicit drug use of any age period.

Sex and Sexuality
<u>Fertility</u>

12. Peak fertility occurs for both groups during _____ and _____.

Sexually Transmitted Diseases

13. AIDS is produced by a virus called the human _____ virus that eventually causes the disease of _____ immune deficiency syndrome.

14. The likelihood of contracting HIV is about _____; the rates for other sexually transmitted diseases is in the range of _____ to _____.

Sexual Attitudes and Behavior

15. Over the course of a _____, a typical _____ has just two partners; a typical _____ has six.

Sexual Identity and Sexual Orientation

16. Genetic research that has studied gene sequences in families with gay brothers or lesbian sisters suggests that a particular gene sequence on the _____ chromosome may be implicated for _____ homosexuality, although no such link appears for _____ homosexuality.

17. In comparison to heterosexual adolescents, lesbian, gay male, and bisexual adolescents are at _____ risk for _____, depression, substance abuse, and _____.

18. Heterosexual _____ have been shown to express more _____ attitudes toward same-sex-oriented people than heterosexual _____.

Cognitive Development in Adulthood

19. Overall _____ _____ (IQ) scores generally remain high throughout most of adulthood, but they often are observed to peak between the ages of _____ and _____.

Beyond Formal Operations

20. Students moved from a thinking style characterized by basic _____ through one that emphasized _____ for many competing points of view to one that _____ self-chosen ideas and convictions.

Postformal Thought

21. One way in which thinking changes as young people move into adulthood is that it becomes more _____ and _____.

Emotional Intelligence

22. Goleman's view of _____ involves concepts–such as empathy, _____, _____, conscientiousness, and competence in social settings–which he believes are more important to success on the job and in personal relationships than intelligence.

Schaie's Stages of Adult Thinking

23. Near the end of life, people may also focus on _____, where they finish the _____ of their lives.

Frameworks for Understanding Adult Development
Stages and Contexts

24. In _____ a blending of _____ and _____ approaches is perhaps the most useful way to conceptualize development.

25. There can be _____ individual variations in how particular people move through their _____ years.

Havighurst's Developmental Tasks

26. In young adulthood, the tasks mostly involve starting a _____ and establishing a _____. In middle adulthood, they center on _____ what was established earlier and on adjusting to _____ changes, as well as to changes in the family.

Erikson's Theory of Development

27. The crisis of _____ versus _____ is the developmental task that is most characteristic of young adulthood.

Levinson's Seasons of a Man's Life

28. During each era, the person constructs what Levinson calls a _____ _____, which is the overall pattern that underlies and unifies a person's life.

The Limitations of Normative Models

29. In the late _____ and _____ most women had little role confusion; the majority had a clear dream: to be a full-time _____.

<u>Gould's Transformations in Early Adulthood</u>

30. Talents, strengths, and _____ that were suppressed during the _____ because they did not fit into the unfolding blueprint of adulthood may _____.

<u>A Closing Comment</u>

31. These theories pay little attention to the _____ of life events.

CRITICAL THINKING QUESTIONS

To further your mastery of the topics, write out the answers to the following essay questions in the space provided.

1. How might age clocks and idiosyncratic events interact to cause stress in a person's life?

2. Why is it so critical to have good exercise and eating habits as young adults, when the body is relatively resilient against injury and disease?

3. What factors do you think are contributing the most to the epidemic spread of HIV/AIDS in developing nations? What measures do you think would be most helpful in stopping this spread?

4. What are some benefits of having children in early adulthood? What are some benefits of having children later in life? What about not having children at all?

5. How does the continuum approach to sexual orientation help to explain incidences or periods of heterosexual behavior by a person who self-identifies as homosexual, and conversely, homosexual behavior by a person who self-identifies as heterosexual?

6. What measures might be taken to help reduce hate crimes committed against homosexual individuals?

7. How might postformal thought better equip a 28-year-old individual to start and maintain a family than a 20-year-old?

8. How does emotional intelligence differ from an intelligence quotient?

9. How have the means by which a woman can balance family versus career responsibilities become more defined since the 1980s?

PRACTICE TEST - POST TEST

Circle the correct answer for each multiple choice question and check your answers with the Answer Key at the end of the chapter.

1. Gina is about to become married to her long-time boyfriend. Her marriage is an example of which of the following?
   a. idiosyncratic events
   b. normative events
   c. age clocks
   d. motivational events

2. Which of the following lets a person know when certain life events should occur, relative to standards of our culture?
   a. normative events
   b. contextual paradigms
   c. age clocks
   d. social norms

3. If Gerald's wife of five years were to suddenly die in a car accident, this would be an example of which of the following?
   a. spontaneous events
   b. life structure
   c. normative events
   d. idiosyncratic events

4. Which of the following is NOT a type of age that is often used to more accurately describe an individual?
   a. biological age
   b. psychological age
   c. social age
   d. emotional age

5. What percentage of 18- to 25-year-olds reports binge drinking at least once a month?
   a. 40%
   b. 50%
   c. 60%
   d. 70%

6. Which of the following is now the second leading cause of preventable death among young adults?
   a. obesity
   b. smoking
   c. alcohol comsumption
   d. illegal drugs

7. How many times greater is the rate of death by accident for males than for females?
   a. 2 times
   b. 2.5 times
   c. 3 times
   d. 5 times

8. Which of the following is a stress-linked disease that exhibits symptoms during young adulthood?
   a. diabetes
   b. ulcers
   c. rheumatoid arthritis
   d. depression

9. Which U.S. law makes it illegal to discriminate against individuals with disabilities in employment, public accommodations, transportation, and telecommunications?
   a. Accommodation of Disabled Americans Act
   b. Disabled Americans Equality Act
   c. Americans with Disabilities Act
   d. Disabled Americans Act

10. What percentage of people reporting having more than five sexual partners in the past year claims either to be decreasing their sexual activity, going for HIV testing on a regular basis, or using condoms always?
    a. 68%   c. 76%
    b. 72%   d. 81%

11. How many married people (out of 5) report having sex twice a week?
    a. 1   c. 3
    b. 2   d. 4

12. Which of the following is most accurate when describing same-sex oriented individuals?
    a. they form friendships that deepen in young adulthood, that may or may not involve sex
    b. they seek out and form intimate relationships that may or may not last
    c. they pursue goals in life and succeed or fail and move on
    d. all of the above

13. In comparison to heterosexual adolescents, homosexual adolescents have a higher risk of all of the following except which?
    a. distress   c. suicide
    b. depression   d. illness

14. What percentage of second-year medical students was found to endorse the belief that homosexuality is a mental disorder?
    a. 4%   c. 9%
    b. 7%   d. 11%

15. Mary is weighing the pros and cons of an important decision. She is trying to integrate opposing ideas and observations. Which of the following best describes her style of thought?
    a. philosophical thought   c. postformal thought
    b. dialectical thought   d. preformal thought

16. Which of the following is NOT an aspect of intellect from which adult thought draws?
    a. logic   c. emotions
    b. intuition   d. experience

17. Which of the following is NOT one of Goleman's four areas of emotional intelligence?
    a. managing emotions
    b. handling emotions
    c. reading emotions
    d. developing emotional self-awareness

18. Wilma is using her intellectual abilities to pursue her chosen career and to decide on a lifestyle. In which of Schaie's stages of adult thinking is she?
    a. achieving period
    b. social responsibility period
    c. acquisitive period
    d. executive period

19. According to Levinson, which of the following is NOT a season of a person's life?
    a. era of adolescence
    b. era of early adulthood
    c. era of middle adulthood
    d. era of late adulthood

20. At which age is a person most likely to assume that doing things his parents' way will bring the best results?
    a. 18
    b. 24
    c. 30
    d. 36

ANSWER KEY

Practice Test – Pretest (with text page numbers)

1.	d 368	6.	d 372	11.	b 382	16.	c 386
2.	b 368	7.	d 373	12.	a 382	17.	b 387
3.	a 369	8.	c 377	13.	c 382	18.	c 390
4.	c 369	9.	a 380	14.	b 384	19.	c 393
5.	b 370	10.	c 380	15.	b 384	20.	b 395

True/False

1.	T	6.	F	11.	T
2.	T	7.	T	12.	F
3.	F	8.	T	13.	F
4.	F	9.	F	14.	T
5.	T	10.	T	15.	F

Matching

1.	d	6.	i
2.	e	7.	f
3.	b	8.	a
4.	g	9.	c
5.	h		

Key Vocabulary Terms

1. Age Clock
2. psychological age
3. sexual orientation
4. homophobia
5. emotional intelligence (EQ)

6. Idiosyncratic events are events in the lifespan that are unanticipated that cause considerable stress and a readjustment of one's life; normative events are events that occur at relatively specific times in the lifespan which most people in a cohort experience.

7. Lesbian refers to a female with a sexual orientation toward other females; gay refers to a male with a sexual orientation toward other males; bisexual refers to a person who is attracted to both males and females.

8. Dialectical thought is thought that seeks to integrate opposing or conflicting ideas and observations; postformal thought is thought that is heavily contextualized and includes consideration of not only logical, but also social and interpersonal issues.

9. <u>Stage models</u> focus on the commonalities of development experienced by individuals; <u>context models</u> focus more attention on the specific experiences that shape an individual's life.

10. <u>Intimacy</u> involves establishing a mutually satisfying, close relationship with another person; <u>isolation</u> involves the inability or failure to achieve mutuality with another person.

Programmed Review
1. personal, social, cultural
2. cultural, age clocks, social norms
3. evaluate, correspond, age clocks
4. 1900, 14%, half
5. biological, social, psychological
6. developmental, within, external
7. childhood, abnormal
8. health, fitness, strength, stamina
9. low activity, overweight, obesity
10. 61%, black, African American
11. 18, 25, smoking
12. late adolescence, early adulthood
13. immunodeficiency, acquired
14. 0.1%, 5, 15%
15. lifetime, woman, man
16. X, male, female
17. higher, distress, suicide
18. men, negative, women
19. intelligence, quotient, 20, 34
20. dualism, tolerance, embraced
21. reflective, complex
22. EQ, motivation, optimism
23. legacy creation, business
24. adulthood, stage, contextual
25. wide, adult
26. family, career, maintaining, physical
27. intimacy, isolation
28. life, structure
29. 1950s, 1960s, homemaker
30. desires, 20s, resurface
31. unpredictability

Practice Test – Post test (with text page numbers)

1.	b 368	6.	a 373	11.	b 380	16.	c 384
2.	c 369	7.	c 373	12.	d 381	17.	b 386
3.	d 369	8.	b 375	13.	d 381	18.	a 387
4.	d 370	9.	c 376	14.	c 382	19.	a 391
5.	b 372	10.	c 379	15.	b 384	20.	b 394

Chapter 13

Young Adulthood: Personality and Sociocultural Development

CHAPTER OUTLINE

◈ Self, Family, and Work
- ◆ The Personal Self
- ◆ Self as Family Member
- ◆ Self as Worker

◈ Forming Close Relationships
- ◆ Adult Friendships
- ◆ Couple Formation and Development
- ◆ Marriage
- ◆ Cohabitation
- ◆ Gay and Lesbian Couples
- ◆ Staying Single

◈ The Family Life Cycle and Adult Development
- ◆ The Family Life Cycle
- ◆ The Transition to Parenthood
- ◆ Coping with Children's Developmental Stages
- ◆ Coping with Single Parenthood

◈ The Occupational Cycle
- ◆ Stages of Occupational Life
- ◆ Gaining a Place in the Workplace
- ◆ Careers and Career Choices
- ◆ Occupational Choice and Preparation
- ◆ Gender and Ethnicity

◈ Work and Gender
- ◆ Changes in Women's Work Patterns
- ◆ The Many Meanings of Work
- ◆ The Role of Women in Careers
- ◆ The Dynamics of Dual-Earner Couples

LEARNING OBJECTIVES

After you have read and studied this chapter, you should be able to answer the following questions.

1. How is the self generally defined by young adults?
2. What is love, and why is it especially important to young adults?
3. What are the main features of the transition that occurs when a person becomes a parent?
4. How do people decide which career or job will be the best choice for them?
5. How have family members' roles changed as women have entered the workforce in increasing numbers?

PRACTICE TEST – PRETEST

Circle the correct answer for each multiple choice question and check your answers with the Answer Key at the end of the chapter.

1. The action of realizing one's full potential by developing one's talents and abilities is referred to as what?
   - a. self-improvement
   - b. self-motivation
   - c. self-actualization
   - d. self-emphasis

2. The classic view of self-development called the Hierarchy of Needs was proposed by which theorist?
   - a. Sternberg
   - b. Piaget
   - c. Rogers
   - d. Maslow

3. The conditions that others impose upon us to cause us to conform to their expectations, thus making us a worthwhile human being, are called what?
   - a. conditional worth
   - b. qualities of worth
   - c. conditions of worth
   - d. consummate worth

4. The proposition that we should warmly accept another person as a worthwhile human being without reservations is called what?
   - a. unconditional positive regard
   - b. unconditional acceptance
   - c. unconditional love
   - d. humanistic regard

5. Which of the following is NOT a typical characteristic of adult friendship?
   - a. positive emotional attachment
   - b. physical intimacy
   - c. need fulfillment
   - d. interdependence

6. What word is used to describe the feeling of closeness that occurs in love relationships?
   a. passion
   b. communication
   c. intimacy
   d. attraction

7. Which of the following components of love refers to physical attraction, arousal, and sexual behavior in a relationship?
   a. decision-commitment
   b. intimacy
   c. companionship
   d. passion

8. During which stage of the stimulas-value-role theory of couple formation do couples determine whether their interests, attitudes, and beliefs are compatible?
   a. ro
   b. stimulas
   c. value-comparison
   d. both a and c

9. Over what percentage of men and women in America will marry at some point in their lives?
   a. 75%
   b. 84%
   c. 90%
   d. 95%

10. According to the 2002 U. S. Census, nearly what percentage of all married couples are "interracial?"
    a. 1%
    b. 2%
    c. 3%
    d. 4%

11. During which of the following decades was the percentage of marriage-age adults only 4%?
    a. 1930s
    b. 1950s
    c. 1970s
    d. 1980s

12. In 2002, what percentage of young adults age 25 to 34 reported living alone?
    a. 10%
    b. 12%
    c. 13%
    d. 15%

13. Which of the following is NOT a major factor in the explosion of single-parent families headed by women?
    a. rising rates of divorce
    b. rising rates of deaths of the father
    c. a tradition of awarding parenthood to the mother
    d. increase in births to unmarried mothers

14. Which of the following is an example of formal workforce preparation?
    a. learning from on-the-job training
    b. learning norms from teachers
    c. learning from television or film
    d. learning from a mentor in the trade

15. Which of the following is NOT a way in which mentors positively assist young workers?
    a. they teach and train
    b. they serve as models of behavior
    c. they sponsor the worker's advancement
    d. they show them loopholes

16. Which of the following fields has emerged to help people select jobs that will be a good match for their interests?
    a. occupational therapy
    b. work-study
    c. clinical psychology
    d. career counseling

17. What percentage of secretaries are women?
    a. 96.6%
    b. 94.3%
    c. 92.8%
    d. 91.0%

18. During which time did men come to be regarded as the "natural" providers for their families?
    a. early 19th century
    b. late 19th century
    c. early 20th century
    d. late 18th century

19. Which of the following is traditionally seen as a female profession?
    a. business
    b. social work
    c. law
    d. medicine

20. How many weeks of unpaid family leave are companies required to give their employees (both male and female) by federal law?
    a. 6 weeks
    b. 8 weeks
    c. 10 weeks
    d. 12 weeks

TRUE/FALSE

For each of the following statements, indicate whether the statement is True or False. Check your answers with the Answer Key at the end of this chapter.

_____ 1.   Modern psychologists believe that one's identity changes over the lifespan, reacting to events and interactions between one's role and one's developing personality.

_____ 2.   A worker whose job emphasizes the intrinsic factors of the work typically reports more job satisfaction.

_____ 3.   According to Sternberg, love has three components which vary in strength between different pairs of people.

_____ 4. During the final stage of the stimulus-value-commitment theory, the couple determines whether they can function in compatible roles such as marriage.

_____ 5. Most cultures define marriage in the exact same way.

_____ 6. According to the text, in traditional Chinese culture, the transition to married life is orchestrated by older relatives who arrange the match, screen the young woman, and negotiate the bride price.

_____ 7. In 2003, the number of couples who were engaged in cohabitation numbered over five million.

_____ 8. The number of single young adults is higher now than it has been for 50 years.

_____ 9. As children develop, the roles and tasks their parents must undertake also change dramatically.

_____ 10. According to Carter, children begin to consider work and careers at a young age, even as early as five years old.

_____ 11. Women and some minority groups are under-represented in lower paying jobs, and over-represented in high paying jobs.

_____ 12. Women and minorities may be subtly (or not so subtly) channeled into certain jobs rather than others.

_____ 13. According to the text, in the early 1900s, many men and women combined their efforts in family businesses and farms.

_____ 14. Women in the professional fields gain more physical and psychological benefits from their jobs than do women who work in more clerical positions.

_____ 15. Women in managerial and professional positions are less willing to take risks than are their male counterparts.

MATCHING

Match the following with the appropriate answer, and check your answers with the Answer Key at the end of this chapter.

1. ____ Conflictual

2. ____ Functional

3. ____ Assimilative

4. ____ Integrative

5. ____ Emotional

6. ____ Accommodative

7. ____ Attitudinal

a. the young adult becomes less dependent on parents for social and psychological support

b. those who incorporate both positive and negative events into their identities

c. the young adult develops attitudes, values, and beliefs that are independent from those held by parents

d. the young adult's separation from parents is accomplished without feelings of guilt

e. those who unrealistically believe themselves to be unchanging

f. the young adult becomes financially independent

g. those who change too much in response to changing circumstances

KEY VOCABULARY TERMS

Label each definition and give an example of each.

1. Realizing one's full potential through the development of one's talents and abilities.

2. The realization of being in love and the establishment of a commitment to maintain it.

3. A variable sequence of periods or stages in a worker's life.

4. A field that attempts to match the talents and interests of individuals to the characteristics of a job.

5. A couple sharing a household in which both contribute to family income as members of the paid labor force.

6. Leave required by law for the purpose of dealing with family affairs and problems.

Explain the difference between the following sets of terms.

7. conditions of worth; unconditional positive regard
8. extrinsic factors; intrinsic factors
9. reciprocity; mutuality
10. intimacy; passion

PROGRAMMED REVIEW

Fill in the blanks in the following programmed review. Then check your answers with the Answer Key at the end of the chapter

1. The role changes of young adulthood typically are _____ and less _____ than those of childhood and adolescence.

Self, Family, and Work

2. Research has shown that the more _____ a father's work experience, the higher his _____ and the more likely he is to have an _____, warm, and positive parenting style.

The Personal Self

3. For Maslow, the ultimate goal of self-development was _____.

4. Life experiences may be _____ into the individual's identity through _____, _____, or a combination of both processes.

Self as Family Member

5. Identity formation continues into adulthood where it often centers on establishing _____ from one's parents and taking on adult _____ that involve _____ and personal _____.

Self as Worker

6. Our work provides an important context in which _____ and _____ develop.

214

7. The fortunate workers whose jobs emphasize _____ factors typically report more job _____ and higher motivation and personal _____ in their jobs.

Forming Close Relationships

8. In early adulthood, most people focus their attention on two developmental tasks–_____ and _____.

Adult Friendships

9. Friendships are usually characterized by positive _____ attachment, need _____ and _____.

Couple Formation and Development

10. Erik _____ proposed that establishing a meaningful _____ relationship was the primary developmental _____ in early adulthood.

11. Most people eventually choose a _____ family lifestyle–one that includes _____ and _____.

12. Those of us who are interested in _____ hope for a relationship marked by _____ love, which includes _____, _____, and _____.

13. According to _____ theory, each person examines the _____ and _____ of the other partner to determine whether the _____ is worthwhile.

Marriage

14. Marriages between two members of the _____ are _____ by _____ in most states.

Cohabitation

15. Both men and women in _____ relationships are more likely than _____ people to have affairs outside the _____.

16. Cohabitation before marriage _____ seem to contribute in universally _____ ways to the quality of a subsequent _____ and may be associated with _____ satisfactory outcomes.

<u>Gay and Lesbian Couples</u>

17. _____ couples prefer _____ relationships, as do heterosexual couples.

18. The vast majority of children raised by _____ parents develop a _____ orientation.

<u>Staying Single</u>

19. During the late _____ when the country was recovering from the Great Depression, _____ people married, and those who did marry did so at _____ ages.

20. Single adults may not feel sufficiently drawn to anyone to undertake one of the most _____ of adult responsibilities–_____.

21. Today, the average age at marriage for women is _____ years and for men it is _____ years. As recently as 1970, the average age at marriage was _____ years for women and _____ years for men.

The Family Life Cycle and Adult Development
<u>The Family Life Cycle</u>

22. _____ is one of a set of significant events in the typical family life cycle and its _____ and _____ compose a major developmental phase for the parents as individuals and for the couple as a system.

<u>The Transition to Parenthood</u>

23. For most new parents, the actual _____ brings an onslaught of _____ and _____ strains.

<u>Coping with Children's Developmental Stages</u>

24. Couples must establish ways of making _____ and resolving _____ that will maintain the _____ and respect of each partner.

<u>Coping with Single Parenthood</u>

25. Since the _____, single-parent families have increased at a rate _____ times faster than traditional two-parent families.

The Occupational Cycle
<u>Stages of Occupational Life</u>

26. A typical pattern is to change _____ and change _____ several times throughout one's working years.

<u>Gaining a Place in the Workplace</u>

27. When young adults start _____, they may experience what could be termed _____ _____.

<u>Careers and Career Choices</u>

28. Holland proposed that individuals can be categorized into six career-related _____ types: _____, investigative, _____, social, _____ and conventional.

<u>Occupational Choice and Preparation</u>

29. People without _____ plans or with varied _____ and _____ may take any job that is available and frequently change jobs.

30. Different types of _____, which also involve many different _____ sets, can be categorized according to their most important dimensions.

<u>Gender and Ethnicity</u>

31. _____ may limit their choices if they question their _____ in the sciences and avoid careers in _____ fields.

Work and Gender

32. As more _____ have entered the U.S. labor force, roles for men and women have changed, both at _____ and at _____.

<u>Changes in Women's Work Patterns</u>

33. In the United States about _____ of physicians, _____ of medical scientists, _____ of lawyers and judges, _____ of economists, and _____ of psychologists were women.

The Many Meanings of Work

34. Many _____ could not make ends meet without _____ from both
    _____.

The Role of Women in Careers

35. The average woman can devote _____ years to full-time child care and still have
    _____ years left to enter the workforce, establish a career, or pursue other interests.

The Dynamics of Dual-Earner Couples

36. During early _____, the needs of young _____ and the struggle to
    _____ a career often collide, forcing the couple to set _____ and resolve
    conflicts.

CRITICAL THINKING QUESTIONS

To further your mastery of the topics, write out the answers to the following essay questions in the space provided.

1. How are Roger's concepts of unconditional positive regard and conditions of worth related to Maslow's concepts of esteem needs and love and belongingness needs?

2. Describe how a job that is challenging, interesting, and involves personal growth can help a person reach a stage of self-actualization?

3. What happens when a person considers his or her job to be boring?

4. Describe how Sternberg's three components of love combine to form different types of love-based relationships.

5. What forms of love are likely to be involved in an arranged marriage?

6. What are the advantages and disadvantages of being a dual-income couple with children?

7. Why does the arrival of the first child put strain on marital relationships?

8. Why might the Personal Responsibility and Work Opportunity Reconciliation Act (PRWORA) actually do little to reverse the welfare and poverty cycle of single parents?

9. What can young adults do to reduce the risk of reality shock upon entering their chosen career?

PRACTICE TEST – POST TEST

Circle the correct answer for each multiple choice question and check your answers with the Answer Key at the end of the chapter.

1. Which of the following is NOT an aspect of adult development?
    a. self as a community member   c. self as a worker
    b. self as an individual   d. self as a family member

2. What was the ultimate goal in Maslow's Hierarchy of Needs?
    a. self-fulfillment   c. self-improvement
    b. self-perfection   d. self-actualization

3. Of the following, which is the most basic of Maslow's Hierarchy of Needs?
    a. safety needs   c. physiological needs
    b. love needs   d. esteem needs

4. Through his own studies and thoughts, Robert has come to realize that he and his parents differ on several important beliefs. Which aspect of independence has Robert accomplished?
    a. functional   c. emotional
    b. attitudinal   d. conflictual

5. What percentage of people identified family roles as the most important components in defining who they are?
    a. 88%   c. 90%
    b. 89%   d. 91%

6. Which of the following is an extrinsic factor of a job?
    a. salary   c. respect earner
    b. hours of work   d. both a and b

7. Victoria and Jared have a love that involves intimacy and decision-commitment. According to the Triangular Theory of Love, which type of love do they share?
    a. romantic love   c. companionate love
    b. consummate love   d. fatuous love

8. Carol and Jason have what is called romantic love. What components of love make up romantic love?
    a. passion, decision-commitment   c. intimacy, passion
    b. intimacy, decision-commitment   d. intimacy, passion, decision-commitment

9. During which stage of stimulus-value-role theory do men and women make initial judgments about each other's appearance and personality?
   a. stimulus
   b. value-comparison
   c. role
   d. both a and b

10. Ten years after marriage, what is the percentage of divorce for people who lived together before marriage?
    a. 30%
    b. 35%
    c. 40%
    d. 45%

11. Which of the following is NOT cited in the text as a major event in the adult life cycle?
    a. marriage
    b. retirement from work
    c. enrollment of youngest child in schoole
    d. buying a house

12. Among all families with children in 2003, what percentage were single-parent families run by a single mother?
    a. 33%
    b. 28%
    c. 26%
    d. 21%

13. Which of the following, passed in 1996, was the first major welfare reform effort in 60 years?
    a. Personal Responsibility and Work Opportunity Reconciliation Act
    b. Aid to Families with Dependent Children Act
    c. Family Welfare Reformation Act
    d. Federal Welfare and Disabled Workers Act

14. 17-year old Kaori has decided that she wants to become a medical doctor. She is in the third stage of whose developmental model of the traditional one-career work cycle?
    a. Rogers
    b. Havighurst
    c. Carter
    d. Holland

15. Which of the following is NOT one of the personality types of the theory of careers?
    a. realistic
    b. investigative
    c. analytical
    d. enterprising

16. Jeremy has several characteristics that might influence his choice of career. He is creative, introspective, and independent. Which of the following careers would best suit Jeremy?
    a. priest
    b. statistician
    c. reporter
    d. beautician

17. Kala wants to be an athletic director. Which of the following personality characteristics is NOT useful for her choice of career type?
    a. high verbal skills
    b. high energy
    c. self-confident
    d. sociable

18. What percentage of married women with children are full-time homemakers?
    a. 7%   c. 9%
    b. 8%   d. 11%

19. Sean and Melody each work to support their family. They are an example of which of the following?
    a. dual-earner couple   c. twice-earner couple
    b. double-income family   d. double-income couple

20. In a recent study (Deutsch, 1999) what percentage of women were found to recognize the necessity of their income, but were still uncomfortable about it?
    a. 55%   c. 65%
    b. 60%   d. 70%

ANSWER KEYS

Practice Test – Pretest (with text page numbers)

1. c 400	6. c 405	11. b 409	16. d 418
2. d 401	7. d 406	12. b 409	17. a 422
3. c 402	8. c 407	13. b 413-414	18. b 423
4. a 402	9. c 407	14. a 417	19. b 424
5. b 405	10. c 407	15. d 417	20. d 425

True/False

1. T	6. F	11. F
2. T	7. T	12. T
3. T	8. T	13. F
4. F	9. T	14. T
5. F	10. F	15. F

Matching

1. d	5. a
2. f	6. g
3. e	7. c
4. b	

Key Vocabulary Terms

1. self-actualization
2. decision/commitment.
3. occupational cycle
4. career counseling
5. dual-earner couple
6. family leave

7. <u>Conditions of worth</u> are conditions others impose upon us if we are to be worthwhile as human beings; <u>unconditional positive regard</u> is Rogers' proposition that we should warmly accept another person as a worthwhile human being without reservation or conditions of worth.

8. <u>Extrinsic factors</u> in work are satisfactions that come in the form of salary, status, and other rewards for the work; <u>intrinsic factors</u> are satisfactions from doing the work in and of itself.

9. <u>Reciprocity</u> in friendship means that the friendship is two-way; <u>mutuality</u> means that the friends care about each other.

10. <u>Intimacy</u> is the feeling of closeness that occurs in love relationships; <u>passion</u> is the component of love that refers to physical attraction, arousal, and sexual behavior in a relationship.

Programmed Review

1. subtler, systematic
2. positive, self-esteem, accepting
3. self-actualization
4. incorporated, assimilation, accommodation
5. independence, responsibilities, work, relationships
6. self, identity
7. intrinsic, satisfaction, involvement
8. work, family
9. emotional, fulfillment, interdependence
10. Erikson, intimate, task
11. traditional, marriage, parenthood
12. marriage, consummate, intimacy, passion, commitment
13. stimulus-value-role, assets, liabilities, relationship
14. same sex, prohibited, law
15. cohabiting, married, relationship
16. does not, positive, marriage, less
17. Homosexual, long-term
18. homosexual, heterosexual
19. 1930s, fewer, later
20. consuming, parenthood
21. 25.3, 27.1, 20.8, 23.4
22. Parenthood, challenges, demands
23. birth, physical, emotional
24. decisions, conflicts, integrity
25. 1970s, 10
26. jobs, companies
27. working, reality shock
28. personality, realistic, artistic, enterprising
29. definite, interests, abilities
30. jobs, skill
31. Women, competence, technology-based
32. women, home, work
33. 28%, 50%, 30%, 53%, 65%
34. married couples, income, spouses
35. 10, 35
36. adulthood, children, establish, priorities

Practice Test – Post test (with text page numbers)

1. a 400	6. d 402	11. d 411	16. c 420
2. d 401	7. c 405	12. c 413	17. d 419
3. c 401	8. c 405	13. a 414	18. c 423
4. b 403	9. a 407	14. b 416	19. a 425
5. c 403	10. c 408	15. c 418	20. c 427

Chapter 14

Middle Adulthood: Physical and Cognitive Development

CHAPTER OUTLINE

◆ Development in Middle Adulthood
- ♦ Prime Time Or The Beginning Of The End?
- ♦ Midlife Crisis: Is It Real?
- ♦ Perceptions And Realities At Midlife

◆ Physical continuity and change
- ♦ Changes In Capabilities
- ♦ The Climacteric
- ♦ Sexuality In The Middle Years

◆ Disease and Health
- ♦ The Cumulative Effects Of Health Habits
- ♦ Stress And Health
- ♦ Ethnicity, Poverty, And Health

◆ Cognitive Continuity And Change
- ♦ Fluid Versus Crystallized Intelligence
- ♦ Experience And Expertise
- ♦ Cognitive Skills In The Workplace

LEARNING OBJECTIVES

After you have read and studied this chapter, you should be able to answer the following questions.

1. How do people in middle age generally approach this period of development – as the best part of life or the beginning of decline?
2. Is there such a thing as the midlife crisis?
3. How does sexuality change when men and women reach middle age?
4. How do habits established earlier in life begin to assert their effects in middle adulthood?
5. How do middle-aged adults adjust to the cognitive decline associated with aging?

PRACTICE TEST - PRETEST

Circle the correct answer for each multiple choice question and check your answers with the Answer Key at the end of the chapter.

1. The command generation refers to people in their:
   a. 20s to 30s
   b. 40s to 60s
   c. 70s to 80s
   d. those above 80

2. Which of the following physical changes is typically experienced more severely in men than in women?
   a. hearing loss
   b. sense of smell
   c. visual acuity
   d. loss of bone mass

3. The broad complex of physical and emotional symptoms that accompany reproductive changes in middle adulthood, affecting both men and women is referred to as the:
   a. menopause
   b. midlife crisis
   c. climacteric
   d. libidinous syndrome

4. The estrogen loss that women experience during middle adulthood causes:
   a. loss of bone mass
   b. changes in genitals
   c. increased coronary heart disease
   d. all of the above

5. Which of the following diseases is among the most common causes of death in middle age?
   a. cancer
   b. respiratory illness
   c. infectious diseases
   d. Alzheimer's disease

6. At every age level throughout the lifespan, the death rate of men is about _____ that of women.
   a. half
   b. one-third
   c. double
   d. triple

7. During middle adulthood, death by suicide accounts for approximately what percentage of deaths?
   a. 20
   b. 15
   c. 8
   d. less than 1

8. After the age of 40, people tend to gain about _____ per year.
   a. one pound
   b. 2 pounds
   c. several pounds
   d. none of the above

9. Over the last several decades, hip and knee replacements are occurring more frequently and at earlier ages due to which of the following?
   a. increases in arthritis rates
   b. increases in early diagnosis
   c. increases in injuries from sports and exercise
   d. increases in obesity

10. Which of the following life events is associated with the highest level of stress?
    a. change to a different line of work
    b. vacation
    c. son or daughter leaving home
    d. minor violation of the law

11. The average life expectancy in the United States is:
    a. 100 years
    b. 90 years
    c. 80 years
    d. 60 years

12. Which of the following is the leading cause of preventable death in the United States?
    a. obesity
    b. smoking
    c. abusing alcohol
    d. exposure to environmental toxins

13. Which of the following statements is true regarding fluid and crystallized intelligence?
    a. crystallized intelligence is not influenced very much by culture
    b. fluid intelligence does not change very much as the adult ages
    c. crystallized intelligence is influence by neurological function
    d. none of the above

14. Since 1900, the life expectancy in the United States has increased _____ years.
    a. about 20
    b. about 30
    c. about 40
    d. about 50

15. Which of the following types of individuals is likely to be the healthiest during middle adulthood?
    a. white man with only a high school diploma
    b. hispanic man with college degree
    c. white woman with college degree
    d. black man with college degree

TRUE/FALSE

For each of the following statements indicate whether the statement is True or False. Check your answers with the Answer Key at the end of this chapter.

_____ 1. The period of middle adulthood occurs at the same time and lasts the same length of time for everyone.

_____ 2. Most decision makers in government, corporations, and society are middle-aged.

_____ 3. Levinson's investigation of midlife crises in males revealed large differences between the experiences of successful middle-class men and unsuccessful lower-class men.

_____ 4. Most researchers nowadays agree with Levinson's view of middle adulthood in men as routinely involving a midlife crisis.

_____ 5. Learning new physical skills becomes increasingly more difficult as middle adulthood progresses.

_____ 6. The personal and psychological adjustments associated with menopause are experienced by women around the world in highly similar ways.

_____ 7. Hormone replacement therapy has been found to be associated with many positive benefits, but absolutely no health risks.

_____ 8. Drugs used to treat erectile dysfunction, such as Viagra and Levitra, are effective for nearly all men who take them.

_____ 9. Studies show that those adults having sex infrequently during middle age generally have conventional ideas about love, sex, and marriage.

_____ 10. In middle age, arthritis affects men, but typically not women.

_____ 11. Research suggests that while stress affects one's mental state, it is not associated with an individual developing an illness.

_____ 12. Young adults can generally outperform adults in middle age on tasks requiring high order cognitive processing.

_____ 13. Brain damage is more likely to affect fluid intelligence than crystallized intelligence.

_____ 14. Aging often involves trade-offs; as one skill declines, another skill improves.

_____ 15.   The old saying that "you can't teach an old dog new tricks" is basically true as far as job training is concerned; older adults who lose their jobs are typically unsuccessful in training for new jobs.

PROGRAMMED REVIEW

Fill in the blanks in the following programmed review. Then check your answers with the Answer Key at the end of the chapter.

Development in Middle Adulthood

1.   The time of life referred to as middle adulthood is a cultural construction and may be shorter or longer for an individual because of different cues associated with aging, including _____ cues and family status, _____ cues, _____ cues, and _____ cues.

Prime Time Or The Beginning Of The End?

2.   Individuals who view middle adulthood as "the prime of life" typically enter this period feeling _____ with their life.

Midlife Crisis: Is It Real?

3.   Research conducted by Daniel Levinson showed that men struggle with a variety of issues during midlife that can be linked to a midlife crisis occurring. These issues relate to being old vs. _____, masculine vs. _____, destructive vs. _____, and alienated to others vs. _____ to others.

Perceptions And Realities At Midlife

4.   Research conducted after that by Daniel Levinson showed that those more likely to experience a midlife crisis do so in order to avoid _____. Midlife crises occur more in a person's _____ than in their _____. They are more likely to occur in _____ people than in _____ people.

Physical continuity and change

5.   By the age of 50, most people have experienced physical changes associated with growing older. For both men and women, there is decreasing _____. For women, there is _____. For men, there is difficulty achieving an _____.

Changes In Capabilities

6. Aging brings on changes to the internal body. The _____ stiffens and shrinks. A person becomes shorter. _____ and _____ lose elasticity and _____ develop. Fat accumulates, especially around the _____.

The Climacteric

7. In women, the reproductive system shuts down when _____ occurs. Less _____ is produced. _____ and _____ stop. Shrinking occurs in the _____ and _____.

8. Many women experiencing menopause develop _____, _____, headaches, _____, and _____.

9. Hormone replacement therapy (HRT) aims to increase the levels of _____ and/or _____ in menopausal women. For many women, HRT reduces the frequency or severity of symptoms, such as _____ and _____.

10. Studies show that in addition to experiencing decreased sexual design, about _____ percent of men over the age of 40 experience some _____.

Sexuality In The Middle Years

11. In middle age, men may experience _____ anxiety and dissatisfaction with middle age. Women may require more time to achieve _____.

12. In the middle years, couples may express _____, which refers to physical affection that may or may not lead to sex, such as _____ and _____.

Disease and Health

13. In middle age, most deaths are due to _____ and _____.

14. At every age level throughout the lifespan, the death rate of men is about _____ that of women. The death rate during middle adulthood is twice that for people with _____ years of schooling or less than for people with more education.

The Cumulative Effects Of Health Habits

15. Since 1985, the percentage of Americans who smoke has dropped from _____ to
    _____. Those who smoke are more likely to belong to _____ groups, be
    living below the _____ level, and have a low level of _____.

16. As one ages, the _____ and _____ become less efficient in their ability to
    clear unusual levels of drugs from the body.

17. The long-term negative health effects of smoking, alcohol abuse, and illegal drug use can be
    compounded by other negative lifestyle issues, including _____,
    _____, and _____.

Stress And Health

18. The effect of stressful events on a person is _____, which means that when
    several stressful events happen at the same time, the impact is _____ than if
    only one or two occur.

19. When people are under stress, they tend to care for themselves less well than when they are
    not under stress; they may _____ less, _____ poorly, experience
    problems _____, drink more _____, and smoke more.

Ethnicity, Poverty, And Health

20. In the 45 to 65 age group, the death rate for blacks is nearly _____ of that for
    whites. Blacks are _____ likely to die from diabetes, heart disease, cancer, high
    blood pressure (hypertension), accidents, and AIDs than are whites. Hispanics are more
    likely than whites to die from _____ and _____ diseases as well as
    diabetes, high blood pressure, and AIDS.

21. Hispanics are less likely to have _____ than either whites or blacks. Twice as
    many Hispanics as whites use _____ as their primary source of health care.

Cognitive Continuity And Change

22. Many aspects of intelligence _____ during middle adulthood. When compared
    with young adults, those in midlife, especially those _____ adults, peak in their
    ability to carry out higher order cognitive abilities.

Fluid Versus Crystallized Intelligence

23. _____ involves abilities used in acquiring new knowledge and skills, including _____, reasoning inductively, and perceiving _____ between objects and events. It is also referred to as _____.

24. _____ involves accumulated knowledge and skills that come with _____ and _____. It is also called _____.

25. The biggest decline in intellectual functioning is seen in tasks involving _____; studies using _____ scans have found that these declines are associated with shrinkage in the _____ regions of the brain.

Experience And Expertise

26. There are two types of knowledge. Factual knowledge, or knowing *what,* is referred to as _____. Action-oriented knowledge, or knowing _____, is referred to as _____.

Cognitive Skills In The Workplace

27. Higher scores on tests of intellectual flexibility are achieved by people who are continually challenged by _____ in their work than those who perform _____ work.

CRITICAL THINKING QUESTIONS

To further your mastery of the topics, write out the answers to the following essay questions in the space provided.

1. Discuss the many physical changes associated with middle adulthood.

2. Describe how modern researchers differ from Daniel Levinson in their views of middle age, specifically regarding the midlife crisis.

3. Explain what Hormone Replacement Therapy is, what it is used to treat, its effectiveness, and any risks or side effects associated with it.

4. Discuss how prevalent cigarette smoking is in the United States and what health problems are known to be associated with cigarette smoking.

5. Discuss differences in the death rates and disease rates for men and women. What factors are likely to contribute to these differences?

6. Discuss how one's socioeconomic status might influence one's health in middle adulthood. What factors related to socioeconomic status have an impact on health and risk of dying?

7. Describe the difference between fluid and crystallized intelligence and how these types of intelligence change across the lifespan.

PRACTICE TEST – POST TEST

Circle the correct answer for each multiple choice question and check your answers with the Answer Key at the end of the chapter.

1. Levinson's research on the midlife crisis in men identified a variety of issues that men deal with during their midlife. Which of the following issues was NOT associated with a midlife crisis occurring?
   a. being young versus old
   b. being masculine versus feminine
   c. being overweight versus fit
   d. being destructive versus constructive

2. Research conducted on the period of middle adulthood after Levinson's research was conducted supported which of the following views of midlife.
   a. crisis model
   b. gender identity model
   c. transition period
   d. mortality focus period

3. Many women experience hot flashes and night sweats, which are triggered by declines in _____.
   a. lung function
   b. muscle mass
   c. cardiovascular function
   d. estrogen level

4. This term is used to refer the loss of bone mass and increased bone fragility:
   a. menopause
   b. osteoporosis
   c. climacteric
   d. general atrophy

5. Hormone Replacement Therapy has been found to be associated with:
   a. increased risk of breast cancer
   b. decreased risk of breast cancer
   c. decreased risk of cardiovascular disease
   d. increased risk of hot flashes

6. In men, which of the following can increase the incidence of erectile dysfunction?
   a. smoking
   b. cardiovascular disease
   c. diabetes
   d. all of the above

7. Which of the following diseases is NOT more common in smokers than non-smokers?
   a. melanoma (skin cancer)
   b. lung cancer
   c. heart disease
   d. none of the above—all are more common in smokers than non-smokers

8. Today ____ percent of American are either overweight or obese.
   a. 50
   b. 55
   c. 65
   d. 75

9. Which of the following life events would be expected to produce the least amount of stress for a typical individual?
   a. death of a spouse
   b. divorce
   c. son or daughter leaving home
   d. pregnancy

10. Illness may follow periods of prolonged stress because stress weakens:
    a. one's heart
    b. one's lungs
    c. one's immune system
    d. none of the above

11. Which of the following types of individuals is least likely to suffer a death in midlife due to disease?
    a. hispanic, low income, man
    b. white, high income, woman
    c. African-American, low income man
    d. all of the above have equal chances

12. Longitudinal studies that have investigated crystallized intelligence have found that knowledge of vocabulary:
    a. decreases as the adult ages
    b. increases as the adult ages
    c. stays about the same as the adult ages
    d. stays about the same until age 60, then decreases dramatically

13. Which of the following jobs is mostly likely to allow the worker occupational self-direction?
    a. an assembly line worker
    b. a housecleaner
    c. a coal miner
    d. a teacher

14. Which of the following would involve procedural knowledge?
    a. learning to type
    b. learning the terms for the parts of a boat
    c. learning the causes of cancer
    d. all of the above

15. Which of the following is more likely to cause death in men than in women?
    a. cancer
    b. suicide
    c. heart disease
    d. all of the above

ANSWER KEYS

Practice Test - Pretest (with text page numbers)

1. b 433	6. c 443	11. c 444
2. a 437	7. c 443	12. a 446
3. c 438	8. a 444	13. d 451
4. d 439	9. d 446	14. b 454
5. a 442	10. a 447	15. c 448

True False

1. F	6. F	11. F
2. T	7. F	12. F
3. F	8. F	13. T
4. F	9. T	14. T
5. T	10. F	15. F

Programmed Review

1. social, physical, biological, psychological
2. satisfied
3. young, feminine, constructive, attached
4. introspection, 50s, 40s, affluent, poor
5. visual acuity, menopause, erection
6. skeleton, shorter, Muscles and skin, wrinkles, midriff
7. menopause, estrogen, Ovulation, menstruation, uterus, breasts
8. hot flashes, night sweats, pain, depression
9. estrogen, progesterone, hot flashes, vaginal changes
10. 50, erectile dysfunction
11. sexual, organism
12. sensuality, hugging, touching
13. cancer and heart disease
14. twice, 12
15. 36, 25, minority, poverty, education
16. liver, kidneys
17. poor nutrition, obesity, lack of exercise
18. additive, much worse
19. exercise, eat, sleeping, alcohol
20. twice, more, infectious, parasitic
21. private health insurance, hospital emergency rooms
22. increase, college educated
23. Fluid intelligence, memorizing, new relationships, cognitive mechanics
24. Crystallized intelligence, education, life experience, cognitive pragmatics
25. speed, MRI, prefrontal
26. declarative knowledge, how, procedural knowledge
27. complexity, routine

Practice Test – Post Test (with text page numbers)

1. c 433	6. d 441	11. b 448
2. c 434	7. d 445	12. b 451
3. d 438	8. c 446	13. d 453
4. b 439	9. c 447	14. a 453
5. a 440	10. c 448	15. d 453

Chapter 15

Middle Adulthood: Personality and Sociocultural Development

CHAPTER OUTLINE

◈ Personality Continuity and Change
  ♦ The Tasks of Middle Adulthood
  ♦ Personal Reactions to Middle Adulthood

◈ Family and Friends: Interpersonal Contexts
  ♦ The Generation That Runs Things
  ♦ Relationships with Adult Children
  ♦ Relationships With Aging Parents
  ♦ Becoming a Grandparent
  ♦ Friendship: A Lifelong Perspective

◈ The Changing Family
  ♦ Divorce and Remarriage
  ♦ Reconstituted Families

◈ Occupational Continuity and Change
  ♦ Job Change and Stress

◈ Continuity and Change in the Structure of Personality
  ♦ The Five Factor Model
  ♦ Stability or Change?

LEARNING OBJECTIVES

After you have read and studied this chapter, you should be able to answer the following questions.

1. What is implied when theorists note that generativity is the primary developmental task of middle adulthood?
2. What differences exist in how men and women react to middle age?
3. How do parents typically respond when their last child leaves home?
4. What stresses result from occupational challenges in middle adulthood?
5. Is personality development in middle adulthood marked more by stability or by change?

PRACTICE TEST - PRETEST

Circle the correct answer for each multiple choice question and check your answers with the Answer Key at the end of the chapter.

1. What percentage of older adults spends their final years of life in nursing homes?
    a. 10
    b. 40

    c. 60
    d. 90

2. Which of the following is NOT one of the Big Five Factors of personality?
    a. agreeableness
    b. intelligence

    c. conscientiousness
    d. openness

3. People who are engaged in similar life tasks, such as caring for a toddler or sending a child off to college, are said to be in the same _____.
    a. cohort
    b. family role

    c. family life cycle
    d. demographic bracket

4. Erik Erikson's view of middle adulthood is one in which individuals deal with the issue of _____ vs. self-absorption.
    a. despair
    b. role identity

    c. intimacy
    d. generativity

5. What percentage of young adults return to their parents' home to live before becoming fully independent adults?
    a. 10 to 20
    b. 30 to 40

    c. 50 to 60
    d. 70 to 80

6. When couples who have been married at least 15 years were asked why they remained married, the number one reason :
   a. for men was financial, but for women was companionship
   b. was "for the sake of the children" for both men and women
   c. for women was financial, but for men was sexual intimacy
   d. was 'because the spouse was their best friend" for both men and women

7. When compared to Erik Erikson's theory of life stages, those of Robert Peck:
   a. placed more of an emphasis on childhood
   b. placed more of an emphasis on adolescence
   c. placed more of an emphasis on young adulthood
   d. placed more of an emphasis on middle adulthood

8. Which of the following activities is least likely to result in role strain?
   a. caring for aging parents
   b. caring for small children
   c. chauffeuring teenagers to school activities
   d. all of the above

9. A give-and-take relationship is also referred to as a _____ one.
   a. risky   c. rational
   b. reciprocal   d. realistic

10. Women's friendships during middle age were _____ than men's friendships.
    a. more focused on similarities
    b. deeper and more focused on reciprocity
    c. more shallow and more focused on activities
    d. less focused on activities

11. Most divorced individuals experience considerable improvements in well-being within:
    a.   6 months   c.   2-3 years
    b.   1 year   d.   5 years

12. In terms of general happiness, when compared to single people, middle-age people who remained married are _____.
    a.   somewhat less happy   c.   about the same
    b.   much less happy   d.   happier

13. Which of the following commonly accompanies job burnout?
    a. absenteeism   c. low morale
    b. psychosomatic illness   d. all of the above

14. A person whose personality is high on the openness dimension is likely to be:
    a. uncreative   c. imaginative
    b. unintellectual   d. all of the above

15. A man who is 40 years old in 2004 can expect to live to the age of ____; a woman who is 40 years old in 2004 can expect to live to the age of ____.
    a. 74; 80
    b. 80; 84
    c. 80; 80
    d. 90; 90

TRUE/FALSE

For each of the following statements indicate whether the statement is True or False. Check your answers with the Answer Key at the end of this chapter.

_____ 1. Research shows that people tend to establish friendships with others who are their own age, rather than establishing friendships with people who are in the same stage in terms of having children and family responsibilities.

_____ 2. Father's influence over children tends to decrease during middle adulthood.

_____ 3. Research has shown that the parent-child relationship is highly similar across families and across cultures.

_____ 4. In the United States today, most older adults spend their last years in nursing homes or other types of special care facilities.

_____ 5. For those who remarry (someone else) after a first marriage has ended in divorce, the chance of that second marriage ending in divorce is about the same as the divorce rate for first marriages.

_____ 6. When couples divorce, it is usually the husband who first raises the issue of divorce and are the initiators of divorce.

_____ 7. Changes related to work, such as career changes or job loss, generally produce high levels of stress and anxiety when they occur during middle adulthood.

_____ 8. Job burnout is more likely to occur during middle adulthood than other times of life.

_____ 9. Research conducted on people's perceptions of how their personality changed or stayed the same over the past six years showed that the majority of people believed that their personality "had changed a great deal."

_____ 10.   Peck's view of the changes that occur during social development across the lifespan was virtually the same as Erikson's view.

_____ 11.   Divorce is more likely to occur during middle adulthood than at any other time of life.

_____ 12.   In 1900, few parents lived long enough to see their child's 16th birthday.

_____ 13.   The majority of stepparents have conflicts with stepchildren that never gets resolved.

_____ 14.   Psychologists today believe that the basic structure of personality is in place for most people by age 30.

_____ 15.   There are substantial gender differences in how friendships are established during middle adulthood.

MATCHING

Match the following types of women with the appropriate description and check your answers with the Answer Key at the end of this chapter.

_____ 1. traditional

_____ 2. innovative

_____ 3. expansive

_____ 4. protesting

a. makes major life changes to expand her horizons in middle age

b. experienced premature adulthood and tries to postpone middle age

c. has identified herself in terms of family and makes the transition to middle age rather easily

d. has devoted herself to career and begins to reassure her life at middle age

Match the following types of men with the appropriate description and check your answers with the Answer Key at the end of this chapter.

_____ 5. Transcendent-generative   a. feels unhappy, ineffective, and alienated

_____ 6. Pseudo-developed man   b. feels fulfilled

_____ 7. Man in midlife crisis   c. feels like his life is falling apart

_____ 8. Transcendent-generative   d. lost or bored

PROGRAMMED REVIEW

Fill in the blanks in the following programmed review. Then check your answers with the Answer Key at the end of the chapter.

Personality Continuity and Change
The Tasks of Middle Adulthood

1. Erik Erikson viewed middle adulthood as a time when people face _____ vs. _____. Some individuals choose to contribute in worthwhile ways to the good of others. People can act in three domains: a _____ domain, by giving and responding to the needs of their children; a _____ domain, by integrating work with family life or by caring for the next generation; and a _____ domain, by contributing to society on a larger scale.

2. Erik Erikson believed that when people fail to develop a sense of generativity, _____ and _____ are the result.

3. Robert Peck argued that Erik Erikson's view of the eight stages of life placed too much emphasis on _____, _____, and _____.

Personal Reactions to Middle Adulthood

4. Traditionally, middle adulthood has stereotypically been viewed as a time when men are focused on _____ and women are focused on _____. However, research shows that in middle adulthood men tend to increase their influence on their _____.

5. During middle adulthood, men may deal with feelings of _____, _____, and low _____.

6. A study of Midwestern women identified three major life transitions. These were _____, _____, and _____.

Family and Friends: Interpersonal Contexts
The Generation That Runs Things

7. Middle-aged adults routinely take on the role of maintaining family history, family rituals, and family celebrations. This role has been referred to as one of _____.

Relationships with Adult Children

8. Many middle-aged couples see their children leave home. This period of time when parents have no children at home is called the _____. However, approximately _____ percent of adult children _____ for at least some time before becoming fully independent.

Relationships With Aging Parents

9. The primary reason that adult children and parents end up sharing the same household is _____.

10. Traditionally, when aging parents need care, the burden of care-taking falls on _____.

Becoming a Grandparent

11. The majority of people become grandparents during _____ and find the experience very _____.

Friendship: A Lifelong Perspective

12. Research shows that young adults have _____ time for friendships than middle-aged adults. The friendships of middle-aged adults were best described as _____.

13. Gender differences in friendships were much larger than _____ differences. Men based friendships on _____. Women based friendships on _____.

The Changing Family

14. Most agree that the _____ family is not dead. However, with the changes in social and personal trends in society, the definition of _____ is changing.

Divorce and Remarriage

15. In the United States, _____ percent of marriages end in divorce. In about _____ percent of divorces, at least one of the parties marries again. The divorce rate for 2nd marriages is about _____ percent.

16. The issue of divorce is usually raised by the _____. However, both parties may view it as a _____.

17. The spouse who initiates the divorce may feel _____, _____, and _____.

18. The adjustment to divorce can bring on stress. Recently divorced men and women have higher rates of _____, _____, and _____.

19. _____ formed after divorce helps decrease the divorced person's attachment to the _____.

20. In the worst case scenario, men may _____ with their children, and women may use _____ as weapons against their ex-spouse.

21. Middle-aged people who remain married report _____ levels of general happiness and satisfaction than those who are single.

Reconstituted Families

22. Nowadays, stepfamilies come about because of _____. In previous decades, stepfamilies occurred most often because of _____.

23. The difficulties experienced in a relationship between a stepparent and stepchildren include _____, adjusting to _____ and _____ and gaining _____.

Occupational Continuity and Change

24. Some middle-aged adults lose jobs because of corporate _____ and _____.

Job Change and Stress

25. The _____ exhaustion that results from working in high-stress professions or trades is referred to as _____. It is more common for those working in the _____ professions.

Continuity and Change in the Structure of Personality
The Five Factor Model

26. The big five factors of personality include: _____, _____, _____, _____, and _____.

<u>Stability or Change?</u>

27. In studies investigating the trait agreeableness, for both men and women, agreeableness
_____ as people moved from early adulthood to _____. It was also
shown that _____ increased after the age of _____. The changes
observed in emotional stability differed for _____ and _____.

CRITICAL THINKING QUESTIONS

**To further your mastery of the topics, write out the answers to the following essay
questions in the space provided.**

1. Discuss the similarities and differences between Peck's and Erikson's views regarding social
   development.

2. How are families affected by aging parents/grandparents? When care-taking of elders is
   handled by the family, on whom does the burden typically fall?

3. Discuss the diverse roles that grandparents play in the lives of their grandchildren.

4. Discuss the differences in how men and women approach marriage and react to divorce.

5. Discuss how blended families or stepfamilies have changed over the last 100 years. What problems are routinely encountered and how do major issues come to be resolved?

6. Describe the typical reaction to job loss in middle adulthood.

7. What does research have to say about how personality changes as people grow older?

8. What are the common myths regarding marriage, divorce and remarriage?

9. What has research shown about the characteristics of a successful marriage?

10. Psychologists have identified five basic aspects of personality. How can each of these aspects of personality vary across people?

PRACTICE TEST – POST TEST

Circle the correct answer for each multiple choice question and check your answers with the Answer Key at the end of the chapter.

1. Which of the following is an accurate statement regarding divorce?
    a. following divorce, women are more likely to marry again than men
    b. following divorce, men are more likely to marry again than women
    c. following divorce, men and women are equally likely to marry again

2. Which of the following sets of personality traits correctly describes the Big Five Factors identified in psychology research?
    a. conscientiousness, openness, extroversion, emotional stability, agreeableness
    b. conscientiousness, altruism, extroversion, emotional stability, agreeableness
    c. altruism, openness, extroversion, emotional stability, agreeableness
    d. conscientiousness, openness, extroversion, emotional stability, altruism

3. Which of the following is NOT among the top seven reasons couples remained married after fifteen years of marriage?
    a. My spouse is my best friend.
    b. My spouse has grown more interesting.
    c. We agree on aims and goals.
    d. We are staying married for our children.

4. Which of the following is NOT an example of what Erik Erikson meant by generativity?
    a. getting involved in charity work   c. caring for children
    b. working to advance in one's career d. becoming closer to aging parents

5. Peck's primary criticism of Erik Erikson's theory of the stages of life is:
    a. Erikson placed too much emphasis on stages occurring during childhood
    b. Erikson placed too much emphasis on stages occurring during middle adulthood
    c. Erikson placed too much emphasis on stages occurring during the last decade of life
    d. none of the above

6. During middle adulthood, men's friendships tend to be based on _____ and women's friendships tend to be based on _____.
    a. work; family   c. similarities; family
    b. reciprocity; similarities   d. similarities; reciprocity

7. Which of the following is true regarding grandparents?
    a. in white families, grandparents are more likely to play a part in raising grandchildren than in families belonging to other ethnic groups
    b. in white families, grandparents are less likely to play a part in raising grandchildren than in families belonging to other ethnic groups
    c. the role of grandparents in raising grandchildren varies very little across families of different ethnic groups

8. Since 1900, the difference in life expectancy between men and women has:
   a. grown smaller   c. stayed the same
   b. become negligible   d. grown larger

9. Which of the following was NOT identified as one of the three major life transitions for women?
   a. death of mother   c. menopause
   b. birth of children   d. children leaving home

10. The divorce rate for 2nd marriages is:
    a. much higher than the divorce rate for first marriages
    b. about the same as the divorcee rate for first marriages
    c. much lower than the divorce rate for first marriages

11. A spouse who initiates a divorce may feel which of the following?
    a. Guilt
    b. anger
    c. sadness
    d. all of the above

12. In terms of the difficulties experienced in stepfamilies:
    a. stepfathers have more difficulty than stepmothers
    b. stepmothers have more difficulty than stepfathers
    c. the difficulty experienced by stepfathers and stepmothers is about the same

13. Researchers believe that many people become dissatisfied with marriage because of:
    a. pressures from in-laws
    b. child-rearing obligations
    c. unrealistic expectations about marriage
    d. financial issues

14. A person who is extroverted is unlikely to be:
    a. talkative   c. shy
    b. outgoing   d. assertive

15. For people who do not marry or have children, _____ provides the primary opportunity for intimacy.
    a. the Internet   c. parents
    b. co-workers   d. friendships

ANSWER KEYS

Practice Test - Pretest (with text page numbers)

1.	a 469	6.	d 477	11.	c 476
2.	b 483	7.	d 462	12.	d 477
3.	c 461	8.	d 465	13.	d 482
4.	d 461	9.	b 468	14.	c 484
5.	b 467	10.	b 473	15.	a 467

True/False

1.	F	6.	F	11.	F
2.	F	7.	T	12.	F
3.	F	8.	T	13.	F
4.	F	9.	F	14.	T
5.	T	10.	F	15.	T

Matching

1.	c	5.	b
2.	d	6.	d
3.	a	7.	c
4.	b	8.	a

Programmed Review

1. generativity, self-absorption, procreative, productive, creative
2. stagnation, boredom
3. childhood, adolescence, young adulthood
4. work, family, children
5. failure, self-estrangement, self-esteem
6. birth of children, children leaving home, menopause
7. kinkeeper
8. empty nest, 30-40, move back in with parents
9. a parent's disability
10. daughters or daughters-in-law
11. middle age, satisfying
12. more, complex
13. age, similarities, reciprocity
14. nuclear, family
15. 50, 75, 50
16. wife (woman), failure
17. sadness, guilt, anger
18. physical illness, alcoholism, depression
19. Ffriendship, ex-spouse
20. lose all contact, their children
21. higher
22. divorce, death of a spouse
23. discipline, habits, personalities, acceptance

24. downsizing, job outsourcing
25. emotional, job burnout, helping
26. conscientiousness, openness, emotional stability, agreeableness, extroversion
27. increased, conscientiousness, 30, men, women

Practice Test – Post Test (with text page numbers)

1. b 476	6. d 473	11. d 476
2. a 483	7. b 471	12. b 478
3. d 477	8. d 468	13. c 474
4. b 467	9. a 464	14. c 484
5. a 462	10. b 474	15. d 477

Chapter 16

Older Adulthood: Physical and Cognitive Development

CHAPTER OUTLINE

- ◈ Aging Today
  - ◆ Ageism and Stereotypes
  - ◆ Four Decades of Later Life

- ◈ The Physical Aspects of Aging
  - ◆ The Changing Body
  - ◆ Health, Disease, and Nutrition

- ◈ The Causes of Aging
  - ◆ Theories of Aging

- ◈ Cognitive Changes in Advanced Age
  - ◆ Understanding Various Aspects of Cognition
  - ◆ Cognitive Decline
  - ◆ Compensating for an Aging Minds

LEARNING OBJECTIVES

After you have read and studied this chapter, you should be able to answer the following questions.

1. Do older adults typically conform to the stereotypes that people hold of the elderly?
2. In what ways are the young-old different from the old-old?
3. What are the typical health problems people face as they age?
4. What theories are used to explain why people grow old and die?
5. What are the differences between normal aging and senility?

PRACTICE TEST - PRETEST

Circle the correct answer for each multiple choice question and check your answers with the Answer Key at the end of the chapter.

1. Ageism refers to:
   a. negative attitudes that older adults have regarding young adults
   b. negative attitudes that older adults have about the aging process
   c. negative attitudes that young adults have regarding older adults
   d. none of the above

2. In colonial America, older adults:
   a. were not trusted
   b. were considered helpless and a burden
   c. received great respect stemming from the biblical tradition
   d. were rarely consulted for their opinions

3. Which of the following sets of terms refers to adults in their 70s, 80s, and 90s in that order?
   a. nonagenarians, octogenarians, septuagenarians
   b. octogenarians, nonagenarians, septuagenarians
   c. septuagenarians, nonagenarians, octogenarians
   d. septuagenarians, octogenarians, nonagenarians

4. The fastest growing segment of the U.S. population is that including:
   a. adults between the ages of 55 and 65
   b. adults between the ages of 65 and 75
   c. adults between the ages of 75 and 85
   d. adults over the age of 85

5. Which of the following is an example of a pathological aging factor?
   a. accidents
   b. illnesses experienced earlier in life
   c. bad health habits, such as smoking
   d. all of the above

6. Which of the following disorders is more commonly known as hardening of the arteries?
   a. atherosclerosis
   b. osteoporosis
   c. hypertension
   d. dementia

7. Which of the following senses is least affected by aging?
   a. taste
   b. hearing
   c. vision
   d. touch

8. Which of the following would be an example of a chronic health problem faced by an older adult?
   a. diabetes
   b. influenza
   c. rash
   d. fever

9. Older adults are most likely to experience which of the following?
   a. increase in brain size
   b. increase in muscle strength
   c. iron deficiency
   d. all of the above

10. The percentage of older adults who are obese has:
    a. remained about the same since 1960
    b. decreased since 1960
    c. increased since 1960

11. Approximately what percentage of older adults living at home experiences problems sleeping?
    a. 100%
    b. 75%
    c. 50%
    d. 25%

12. Which of the following is true of stochastic theories of aging?
    a. aging is viewed as resulting from random wear-and-tear on the body
    b. aging is viewed as guided by genetic programming
    c. aging is viewed as occurring largely the same for all individuals
    d. none of the above

13. Free radicals are:
    a. the ends of chromosomes
    b. unstable oxygen molecules left over from cellular processes
    c. nutrients that cannot be absorbed by the body
    d. cells in the immune system useful in fighting off disease

14. This term is used to refer to one's general thinking, reasoning, and memory processing:
    a. stochastic staging
    b. biological clock
    c. social perceptions
    d. cognition

15. Which of the following is an example of working memory?
    a. remembering the meaning of a word
    b. recalling the details of a life event
    c. keeping a friend's phone number in mind by repeating it
    d. multiplying 22 x 11 without pencil or paper

TRUE/FALSE

For each of the following statements indicate whether the statement is True or False. Check your answers with the Answer Key at the end of this chapter.

_____ 1. Today's older adults generally have a higher education level than the younger population.

_____ 2. Among Native American cultures throughout the hemisphere, older adults are held in high esteem.

_____ 3. At the time that the U.S. Constitution was written, Benjamin Franklin had less influence than other statesmen because he was the youngest.

_____ 4. The percent of adults over the age of 65 is about the same across the countries of the world.

_____ 5. Most adults over the age of 85 are frail.

_____ 6. Maintaining a positive attitude is a challenge for adults over the age of 65.

_____ 7. Older adults are an inch or more shorter than they were during their early adult life.

_____ 8. High intensity exercise training is recommended for older adults to prevent declines in strength and mobility.

_____ 9. Older individuals adapt less well to changes in temperature than younger adults.

_____ 10. Older adults have trouble ignoring irrelevant stimuli.

_____ 11. Developing dementia is part of the normal aging processing, which means that even healthy adults will eventually develop dementia if they live long enough.

_____ 12. The average life expectancy is longer for African-American men than African-American women.

_____ 13. A person's metabolism slows as he or she ages.

____ 14.   Around the world, atherosclerosis is much more common in non-Western countries than in Western countries.

_____15.   Those living in Western countries consume more fat than those living in non-Western countries.

_____16.   Most studies find little or no difference in the short-term memory performance of young and older adults.

_____17.   Wisdom is seen equally often among young adults and older adults.

_____18.   Alzheimer's disease can now be cured with several new drug therapies.

_____19.   One of the health conditions that many older adults face is Type II diabetes.

_____20.   Although older workers may be slower to perform some tasks than younger workers, older workers may value accuracy more than younger workers.

MATCHING

Match the issues facing individuals in each of the following decades of life. You can check your answers with the Answer Key at the end of this chapter.

1.   _____60s   a.   retaining one's abilities and keeping a positive attitude
2.   _____70s   b.   coping with role changes, often related to retirement
3.   _____80s   c.   coping with increasing frailty and maintaining social contacts
4.   _____90s and above   d.   coping with illness, the loss of loved ones, and social isolation

Match each type of memory to its description. You can check your answers with the Answer Key at the end of this chapter.

5.   _____sensory memory   a.   knowledge of facts and vocabulary
6.   _____short-term memory   b.   recollection of past events
7.   _____working memory   c.   brief retention of a sensory event
8.   _____episodic long-term memory d.   memory for information one is actively thinking about
9.   _____semantic long-term memory e.   mental processing carried out in short-term memory

PROGRAMMED REVIEW

Fill in the blanks in the following programmed review. Then check your answers with the Answer Key at the end of the chapter.

Aging Today
<u>Ageism and Stereotypes</u>

1. In the Western societies, many people hold _____ attitudes toward older adults. Such attitudes are considered _____.

2. A survey of popular movies found that older women are more often portrayed as _____, _____, and _____ than older men.

3. Attitudes toward older adults are both ambivalent and contradictory. Older adults are viewed as wise and _____, kind and _____, and concerned for others and _____ and _____.

4. In Japan, _____ out of four older adults live with their children. In public, people _____ with respect when they pass by an older person. Respect for elders in Asian cultures, which is referred to as _____, is observed less among _____ adults and those who live in _____.

5. In the colonial period of the United States, the median age of the population was _____ and only _____ percent of people reached the age of 65. Today, the median age of the population is _____ and one in _____ people is at least 65 years of age.

<u>Four Decades of Later Life</u>

6. In the United States today, a 65-year-old can expect to live another _____ years. A 75 year old can expect to live another _____ years.

7. Adults over the age of 60 represent several different cohorts of individuals. Septuagenarians are adults in their _____. Octogenarians are adults in their _____. Nonagenarians are adults in their _____.

8. People who survive to their 90s typically experience _____ cognitive decline and are often _____, more _____, and more _____ than people 20 years younger.

The Physical Aspects of Aging

9. The cumulative effects that result from _____ events and _____ choices that may accelerate aging are referred to as _____.

The Changing Body

10. Aging may increase the number of _____ on the trunk, face, and scalp. Brown spots may appear on the skin. These are called _____. Wrinkles appear, which occur when _____ is lost under the skin.

11. Decreased lung functioning may also reduce the supply of _____ to the _____, which can reduce _____ and _____, fine motor coordination, and reaction time.

12. Older adults commonly experience problems sleeping. Some experience an inability to sleep, which is referred to as _____. Some frequently wake up due to interruptions in their breathing, which is called _____.

13. Older adults experience vision problems, including problems distinguishing fine detail, which is referred to as _____. The lens becomes less flexible resulting in problems with _____. An extremely cloudy lens may be a _____. When pressure within the eye increases, _____ may be present.

14. As people age, the brain's size _____. The loss of weight seems to be related to fewer _____ among neurons, rather than fewer total _____. Changes are greatest in the _____ cortex.

Health, Disease, and Nutrition

15. Chronic conditions are _____ or _____ conditions that never go away completely. The most common chronic conditions facing older adults are _____, _____, and _____.

16. The most common dietary deficiencies in old age are _____, _____, _____, and _____.

The Causes of Aging

17. Those who are economically disadvantaged live in more _____ environments, have _____ nutrition, have more _____ access to health care, and are more likely to engage in _____ habits.

<u>Theories of Aging</u>

18. The universal biological processes of aging, which is not connected to disease, is referred to as _____. There are two types of theories of these processes -- _____ and _____.

Cognitive Changes in Advanced Age

19. Mental skills remain _____ intact as people age, despite the common misperception that aging will automatically result in mental _____.

<u>Understanding Various Aspects of Cognition</u>

20. Cognition is a general term used to describe overall _____ functioning, which includes thinking, _____, and reasoning.

21. Older adults typically take about _____ percent longer to complete a task than do younger people. Often older adults will learn new _____ to compensate for their loss of speed.

22. Sensory memory is very brief _____ or _____ memory that holds sensory input while it is being processed.

23. Older adults are less efficient in _____, _____, and _____ material to be learned.

24. Older adults experience more decline in their ability to retrieve _____ memories than _____ memories.

25. Wisdom refers to a(n) _____ knowledge system that focuses on the _____ of life. It is rarely seen in _____ adults, because it is gained through _____ experiences.

<u>Cognitive Decline</u>

26. Senility, also known as _____, refers to chronic _____, _____, and accompanying _____ changes.

27. Two common causes of dementia are _____ and _____ disease.

28. A blockage of blood to a region in the brain, which causes brain damage, is called a
    _____.   The obstruction itself is referred to as a(n) _____.
    Sometimes people experience temporary mini-strokes, referred to as _____.
    One of the leading causes of strokes is _____, which is the build up of fatty
    plaques on the lining of the _____.

29. The eighth leading cause of death in adults over the age of 65 is _____. The
    onset of the disease is usually _____ and _____. A person may
    have trouble recognizing _____ or _____ and performing routine
    _____.

CRITICAL THINKING QUESTIONS

**To further your mastery of the topics, write out the answers to the following essay
questions in the space provided.**

1. What stereotypes of older adults persist in the United States today?

2. Discuss the differences in how older adults are viewed and treated across cultures.

3. What are the chronic conditions that are commonly experienced by older adults? What
    lifestyle factors contribute to these conditions?

4. Contrast stochastic theories of aging with biological clock theories of aging. What aspects of aging does each theory explain well and what aspects are not explained well?

5. Discuss the memory abilities of the typical older adult. How does memory function change as a person ages?

6. What is Alzheimer's disease? How is one typically diagnosed? What is known about its causes?

7. What is wisdom? How does it differ from other forms of knowledge, presumably stored in memory?

8. What are the sleeping patterns of older adults? What sleeping problems do aging adults typically face?

PRACTICE TEST – POST TEST

Circle the correct answer for each multiple choice question and check your answers with the Answer Key at the end of the chapter.

1. The tradition of respecting older adults in Asian cultures, such as those inn China and Japan is referred to as:
    a. discrimination
    b. ageism
    c. elder disabuse
    d. filial piety

2. In the United States today, the median age of the population is about:
    a. 25 years
    b. 35 years
    c. 45 years
    d. 65 years

3. What percentage of adults 85 years of age or older live in nursing homes?
    a. 2
    b. 10
    c. 19
    d. 33

4. Which of the following changes are common as we age?
    a. loss of muscle mass
    b. loss of fat under the skin
    c. weakening of the immune system
    d. all of the above

5. Many older adults find it more difficult to maintain their balance. This reflects aging-related changes in the:
    a. visual system
    b. vestibular system
    c. cardiovascular system
    d. central nervous system

6. Older adults sometimes suffer from a condition that makes their bones hollower and more brittle and may lead to a bent or stooped posture. This condition is:
    a. arthritis
    b. atherosclerosis
    c. muscular atrophy
    d. osteoperosis

7. Abnormally high blood pressure is referred to as:
    a. atherosclerosis
    b. hypertension
    c. osteoporosis
    d. glaucoma

8. Which of the following is NOT a chronic condition affecting older adults?
    a. hypertension
    b. influenza
    c. arthritis
    d. osteoporosis

9. The loss of flexibility in the lens of the eye is responsible for:
    a. problems with depth perception
    b. cataract
    c. glaucoma
    d. all of the above

10. Older adults sleep about _____ hours a night.
    a. 4   c. 8 to 8 1/2
    b. 6 to 6-1/2   d. 9 to 10

11. This term is used to refer to the universal biological processes associated with aging, which are not associated with disease:
    a. dementia   c. apnea
    b. senescence   d. none of the above

12. Advocates of this theory of aging assume that the pace and process of aging are determined by genetic factors.
    a. stochastic theories of aging
    b. biological clock theories of aging
    c. nature-nurture theories of aging
    d. none of the above

13. Which of the following types of memory is likely to change the most as a person ages?
    a. sensory memory
    b. semantic long-term memory
    c. short-term memory
    d. working memory

14. Which of the following is NOT true regarding Alzheimer's disease?
    a. it can be caused by strokes
    b. in some cases, genetic factors may play a role
    c. symptoms tend to develop gradually
    d. it is progressive and always fatal

15. Which of the following is true regarding strokes?
    a. they can be caused by atherosclerosis
    b. they result in brain damage
    c. having hypertension is a risk factor
    d. all of the above

ANSWER KEYS

Practice Test - Pretest (with text page numbers)

1. c 490	6. a 505	11. c 499
2. c 492	7. a 499	12. a 507
3. d 495	8. a 501	13. b 506
4. d 495	9. c 505	14. d 508
5. d 497	10. c 502	15. d 509

True/False

1. F	6. T	11. F	16. T
2. T	7. T	12. F	17. F
3. F	8. T	13. T	18. F
4. F	9. T	14. F	19. T
5. T	10. T	15. T	20. T

Matching

1. b	6. d
2. d	7. e
3. c	8. b
4. a	9. a
5. c	

Programmed Review

1. negative, ageism
2. unattractive, unfriendly, unintelligent
3. senile, grouchy, inactive, unsociable
4. three, bow, filial piety, young, cities
5. 16, 2, 35.3, eight
6. 18.2, 11.5
7. 70s, 80s, 90s
8. minor, healthier, agile, active
9. earlier, lifestyle, pathological aging factors
10. warts, liver spots, fat
11. oxygen, muscles, strength, endurance
12. insomnia, sleep apnea
13. visual acuity, depth perception, cataract, glaucoma
14. shrinks, connections, neurons, frontal
15. lasting, recurrent, hypertension, arthritis, heart disease
16. iron, calcium, vitamin A, vitamin C
17. dangerous, poorer, limited, destructive
18. senescence, stochastic, biological clock
19. largely, declines
20. intellectual, memory
21. 50, strategies
22. visual, auditory

23. organizing, rehearsing, encoding
24. episodic, semantic
25. expert, practicalities, young, life
26. dementia, confusion, forgetfulness, personality
27. strokes, Alzheimer's
28. stroke, infarct, transient ischemic attacks, atherosclerosis, arteries
29. Alzheimer's disease, gradual, continuous, objects, people, tasks

Practice Test – Post Test (with text page numbers)

1. d 492	6. d 498	11. b 506
2. b 492	7. b 499	12. b 507
3. c 495	8. b 501	13. d 509
4. d 498	9. a 500	14. a 515
5. b 498	10. b 499	15. d 514

Chapter 17

Older Adulthood: Personality and Sociocultural Development

CHAPTER OUTLINE

◈ Personality and Aging
   ◆ Developmental Tasks in Older Adulthood
   ◆ Emotional Development in Older Adulthood
   ◆ Continuity and Change in Older Adulthood
   ◆ Successful Aging

◈ Retirement: A Major Change in Status
   ◆ Adjusting to Retirement
   ◆ Retirement Options

◈ Family and Friends: Interpersonal Contexts
   ◆ When Parenting Is Over
   ◆ Caring for an Ill Spouse
   ◆ Widows and widowers

◈ U.S. Social Policy and Older Adulthood
   ◆ The Demographics of Aging
   ◆ Lifestyle Options for Older Adults
   ◆ Goals for the Care of Older Adults

LEARNING OBJECTIVES

After you have read and studied this chapter, you should be able to answer the following questions.

1. What did Erik Erikson mean when he identified the critical conflict of older adulthood as one of integrity versus despair?
2. What changes – good and bad – does retirement typically bring?
3. How do older adults typically cope with loss?
4. What are the pros and cons associated with the two major government supported social programs for older adults – Social Security and Medicare?
5. What options are available when older adults need assistance in living, and how should families choose among them?

PRACTICE TEST - PRETEST

Circle the correct answer for each multiple choice question and check your answers with the Answer Key at the end of the chapter.

1. Which of the following describes how the emotional relationships of older adults change as they grow older?
    a. they decrease in intensity
    b. they increase in intensity
    c. they stay the same in terms of intensity

2. Which of the following is NOT one of the six components of adult well-being?
    a. self-acceptance
    c. autonomy
    b. personal growth
    d. parenthood

3. As women age they tend to become more:
    a. domineering
    c. aggressive
    b. instrumental
    d. all of the above

4. A study of Americans 65 or older found that _____ percent rated their health and well-being as good to excellent.
    a. about 10
    c. about 50
    b. about 40
    d. about 75

5. Research shows that young adults gain the most satisfaction from making advancements in their work. How do older adults compare?
    a. older adults also gain the most satisfaction from making advancements in their work
    b. older adults gain more satisfaction from work advancements than do young adults
    c. older adults gain less satisfaction from work advancements than do young adults

6. What percentage of American adults retires during the traditional time period – between the years of 62 and 65?
   a. 15%
   b. 33%
   c. 67%
   d. 90%

7. In the U.S., _____ percent of adults 65 years of age or older live below the poverty line.
   a. 90
   b. 70
   c. 40
   d. 10

8. Since 1950, the percentage of men over the age of 65 who are still in the workforce has:
   a. stayed about the same
   b. increased
   c. decreased

9. The number of older men whose spouses die during older adulthood is about _____ the number of older women whose spouses die.
   a. 4 times
   b. twice
   c. one quarter of
   d. one half of

10. What percent of women over the age of 85 are widowed?
    a. 10
    b. 40
    c. 85
    d. 95

11. This term is used to refer to a measure of how well prepared a person is to retire:
    a. resiliency index
    b. retirement maturity
    c. magical mastery
    d. none of the above

12. Approximately what percentage of older adults spends their last years in nursing homes?
    a. under 5 %
    b. between 5 and 10%
    c. between 50 and 60%
    d. between 75 and 80%

TRUE/FALSE

For each of the following statements indicate whether the statement is True or False. Check your answers with the Answer Key at the end of this chapter.

_____ 1.   Erik Erikson's view of the stage of life representing older adulthood is one focused on the issues of identity versus role confusion.

_____ 2.   Research has confirmed that an older adult's emotional and social world is one of narrowness and emptiness.

_____ 3.   Older adults report gaining more emotional satisfaction with their interpersonal relationships than they did at earlier times in their lives.

_____ 4.   Most older adults spend their later years in sadness and despair.

_____ 5. Both men and women become more aggressive as they age.

_____ 6. Older adults tend to have more friends than they did when they were younger adults.

_____ 7. Even retired business executives are found to have the most difficult time finding activities to fill up their leisure time.

_____ 8. Older adults tend to be wealthier than young adults.

_____ 9. Older men are more likely to be poor than older women.

_____ 10. Some companies provide counselors to assist employees dealing with the adjustment of retirement.

_____ 11. Older married couples report being more satisfied with their marriages after their children leave home.

_____ 12. The age at which most Americans will be able to retire in the future is likely to increase.

_____ 13. Baby boomers will retire in large numbers starting in 2050.

_____ 14. Over the coming decades, the percentage of older adults who belong to minority groups is expected to decrease.

_____ 15. While AARP aims to protect the interests of older adults, the organization known as the Gray Panthers aims to limit the success of organizations like AARP.

PROGRAMMED REVIEW

Fill in the blanks in the following programmed review. Then check your answers with the Answer Key at the end of the chapter.

1. Social passages typically involve changes in _____ and _____. Those entering older adulthood typically experience losses of _____, _____, and _____.

Personality and Aging
Developmental Tasks in Older Adulthood

2. Erik Erikson viewed the final developmental task that people face as one that focuses on _____ versus _____.

3. Adjustments made during older adulthood may challenge one's established _____, which is a person's consistent view of their physical, psychological, and social attributes. In terms introduced by Jean Piaget, a person must _____ new events and changing circumstances into one's _____ and change one's self when major life events cannot be _____.

4. Following Piaget's view, people who refuse to accommodate may end up _____ reality. On the other hand, accommodating too readily may also have negative consequences; a person may become _____, _____, or _____.

5. A study of older adults in their 70s and 80s found that it is difficult for older adults to maintain a sense of personal identity in the face of major changes in health status and living arrangements. Those who did the best tended to focus on the _____ rather than the _____.

Emotional Development in Older Adulthood

6. Research shows that older adult's emotional and social world is not one of _____ and _____, but is a period of _____.

7. Older adults' heightened awareness of the _____ of human life leads them to invest _____ in close emotional relationships.

8. Older adults experience _____ and _____ at levels similar to younger adults. Studies comparing cultures showed that older adults experience fewer _____, less _____, and more _____ control than young adults.

Continuity and Change in Older Adulthood

9. Stage theorists believe that as one ages new _____ or _____ are built on earlier stages.

10. Some researchers believe that people strive to maintain _____ because it makes them feel more _____.

11. Carol Ryff and colleagues proposed that psychological well-being in adulthood is comprised of six components: 1) _____; 2) _____; 3) _____; 4) _____; 5) _____; and 6) _____.

12. Some people, such as _____, become more introverted as they _____; however, other personality characteristics, such as _____ and _____ remain consistent throughout adulthood.

13. Some researchers found that younger adults are more likely to use _____ coping styles that focus on _____ problems; older adults tend to be _____ and focused on _____.

14. An _____ adult is more likely than a _____ adult to use humor and to be accepting when they are faced with setbacks in life.

15. As women age, they tend to become more _____, _____, and _____.

16. The parental imperative refers to the fact that traditional social pressures call for _____ to be nurturing and for _____ to be financially responsible.

Successful Aging

17. In a study of older Americans in 2002, _____ percent of adults 65 or older rated their health and well-being as _____ to _____.

18. When older adults compare themselves to a person who is much worse off, their mental health is generally _____ than those who do not engage in this type of _____.

19. Younger adults gain the most satisfaction from their _____ and _____ in work. Older adults define their psychological well-being in terms of being a _____ person and have good _____ with others.

Retirement: A Major Change in Status

20. In traditional families with a stay-at-home mom and working dad, the retirement of dad results in _____ for dad and in a significant reduction of _____ for mom.

21. If retirement comes _____, then an individual who has been dedicated to his or her work will find the transition to be _____.

<u>Adjusting to Retirement</u>

22. Adjusting to retirement is more difficult for people who are _____ educated, financially _____, and who are involved in _____ social or political outlets.

<u>Retirement Options</u>

23. Since 1950, retirement patterns have shifted. In 1950, about _____ percent of all men over 65 were still working; however, in the 1980s and early 1990s, only about _____ percent were working or looking for work.

24. In 2003, the _____ percent of men and _____ percent of women between 65 and 69 were still in the workforce.

25. If current trends continue, many of the _____ million baby boomers will not be able to retire until the age of _____ or later.

26. Recent retirees experience a(n) _____ in life satisfaction. About _____ percent report an improvement in their mental and physical health, and _____ percent report no change.

Family and Friends: Interpersonal Contexts
<u>When Parenting Is Over</u>

27. Happy marriages that survive into later adulthood are more _____ and _____.

28. By 1997, approximately _____ percent of children under the age of 18 in the United States lived in a household headed by a _____.

Caring for an Ill Spouse

29. Caring for a spouse with Alzheimer's disease is especially difficult because the ill spouse experiences changes in _____ and may behave in ways that are _____ and/or _____.

Widows and widowers

30. By the age of 85, _____ percent of women are widows. After a spouse's death, _____ live longer than _____, and widows are _____ likely than widowers to remarry.

31. Women in older adulthood are _____ likely than men to live alone. The majority of older adults have at least one _____ living within _____ miles.

U.S. Social Policy and Older Adulthood
The Demographics of Aging

32. By 2050, the percentage of older adults in the United States who are white will be about _____ percent, which is a decline from _____ percent in 2003.

33. Financial experts anticipate a significant strain on social security and _____ will be due to the large numbers of _____ retiring.

Lifestyle Options for Older Adults

34. Only about _____ percent of adults over the age of 65 reside in nursing homes. Of people living in nursing homes, _____ percent are over the age of 85. Most are _____ and have some form of mental impairment.

Goals for the Care of Older Adults

35. Two organizations that exist to advance the interests of older adults are _____ and the _____.

CRITICAL THINKING QUESTIONS

To further your mastery of the topics, write out the answers to the following essay questions in the space provided.

1. What are the six components of adult well-being according to Carol Ryff and colleagues? What are the differences between people who score high versus low on each component?

2. Describe how individuals adjust to retirement. What factors would be related to one having a smooth versus difficult adjustment?

3. Discuss who is and is not likely to be poor in later adulthood. What factors lead to these differences for men and women? What factors might be related to differences for different ethnic groups?

4. What role do friendships play in the lives of older adults? How do friends change as we age?

5. What is a baby boomer? What impact will baby boomers have on the demographic profile of the working and retired population in the United States? How will baby boomers affect social security and Medicare funds?

6. Describe the function of a traditional nursing home and an assisted living facility. What types of older adults are most likely to be in each place?

PRACTICE TEST – POST TEST

Circle the correct answer for each multiple choice question and check your answers with the Answer Key at the end of the chapter.

1. As people age _____ become more introverted.
   a. men more so than women
   b. women more so than men
   c. men and women at comparable rates

2. Which of the following statements describes a person who scores low on the autonomy component of adult well-being?
   a. relies on one's self for important decisions, rather than relying on others
   b. is concerned about the expectations and evaluations of others
   c. is able to resist social pressures to think and act in certain ways
   d. regulates behavior from within

3. This is a coping style of very old men that is characterized by dealing with reality through projection and distortion:
   a. parental imperative   c. magical mastery
   b. desperation avoidance   d. reality ambibalence

4. When older adults use social comparison, they may:
   a. feel less negatively about their own physical health problems
   b. minimize their own psychological distress
   c. increase their sense of well-being in general
   d. all of the above

5. Which of the following factors is the least related to whether one is satisfied with life in older adulthood?
   a. age   c. marital status
   b. adequacy of housing   d. amount of social interaction

6. Research shows that in America approximately _____ percent of people retire and then continue to work.
   a. 10   c. 33
   b. 20   d. 50

7. About _____ percent of retirees rely on social security benefits as their sole source of income.
   a. 15
   b. 33
   c. 47
   d. 75

8. Which of the following is a reason that more older women are poor than older men?
   a. women live longer than men
   b. women receive less in social security benefits than men
   c. women accumulate less savings over their lifetimes
   d. all of the above

9. To what extent are men and women over the age of 85 whose spouses die likely to remarry?
   a. women and men are equally likely to remarry
   b. women are more likely than men to remarry
   c. women are less likely than men to remarry

10. Since 1900, the number of older adults in the population has
    a. stayed about the same
    b. decreased
    c. increased

11. Social Security benefits include which of the following?
    a. healthcare benefits
    b. cash payments
    c. both healthcare benefits and cash payments

12. The full name of the organization known as AARP is which of the following?
    a. Association of American Retired People
    b. Against Antagonism of Retired Persons
    c. All American Retired People
    d. American Association of Retired Persons

ANSWER KEYS

Practice Test - Pretest (with text page numbers)

1.	b 524	5.	c 529	9.	c 535
2.	d 526	6.	b 530	10.	c 536
3.	d 528	7.	d 531	11.	c 533
4.	d 528	8.	c 532	12.	a 542

True/False

1.	F	6.	F	11.	T
2.	F	7.	F	12.	T
3.	T	8.	T	13.	F
4.	F	9.	F	14.	F
5.	F	10.	T	15.	F

Programmed Review

1. role, social position, power, responsibility, autonomy
2. integrity, despair
3. identity, assimilate, self-concept, assimilated
4. denying, hysterical, impulsive, hypersensitive
5. past, present
6. narrowness, emptiness, continued emotional growth
7. frailty, more
8. joy, happiness, mood swings, agitation, emotional
9. life structures, organizations
10. consistency, secure
11. self-acceptance, positive relations with others, autonomy, environmental mastery, purpose in life, personal growth
12. men, age, openness, emotional stability
13. active, specific, passive, emotions
14. older, younger
15. aggressive, instrumental, domineering
16. women, men
17. 73, good, excellent
18. better, social comparison
19. achievements, advancements, caring, relationships
20. leisure time, autonomy
21. suddenly, difficult
22. less, strained, few
23. 50, 12
24. 33, 23
25. 76, 70
26. increase, 33, 50
27. egalitarian, cooperative
28. 5.5, grandparent
29. personality, disruptive, socially embarrassing

30. 80, widows, widowers, less
31. more, child, 10
32. 61, 83
33. Medicare, baby boomers
34. 4.3, 50, single
35. AARP, Gray Panthers

Practice Test – Post Test (with text page numbers)

1. a 526	5. a 528	9. c 536
2. b 526	6. c 530	10. c 539
3. c 528	7. b 531	11. b 539
4. d 528	8. d 531	12. d 544

Chapter 18

Death and Dying

CHAPTER OUTLINE

- Thoughts and Fears of Death
  - Denial of Death
  - Reactions to Death
  - Managing the Anxiety Associated with One's Own Death

- Confronting One's Own Death
  - Death as the Final Developmental Task
  - Stages of Adjustment
  - Coping with Terminal Illness
  - Alternative Trajectories

- The Search for a Humane Death
  - Hospice
  - The Right to Die

- Grief and Bereavement
  - Grieving
  - Patterns of Grief
  - Bereavement in Cross-Cultural Perspective
  - Rituals and Customs
  - The Death of a Child
  - Grieving When a Child Dies

- Completing the Life Cycle

LEARNING OBJECTIVES

After you have read and studied this chapter, you should be able to answer the following questions.

1. How do most individuals manage the anxiety associated with the death of a loved one?
2. How can a terminally ill person best cope with the knowledge that death is imminent?
3. What characterizes a humane death, and how can we make death more humane?
4. What factors generally influence how people deal with grief?
5. What special circumstances are associated with the death of a child?
6. How can death be considered as part of the lifespan?

PRACTICE TEST - PRETEST

Circle the correct answer for each multiple choice question and check your answers with the Answer Key at the end of the chapter.

1. The first hospice care was established in:
    a. the United States
    b. Canada
    c. England
    d. France

2. People's attitudes about themselves are referred to as their:
    a. reflective self
    b. self worth
    c. reflective attitude
    d. self-esteem

3. Which of the following did Kübler-Ross's research on death and dying NOT show?
    a. After a patient was diagnosed as terminally ill, doctors and nurses spent more time talking to the patient
    b. After a patient was diagnosed as terminally ill, doctors and nurses avoided all but necessary contact with the patient
    c. After a patient was diagnosed as terminally ill, doctors and nurses provided less routine care to the patient
    d. None of the above – all were observed in the research

4. Which of the following is the first of the five stages of death and dying described by Kübler-Ross?
    a. anger
    b. bargaining
    c. depression
    d. denial

5. For which of the following groups of individuals is the suicide rate the highest?
    a. white women
    b. white men
    c. women of color
    d. men of color

6. Submissive death is one in which:
   a. palliative care is unavailable
   b. the family withdraws life support
   c. the ill person neglects his or her own needs
   d. death occurs suddenly

7. The death of a person who has been taking large amounts of illegal drugs and who at the same time has been engaging in dangerous activities, such as driving or mountain climbing, might be a case of :
   a. submissive death
   b. euthanasia
   c. naïve suicide
   d. suicidal erosion

8. Which of the following is NOT true regarding hospice care?
   a. hospice care is usually covered by insurance
   b. hospice care is designed to help the ill person live as independently as possible
   c. hospice care is designed to help the family of the ill person understand the process of dying
   d. hospice care originated in the late 1800s in New England

9. This term is used to describe when terminally ill patients are provided with "death machines" with which they can self-administer a lethal drug:
   a. active euthanasia   c. passive euthanasia
   b. palliative care   d. assisted suicide

10. A person who would like to make his or her wishes known regarding the extent to which "heroic measures" should be taken to maintain his or her life in the event of irreversible illness or injury should:
    a. make arrangements for hospice care
    b. contact a medical doctor
    c. make a living will
    d. make arrangements for palliative care

11. Which of the following types of individuals is most likely to experience chronic grief?
    a. a person whose loved one has been diagnosed with a terminal illness
    b. a person who has lost a brother, a spouse, and a close friend to death in the last year
    c. a person who has lost a loved one to a sudden unexpected death
    d. all of the above

12. In which culture is there a celebration in which deceased loved ones are reintegrated into the family as ancestors?
    a. Japanese   c. Chinese
    b. Egyptian   d. Mexican

13. Terror Management Theory assumes that _____ is triggered by the awareness that death is inevitable.
    a. a sense of hopelessness   c. grief
    b. low self-esteem   d. anxiety

14. Grieving involves which of the following pairs of tasks?
    a. healing and renewal   c. shock and healing
    b. renewal and acceptance   d. shock and acceptance

15. Which of the following is NOT something generally involved in hospice care?
    a. making sure the ill person is comfortable
    b. pain management
    c. talking with family members about the ill person's experiences
    d. delivering a lethal dose of medication when the end is near

TRUE/FALSE

For each of the following statements indicate whether the statement is True or False. Check your answers with the Answer Key at the end of this chapter.

_____ 1.   In the United States, women commit suicide at a higher rate than men.

_____ 2.   In the United States, euthanasia, from a legal perspective, is murder.

_____ 3.   At the end of his life, Freud became terminally ill and killed himself.

_____ 4.   When asked, young people report that they would prefer a sudden death.

_____ 5.   The amount of anxiety experienced when death is considered is relatively the same across cultures.

_____ 6.   Hospice workers not only provide direct care to dying patients, but also help the family members of patients to understand patients' needs and experiences.

_____ 7.   Kübler-Ross's research on death and dying identified five stages of coping that are universal.

_____ 8.   Historically, the topic of how people deal with death has received a great deal of attention.

_____ 9.   Palliative care is aimed curing the life-threatening illness.

_____ 10.   The ways in which people experience grief vary a great deal across cultures.

_____ 11.   Terror management theory addresses how individuals gain self-esteem.

____ 12. Grieving the loss of a child is the same regardless of how old the child is.

____ 13. A medical power of attorney is another term for a living will.

____ 14. One of the stages that occurs in all people facing a terminal illness is elation.

____ 15. One can experience grief before the death of a loved one actually occurs.

KEY VOCABULARY TERMS

Explain the difference between the following sets of terms.
1. active euthanasia; passive euthanasia
2. suicidal erosion; assisted suicide
3. palliative care; end of life care
4. living will; medical power of attorney
5. chronic grief; bereavement overload

PROGRAMMED REVIEW

Fill in the blanks in the following programmed review. Then check your answers with the Answer Key at the end of the chapter.

Thoughts and Fears of Death

1. In the past, developmental psychologists have _____ the topic of death. Perhaps, this is because it was _____ to study or because there was a belief that it was _____ to study.

Denial of Death

2. Prior to the latter half of the _____ century, death occurred at home or outside of hospitals. After this time, death became a _____ marvel. In Western nations today, most people die _____.

3. Kübler-Ross conducted her research on death and dying in the mid-_____. She found that once a diagnosis of a terminal illness was made, _____ and _____ talked _____ to the patient and did not tell the patient that he or she was in a terminal state, even if the patient_____

4. Research suggests that there _____ individual differences in how
   _____ people are about death. Those with a strong belief in a(n)
   _____ are less anxious. Those who have been _____ and in control
   of their lives up to the point of an illness tend to have lower levels of anxiety.

Managing the Anxiety Associated with One's Own Death

5. Research has repeatedly shown that people with strong _____ beliefs have less
   _____ and _____ about death.

6. According to terror management theory, the universal need for _____ is
   motivated by the universal reaction against the _____ triggered by our
   awareness of _____.

7. In _____ cultures, the anxiety about death is greater than in _____
   cultures.

Confronting One's Own Death

8. When people are asked to imagine that they have only 6 months to live, _____
   people report they would like to spend their remaining time involved in inner-focused
   pursuits, such as contemplation and meditation, while _____ people report they
   would like to spend their remaining time involved in activities, such as traveling.

Death as the Final Developmental Task

9. When people have time to face their impending death, they can engage in a kind of life
   _____, reliving past _____ and _____. This results in
   a strong sense of self-awareness.

Stages of Adjustment

10. The five stages of coping with dying identified in the research conducted by
    _____ showed that people commonly go through stages of denial,
    _____, _____, depression, and _____. Although the
    stages are common, they are not _____.

11. Most people providing care for a family member who is terminally ill report feeling
    _____ in their task.

Coping with Terminal Illness

12. A study of those caring for a terminally ill person found that _____ of people were "on duty" 24-hours a day and spent at least _____ hours per week providing care to the person.

13. The majority of caregivers in the study indicated that the _____ of the ill person brought a sense of _____ to them and the dying person.

14. If death is _____, then there is little opportunity for life _____ and integration.

Alternative Trajectories

15. In the United States today, the ideal life is viewed as one in which a person lives to the age of _____, puts their affairs in order, and dies _____ without pain, perhaps while _____.

16. Those suffering from AIDS may face strong emotions that those suffering from other terminal illness do not face, such as _____ and _____.

17. The rate of suicide is highest among _____ aged _____ or older. The suicide rate for women is _____ that of men.

18. A person may hasten their own death by simply not caring for themselves, which is called _____, or may engage in high-risk activities, such as excessive drinking and drug abuse, which is called _____.

19. After the age of 85, the suicide rate of men is about _____ times that of women.

20. For men who lose a spouse, suicide is most likely to occur during _____ after the spouse dies.

The Search for a Humane Death

21. Research has shown that patients with congestive heart failure who are more _____ are _____ likely to die from their illness. People who attempt to _____ their environment tend to live longer.

22. If there is adequate time to prepare for death, more fear surrounds _____ death will occur than _____ it will occur.

Hospice

23. The first hospice was started in _____ in _____. Hospice is designed to help people with a terminal illness live out their days as fully and _____ as possible.

24. Eighty percent of hospice care is provided in _____ and _____. It is usually covered by _____ and _____ cost-effective than hospitalization.

25. Hospital personnel tend to view death as _____. Hospice personnel view death as a(n) _____ and _____ stage of life.

The Right to Die

26. Mercy killing or _____ was practiced as early as ancient _____.

27. Professional organizations, such as the _____ oppose the use of _____.

Grief and Bereavement

28. Dealing with the emotional reactions to the loss of a loved one is referred to as _____. Different rituals and customs are used across _____ for the purpose of dealing with grief.

Grieving

29. Immediately after the death of a loved one, people tend to experience _____ which usually lasts for _____.

30. Two tasks are involved in grieving: 1) _____, which involves adjusting to the sense of loss and new roles needing to be assumed because of the loss of the loved one and 2) _____ , which involves establishing new life patterns with a future-oriented focus.

31. People who experience the loss of several family members or friends in a relatively short span may experience _____, which is a _____ reaction often characterized by depression.

32. Sometimes individuals experience _____ which involves an ingrained _____ mourning process in which a person never recovers.

Patterns of Grief

33. The Leiden Bereavement Study was conducted in _____ and found _____ in how people dealt with grief.

Bereavement in Cross-Cultural Perspective

34. In Western culture, people are expected to grieve for a time and then to return to normal functioning _____. In other cultures, individuals maintain a continuing bond with _____.

Rituals and Customs

The Death of a Child

35. In 1900 in the United States, the death rate for children under the age of 5 was _____ percent; by 1999, it had dropped to _____ percent.

Grieving When a Child Dies

36. In a study of the families who had lost a child in the Arab-Israeli conflict, _____ were more likely than _____ to see the forces surrounding their children's death as externally controlled and expressed greater feelings of _____.

Completing the Life Cycle

37. In _____ culture, it is common to name a child after a deceased relative. In _____ culture, the death of a grandparent may bring on family pressure for a grandchild to marry or to have child.

CRITICAL THINKING QUESTIONS

To further your mastery of the topics, write out the answers to the following essay questions in the space provided.

1. Describe how the issue of death is dealt with across cultures.

2. Describe the research conducted by Kübler-Ross. What did it show about how individuals cope with a terminal illness? What changes in the medical field have occurred because of her findings?

3. What are the basic assumptions of terror management theory and how do they relate to how individuals deal with the issue of death?

4. Discuss the differences among suicide, suicidal erosion and submissive death.

5. What is the role of hospice when one faces a terminal illness?

6. Describe the nature of grief. How does grief stemming from the death of a child differ from that stemming from the death of any other loved one?

7. Why is it difficult for researchers to determine how many deaths each year stem from individuals feeling suicidal?

PRACTICE TEST – POST TEST

Circle the correct answer for each multiple choice question and check your answers with the Answer Key at the end of the chapter.

1. After the work of Kübler-Ross, the amount of training received by doctors and nurses in the treatment of the terminally ill has:
   a. stayed the same
   b. decreased
   c. increased

2. Which of the following lists the five stages of death and dying described by Kübler-Ross in the correct order?
   a. denial, anger, bargaining, depression, acceptance
   b. depression, denial, anger, bargaining, acceptance
   c. anger, depression, denial, bargaining, acceptance
   d. anger, denial, bargaining, depression, acceptance

3. Which of the following describes the levels of anxiety about death individuals in individualistic and collectivistic cultures experience?
   a. those in individualistic and collectivistic cultures experience similar levels of anxiety about death
   b. those in individualistic cultures experience lower levels of anxiety about death than those in collectivistic cultures
   c. those in collectivistic cultures experience lower levels of anxiety about death than those in individualistic cultures
   d. those in individualistic and collectivistic culture experience lower levels of anxiety about death than those in other types of cultures

4. This term is used to describe the situation where people fail to take care of themselves and essentially contribute to their own premature death:
   a. suicidal erosion   c. anticipatory suicide
   b. anticipatory death   d. submissive death

5. Which of the following accurately describes the relationship between religious beliefs and anxiety about death?
   a. those with strong religious beliefs have the same level of anxiety about death than those who do not have strong religious beliefs
   b. those with strong religious beliefs actually have more anxiety about death than those who do not have strong religious beliefs
   c. those with strong religious beliefs actually have less anxiety about death as those who do not have strong religious beliefs

6. For adults over the age 85, which of the following is true?
   a. men are 10 times more likely to commit suicide than women
   b. women are 10 times more likely to commit suicide than men
   c. men are 4 times more likely to commit suicide than women
   d. women are 4 times more likely to commit suicide than men

7. Which of the following accurately describes the relationship between living longer and attempting to control one's environment?
   a. those who attempt to control their environment tend not to live as long as those who relinquish control
   b. those who attempt to control their environment tend to live longer than those who relinquish control
   c. no relationship between control and how long one lives has been established

8. The primary goal of hospice is designed to manage which of the following types of pain?
   a. mental   c. physical
   b. spiritual   d. all of the above

9. At the end of his life, Sigmund Freud:
   a. was the recipient of active euthanasia
   b. succumbed to a submissive death
   c. took part in suicidal erosion
   d. none of the above

10. The loss of a loved one usually involves which of the following?
   a. Shock   c. chronic grief
   b. anticipatory grief   d. sleep disturbances

11. The type of care that is designed to address the circumstances associated with impending death is:
   a. assisted suicide   c. end of life care
   b. active euthanasia   d. passive euthanasia

12. In 1900, the death rate in the United States for children under the age of 5 was
   a. 50%   c. 30%
   b. 60%   d. 10%

13. In 1999, deaths of children under the age of 19 in the U.S. were most common in which of the following groups?
    a. infancy (under 1 year)
    b. 1- 4 years of age
    c. 5 to 9 years of age
    d. 10 to 14 years of age

14. When a person faces a terminal illness, they sometimes look for ways to buy time, making promises to God for more time or relief of pain. This is referred to as:
    a. denial
    b. acceptance
    c. grieving
    d. bargaining

15. When one takes concrete steps to end a terminally ill person's life, such as administering a lethal dose of drugs to the ill person, it is referred to as:
    a. active euthanasia
    b. suicidal erosion
    c. passive euthanasia
    d. assisted suicide

ANSWER KEYS

Practice Test - Pretest (with text page numbers)

1. c 559	6. c 557	11. b 566
2. d 552	7. d 557	12. d 566
3. a 551	8. d 559	13. d 552
4. d 555	9. d 561	14. a 565
5. b 557	10. a 561	15. d 559

True/False

1. F	6. T	11. T
2. T	7. F	12. F
3. F	8. F	13. F
4. T	9. F	14. F
5. F	10. T	15. T

Key Vocabulary Terms

1. Active euthanasia is taking steps to bring about another person's death; passive euthanasia is withholding or disconnecting life-sustaining equipment so that death can occur naturally.
2. Suicidal erosion is an indirect form of suicide by engaging in high-risk activities; assisted suicide is providing people with a terminal illness the means to end their own life.
3. Palliative care is care that attempts to prevent or relive the emotional distress and physical difficulties associated with a life-threatening illness; end of life care is care that specifically addresses the concerns and the circumstances associated with impending death.
4. A living will is a legal directive indicating that the person does not wish for extraordinary measures be taken to sustain life in the case of a terminal illness; medical power of attorney is a legal document that one makes to authorize another individual to make medical decisions for him or her in the event of a life-and-death circumstance.
5. Chronic grief is an ingrained pathological mourning process in which the person never overcomes the grief; bereavement overload is a stress reaction experienced by people who lose several friends or loved ones during a short period of time.

Programmed Review

1. ignored, difficult, inappropriate
2. 20th, technological, in hospitals
3. 1960s, doctors, nurses, less, asked
4. are, anxious, afterlife, healthy
5. religious, depression, anxiety
6. self-esteem, anxiety, death
7. individualistic, collectivistic
8. older, younger
9. review, pleasures, pains
10. Elizabeth Kübler-Ross, anger, bargaining, acceptance, universal
11. inadequate
12. half, 46

13. death, relief
14. sudden, review
15. 85, suddenly, sleeping
16. anger, guilt
17. white men, 75, 1/4th
18. submissive death, suicidal erosion
19. 10
20. the first year
21. disengaged, more, control
22. how, when
23. England, 1967, independently
24. homes, nursing homes, insurance, more
25. the enemy, normal, natural
26. euthanasia, Greece
27. American Medical Association, assisted suicide
28. grief work, cultures
29. shock, several days
30. healing, renewal
31. bereavement overload, stress
32. chronic grief, pathological
33. Holland, wide variation
34. as soon as possible, the deceased
35. 30, 1.4
36. mothers, fathers, hopelessness
37. Jewish, Chinese

Practice Test – Post Test (with text page numbers)

1. c 551	6. a 558	11. c 563
2. a 555	7. b 559	12. c 567
3. c 553	8. d 559	13. a 567
4. d 557	9. a 560	14. d 555
5. c 552	10. a 564	15. a 560